IMAGES
of America

CUSTER COUNTY

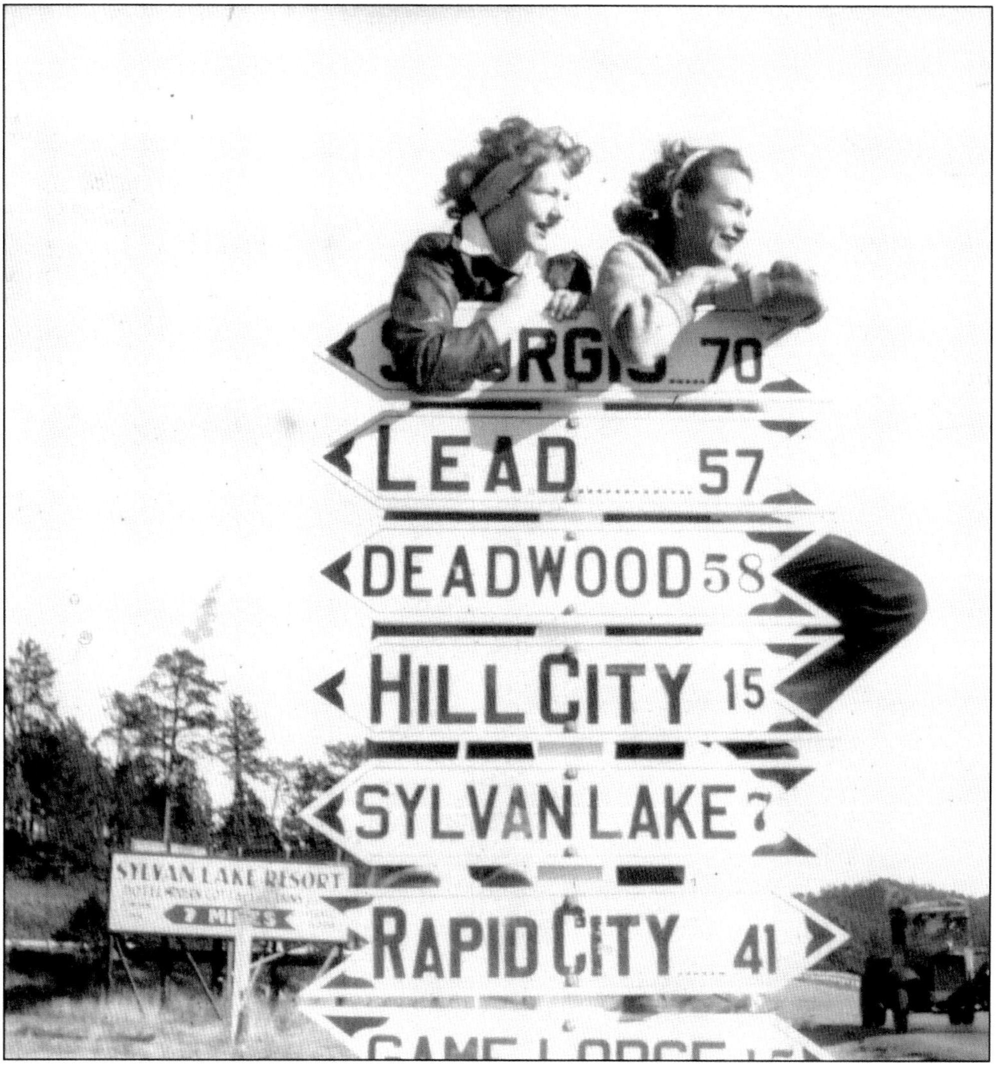

Oleta Harley and Norma Sutherland add beauty to this directional sign. (Author's collection.)

IMAGES
of America

CUSTER COUNTY

Peggy A. Sanders

ARCADIA
PUBLISHING

ISBN 978-0-7385-3438-1

Published by Arcadia Publishing
Charleston, South Carolina

Printed in the United States of America

Library of Congress Control Number: 2005926130

For all general information, please contact Arcadia Publishing:
Telephone 843-853-2070
Fax 843-853-0044
E-mail sales@arcadiapublishing.com
For customer service and orders:
Toll-Free 1-888-313-2665

Visit us on the Internet at www.arcadiapublishing.com

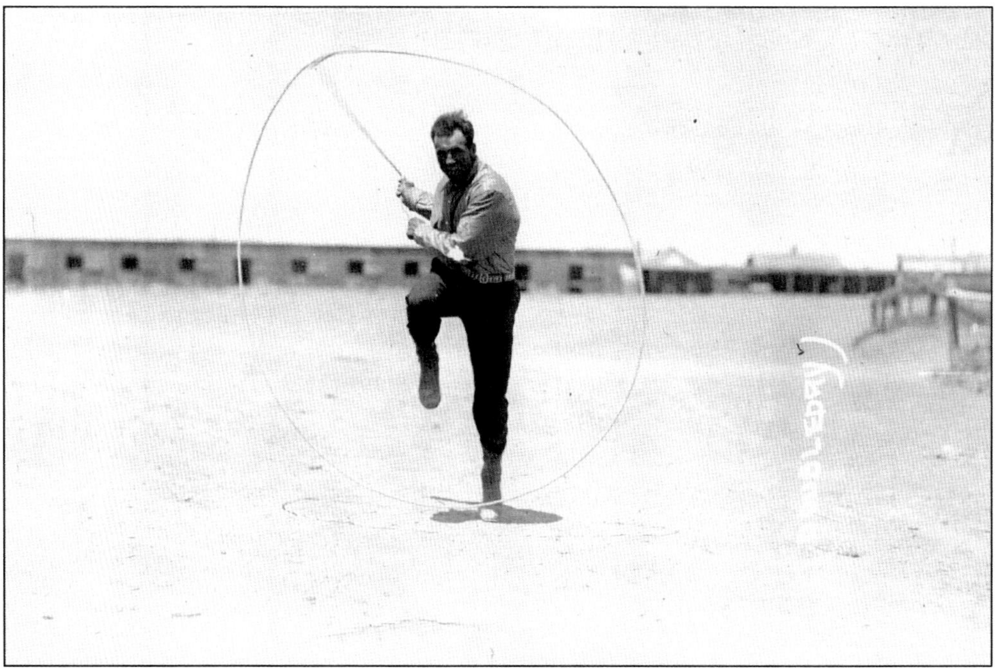

Al Stringham became a trick-roping performer and traveled to many rodeos in the Southwest. He and his wife, Lillie, lived on the rock house ranch south of Pringle from 1931 to 1959. (Courtesy of Wayne Kewley.)

CONTENTS

Acknowledgments		6
Introduction		7
1.	Friends and Neighbors	9
2.	Town and Country	33
3.	Making a Living	41
4.	Families Are Forever	55
5.	Daily Lives	73
6.	Changing Faces	85
7.	Anchors of the County	99

ACKNOWLEDGMENTS

Each photograph in this book is a gift to those who cherish history. We thank the following for their contributions: Chris Jensen, Wayne Kewley, Jim and Marlene Galloway, Wade Fleming, Ed Streeter, Anita (Shortie) Gallentine, Nelda Carroll, Glen Smith, Don Sieger, Pat Roseland, Carl E. Clements, Avelda Walker, Leona McMaster, Leonard and Oonagh Wood, Dolly Evans, Rick Mills, the Hermosa Arts and History Association, Susan Davis, Gene and Joyce Phillips, Mary Brady, Bonnie Doughty, Irv and Geraldine Evans, Helen and Guy Van Nice, Bob and Carol Harley, Ferol McClaren, Charlotte McClaren, Edna Wulff, Russell Wyatt, Gene Miller, and Gary Holst.

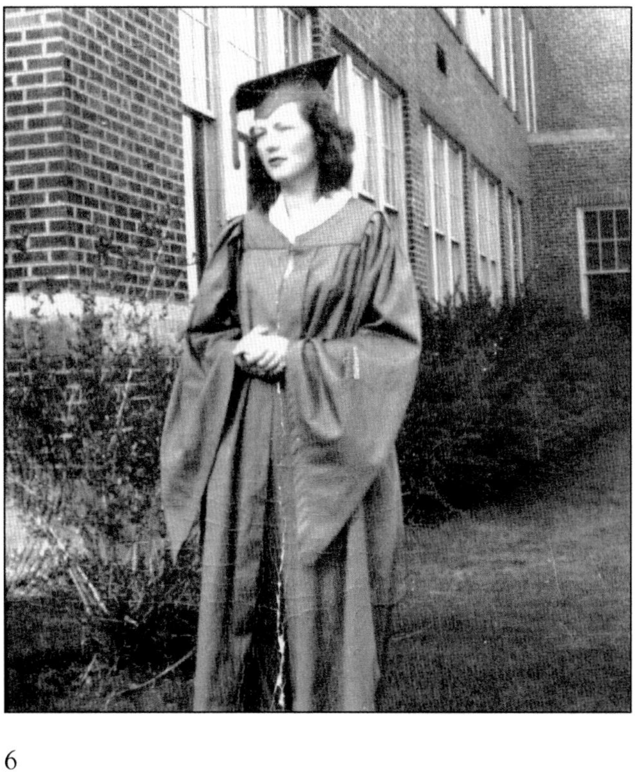

Seen here is the author's mother, Oleta Harley, who was part of the Custer High School class of 1946. (Author's collection.)

Introduction

Well before South Dakota became a state in 1889, the Dakota Territorial Legislature, in 1875, established three counties in the Black Hills: Custer, Pennington, and Lawrence. Custer County actually came into existence two years later, in 1877. Custer City became the county seat in 1879 after much wrangling, including contested elections, between Hayward and Custer City. When county boundaries were firmly fixed in 1881, Hayward became part of Pennington County. By 1883, the ranchers on the southern end of Custer County wanted to be separated into their own county. They proclaimed that the miners of Custer County had few common interests with the ranchers, and the people would therefore be better served with two governments. Custer County was divided in 1883 into Fall River and Custer Counties. By 1890, Custer County had 4,891 residents. Of those, 790 lived in Custer City.

Mining had been done in various parts of the county before, and once the railroad came to Custer County in 1885, mining became an integral part of the economy. In addition to gold, other products mined over the years include mica, tin, quartz, slate, sandstone, granite, silver, coal, and feldspar. Fairburn agates, which originate in limestone, are another of Custer County's legacies.

Logging follows forests, and there are plenty of trees in parts of the county. Solid trees make for sturdy lumber that was in demand from the miners and continues to be a necessity today. Hundreds of families in Custer County have made their livings from logging, sawmills, and associated services. A common sight on many area homesteads was a small sawmill that served local needs. The mills used to burn their sawdust to dispose of it. That aroma is forever tied to the memory of Custer City, in particular.

Farming is more prevalent in the eastern part of Custer County, where the land is flatter and the altitude is more conducive to growing crops. Attorney C. A. (Charles) Nystrom from Buffalo Gap was a huge booster of irrigation and was highly influential in promoting the construction of Angostura Dam, as early as 1913. Angostura was first funded in the Water Conservation and Utilization Act of August 11, 1939, and was reauthorized by the Flood Control Act of 1944, Public Law 534. Construction of the Angostura Dam began on August 23, 1946, and was completed on December 7, 1949. The first delivery of irrigation water was made in 1953. The project contains the largest contiguous section of irrigated farmland in Custer County, 4,000 acres east of Buffalo Gap on an area known as Harrison Flat. An additional 8,000 acres of the irrigation project are located in Fall River County, to the south of Custer County. Smaller areas of farm ground, particularly hay crops, dot the county. In years of plentiful moisture, grass hay is abundant and is harvested throughout the hills and valleys.

Tourism grew over the years with a big jump in 1927, when Pres. Calvin Coolidge came to the Black Hills for the summer. He and his entourage stayed at the State Game Lodge, which had been built in 1921. They attended church in Hermosa during their summer stay. They traveled throughout the hills, and the national exposure received from the publicity propped up the tourism economy. Coolidge dedicated Mount Rushmore on August 10, 1927. The granite mountain was selected on a horseback ride with Gutzon Borglum and his son Lincoln, along with state forester Theodore Shoemaker and Ray Sanders, a horseman at the State Game Lodge.

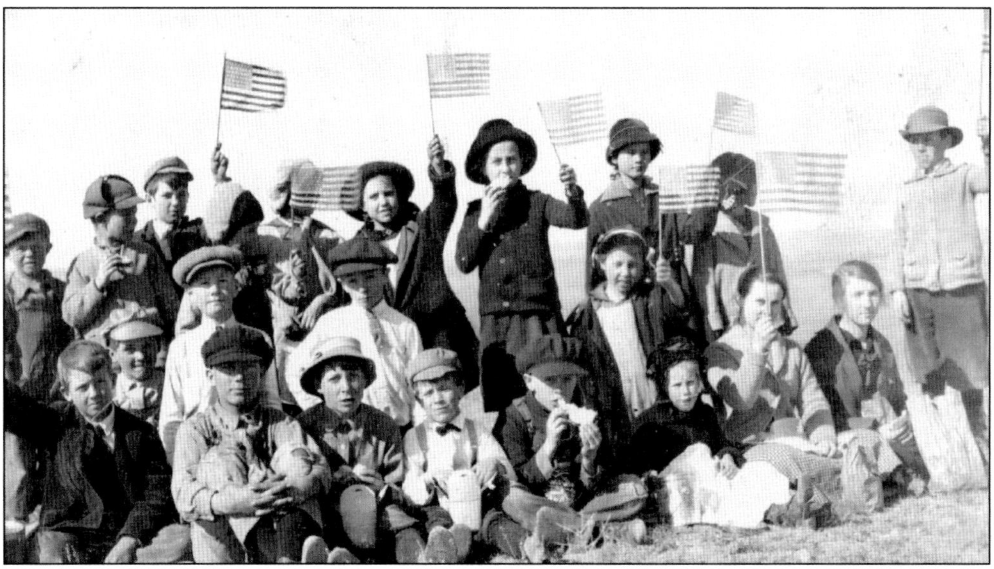

Happy birthday, George Washington. The students of Buffalo Gap School are pictured on February 22, 1916. (Courtesy of Jim and Marlene Galloway.)

One

Friends and Neighbors

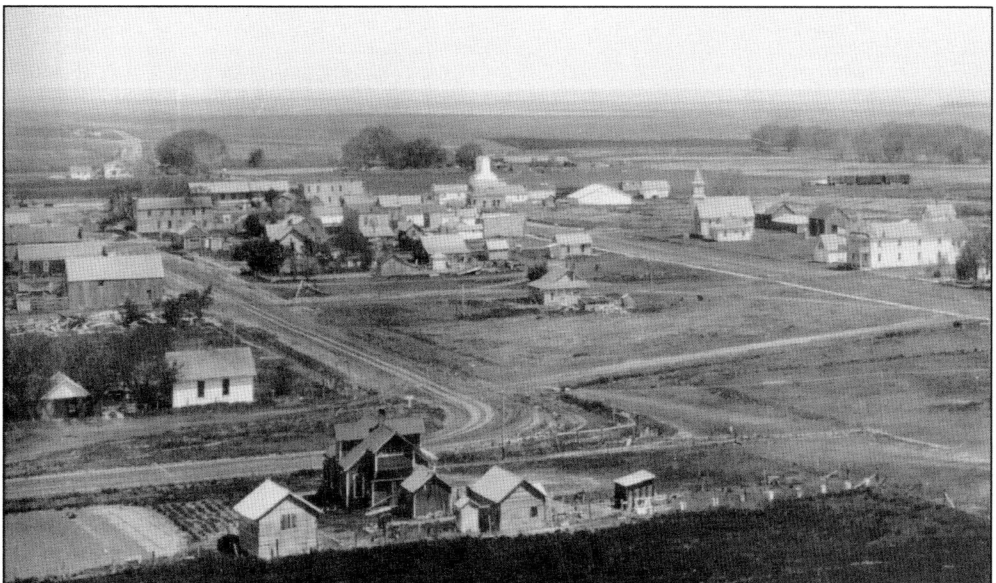

This is an early view of Buffalo Gap. The house in the foreground was built by Edwin L. Kohl in 1910. Kohl owned and operated a general store in Buffalo Gap for many years. He also showed silent movies in the city auditorium for community entertainment. (Courtesy of Jim and Marlene Galloway.)

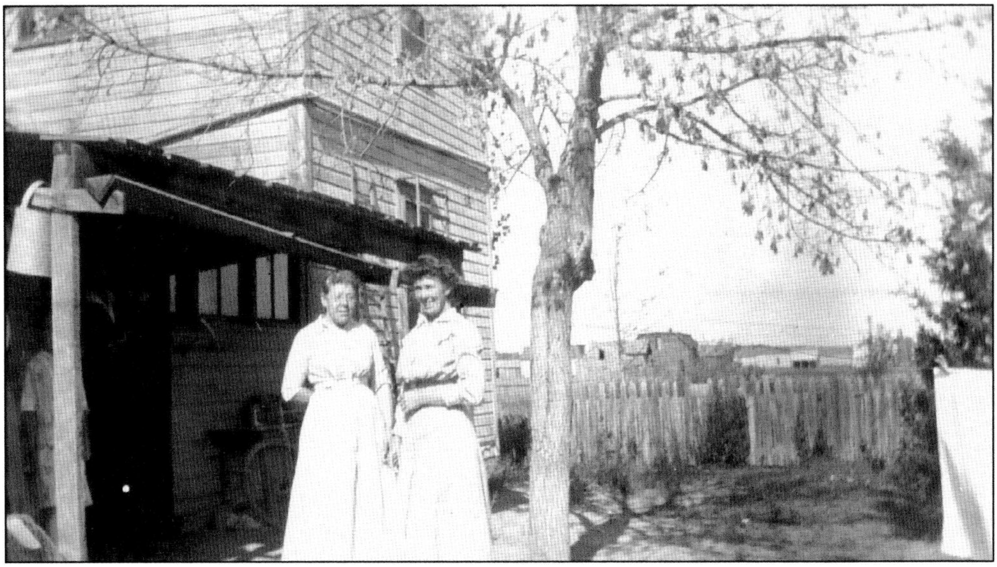

In this 1916 photograph, Lydia (Raymer) Stabler, on the left, and her daughter-in-law Winifred (Spicer) Stabler are standing near the Stabler home in Buffalo Gap. (Courtesy of Jim and Marlene Galloway.)

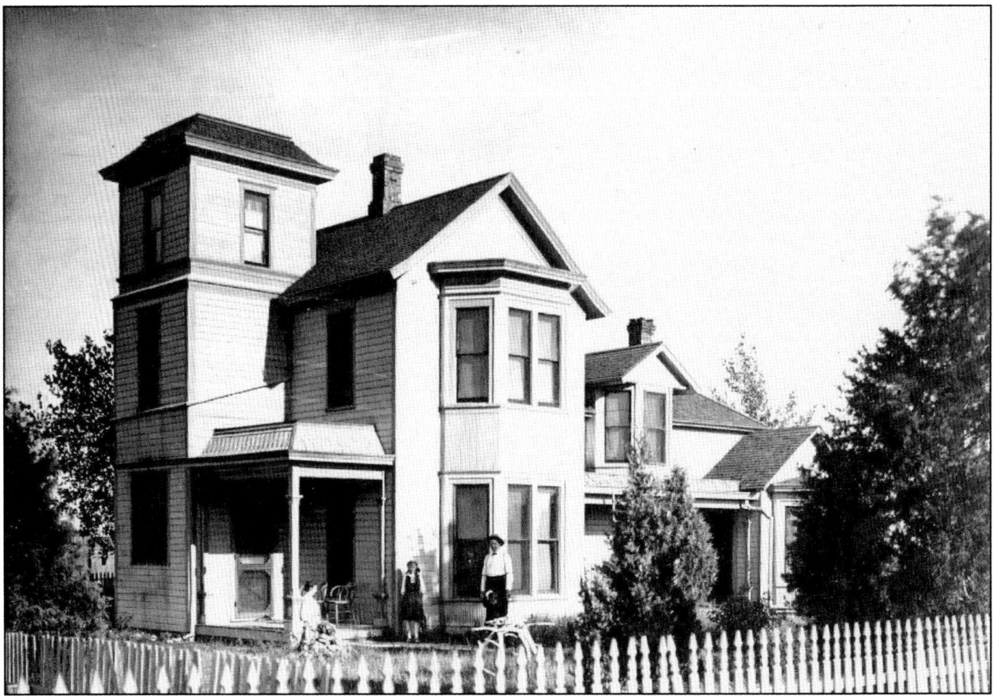

The Stabler family was one of the early families involved with Wind Cave. After the government took over the cave, the Stablers moved to Buffalo Gap and Charles built this house in 1907. Block 11, lot 27, on which the house sits, was first sold by the Pioneer Town Site Company, a Nebraska corporation, in 1904 to Willis Flewellin and William A. Brooks for $35. They sold it to Charles Stabler for $400 in 1907. (Courtesy of Jim and Marlene Galloway.)

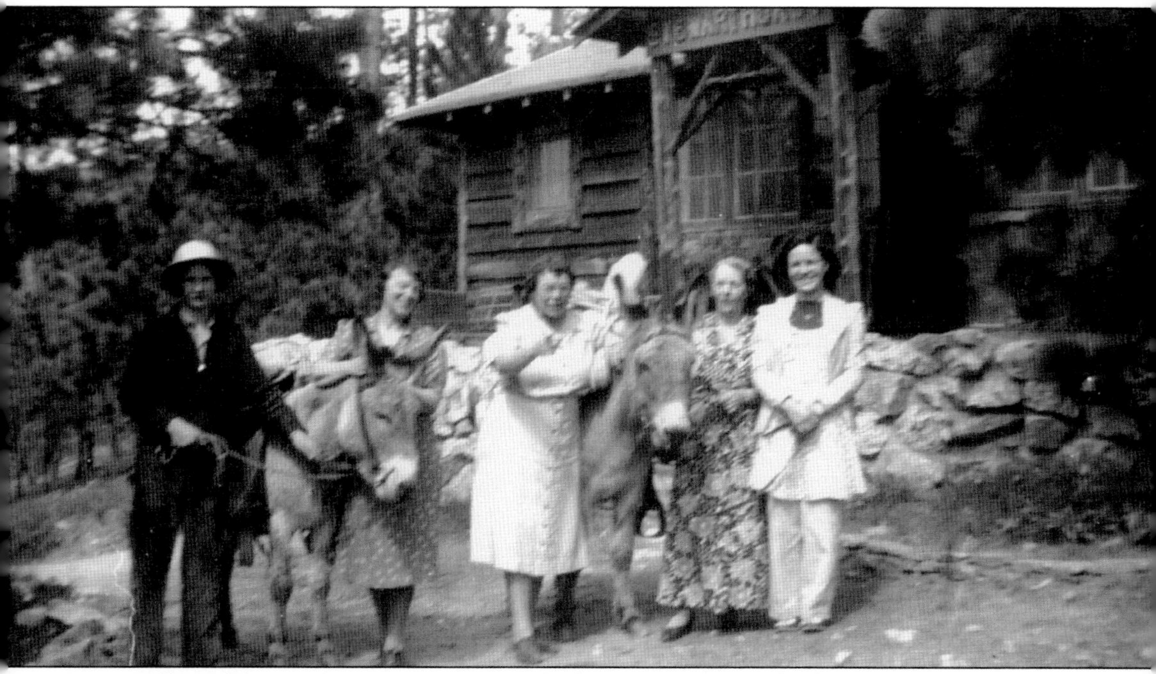

Sisters Belle and Queena Stewart ran a group of cabins near Sylvan Lake during several summers. Harold Sieg, Mrs. Cavey, and Alice Sandy were employed by the Stewarts. In this photograph, from left to right, Harold Sieg, Belle Stewart, Queena Stewart, Mrs. Cavey, and Alice Sandy are shown with the burros used to haul supplies to Belle on Harney Peak, where she stayed the summer of 1941. (Courtesy of Alice Gregerson.)

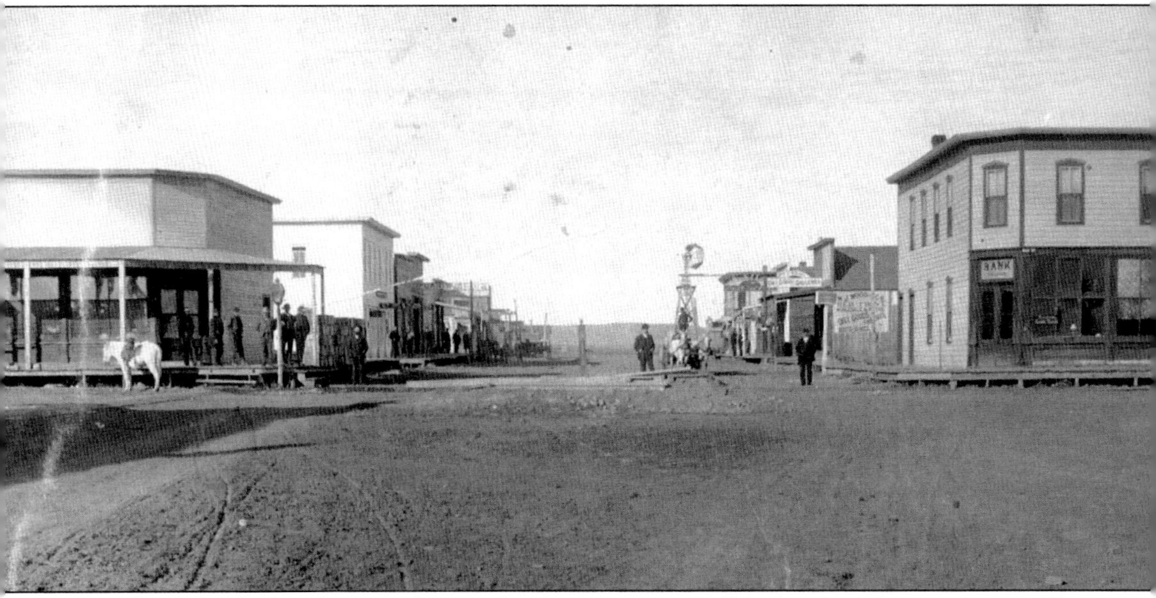

Saloons, banks, hotels, general stores, hardware stores—Buffalo Gap had these and many other businesses. A devastating fire on November 8, 1891, burned most of the town's buildings. The photograph is undated, and it is unclear whether these were the buildings that burned or if they were built after the fire. (Courtesy of Shortie Gallentine.)

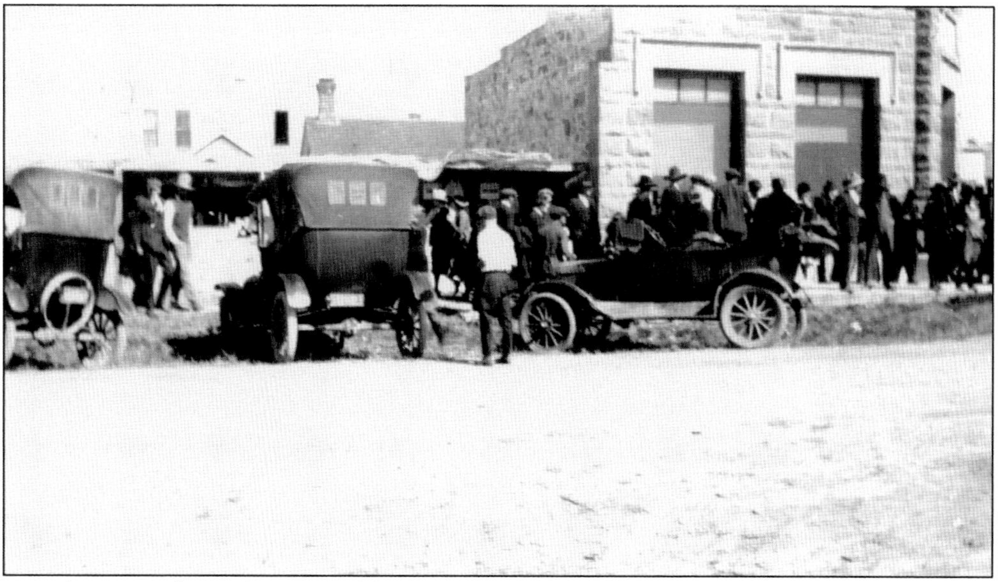

Grand opening day at the new building of Citizens Bank in 1910 brought a crowd to town. John Davidson of Smithwick, South Dakota, was the bank president at the time. (Courtesy of Jim and Marlene Galloway.)

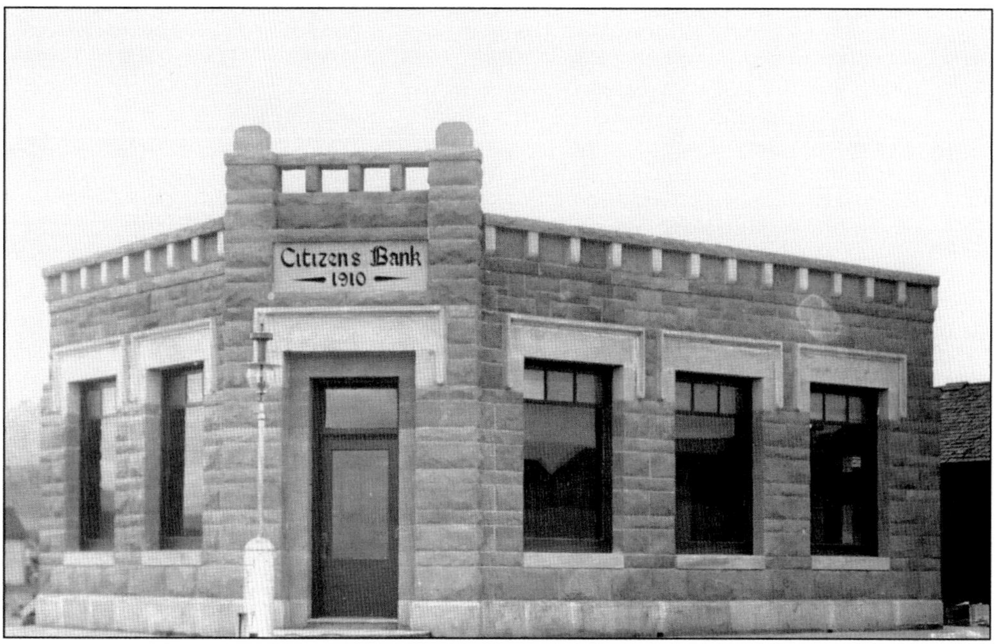

The bank was built of native sandstone, and though the business is closed, the vacant building still stands in good repair at Second and Main Streets. (Courtesy of Jim and Marlene Galloway.)

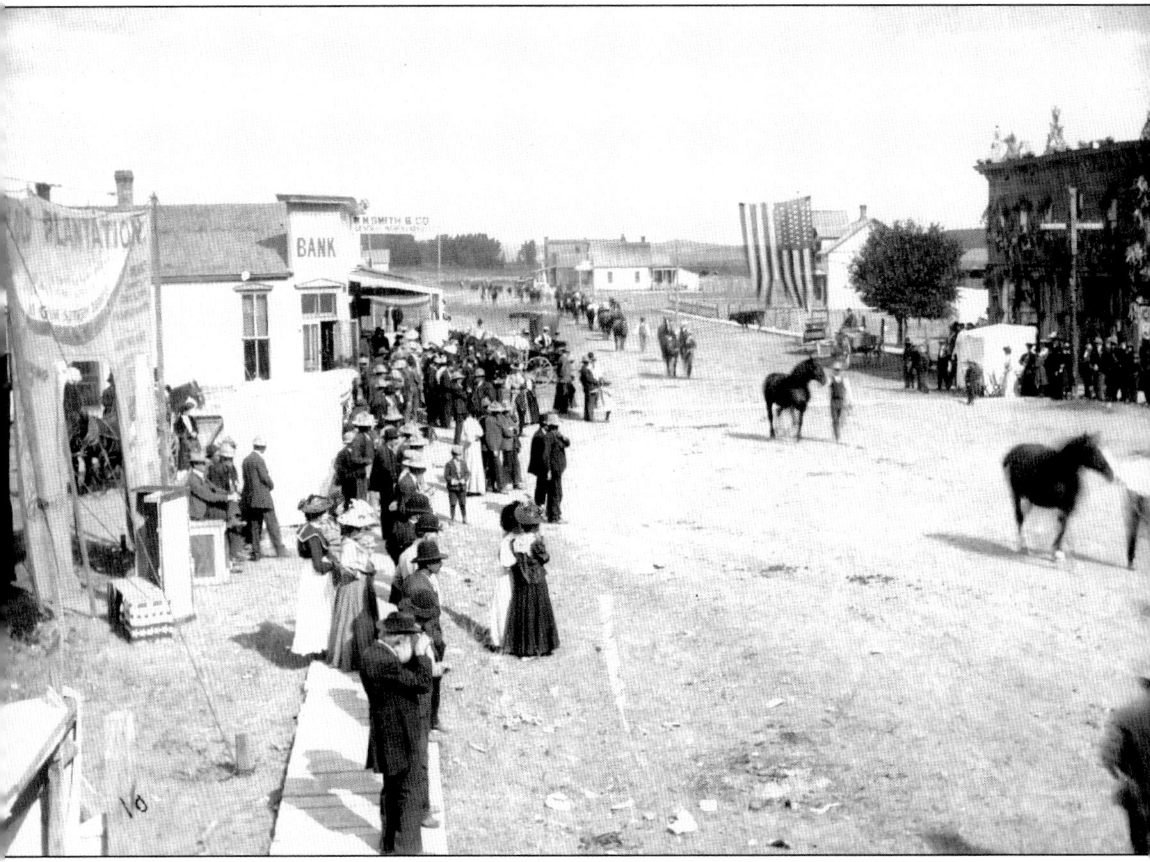

Fairs and parades were annual events in towns all around the area; they had a cooperative agreement to plan the dates, so there was no conflict among the towns. This one was in Buffalo Gap. (Courtesy of Shortie Gallentine.)

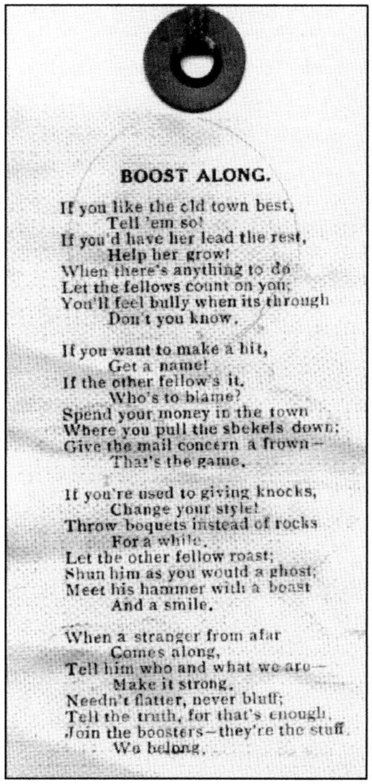

BOOST ALONG.

If you like the old town best,
Tell 'em so!
If you'd have her lead the rest,
Help her grow!
When there's anything to do
Let the fellows count on you;
You'll feel bully when its through
Don't you know.

If you want to make a hit,
Get a name!
If the other fellow's it,
Who's to blame?
Spend your money in the town
Where you pull the shekels down;
Give the mail concern a frown—
That's the game.

If you're used to giving knocks,
Change your style!
Throw boquets instead of rocks
For a while.
Let the other fellow roast;
Shun him as you would a ghost;
Meet his hammer with a boast
And a smile.

When a stranger from afar
Comes along,
Tell him who and what we are—
Make it strong.
Needn't flatter, never bluff;
Tell the truth, for that's enough.
Join the boosters—they're the stuff
We belong.

This encouraging poem was on the back of the fair entry tag that appears below. (Courtesy of Jim and Marlene Galloway.)

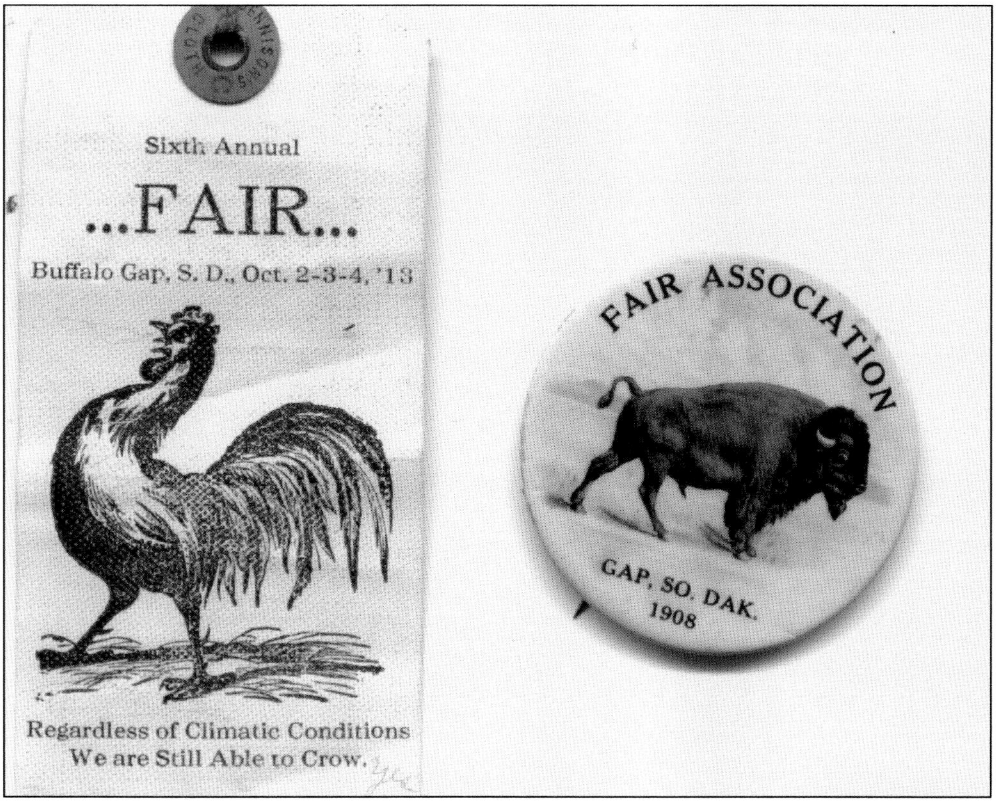

The 1908 Buffalo Gap fair button was good for advertising. (Courtesy of Jim and Marlene Galloway.)

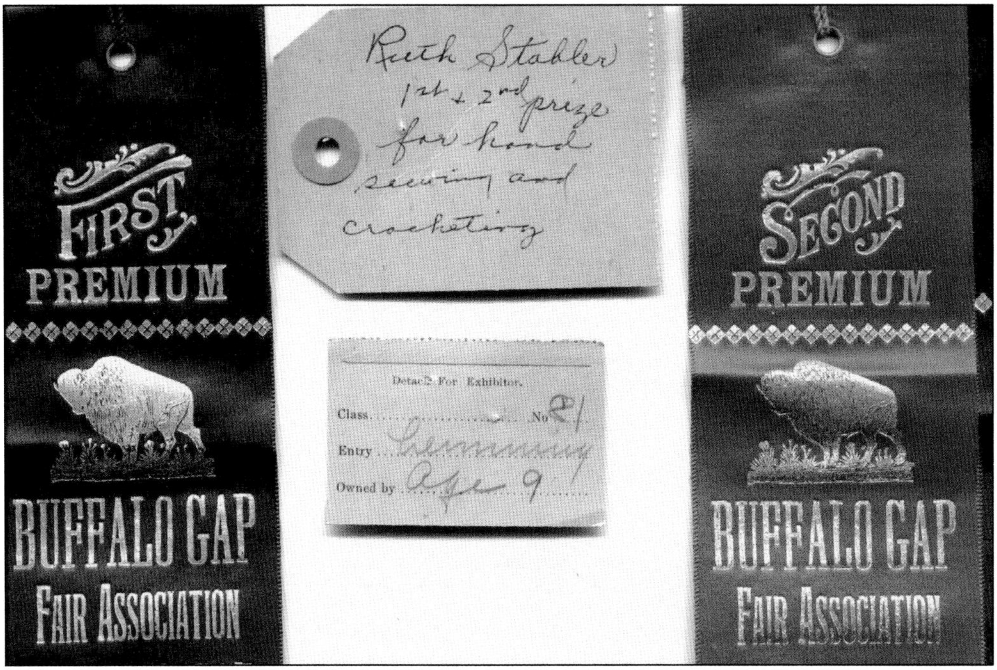

At age nine, Ruth Stabler won first- and second-prize ribbons for her handiwork. (Courtesy of Jim and Marlene Galloway.)

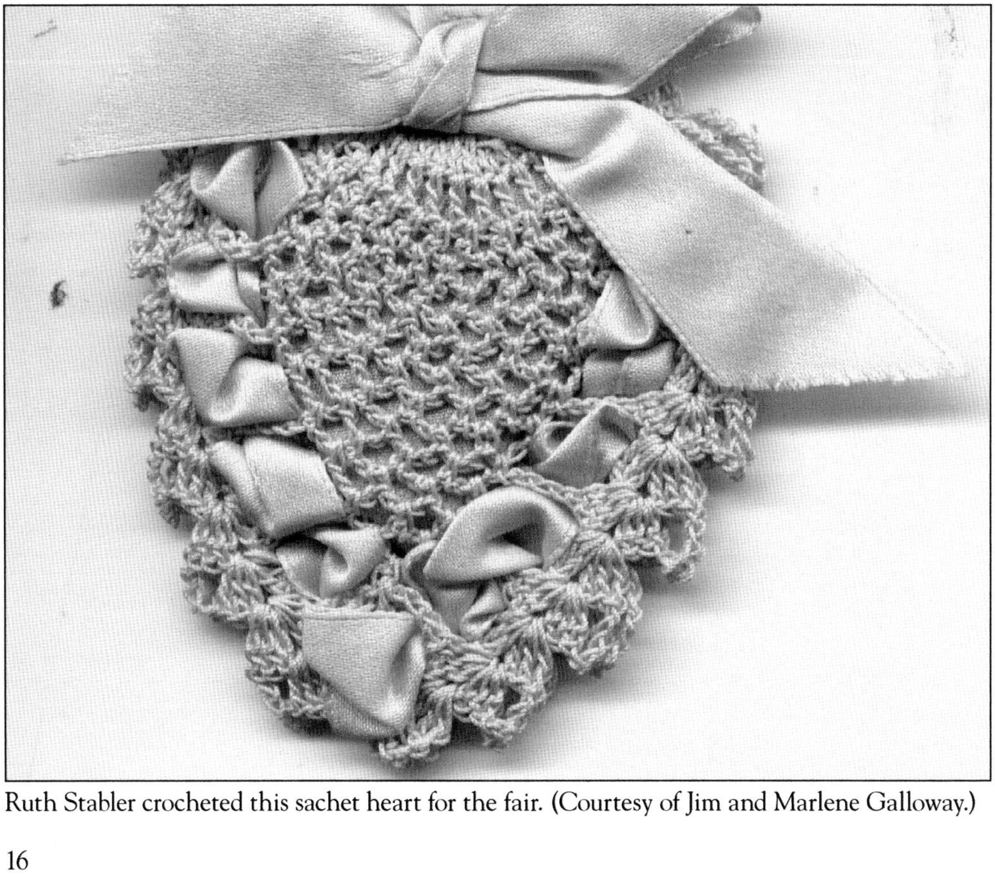

Ruth Stabler crocheted this sachet heart for the fair. (Courtesy of Jim and Marlene Galloway.)

This half-skirt showcases Ruth Stabler's hand-sewing ability and more of her crochet skills. (Courtesy of Jim and Marlene Galloway.)

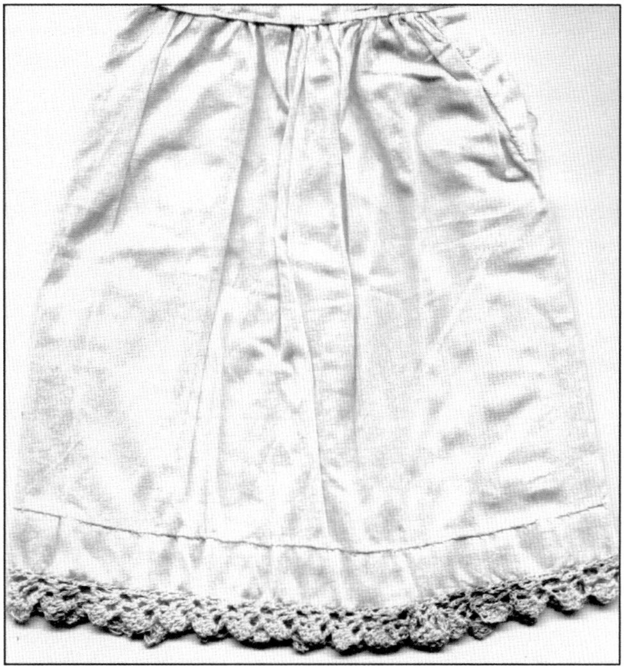

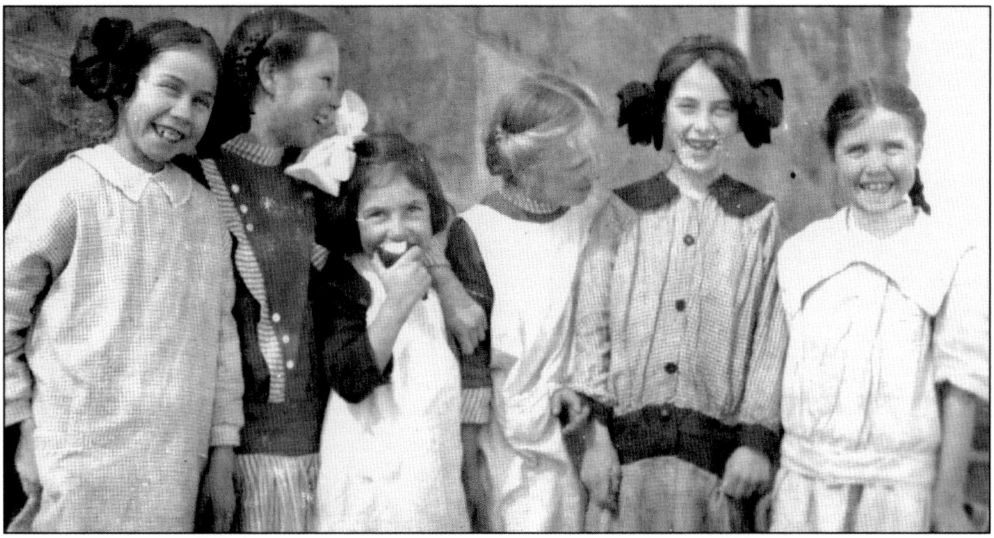

Ruth Stabler, the young artisan, is the little girl second from the right with the dark bows in her hair and the big smile on her face. She is joined by her Buffalo Gap school friends on April 1, 1915. The other girls are, from left to right, Onalie Kohl, Ruth Miller, Dorothy Sewright, Mildred Miller, and Iva Davis. (Courtesy of Jim and Marlene Galloway.)

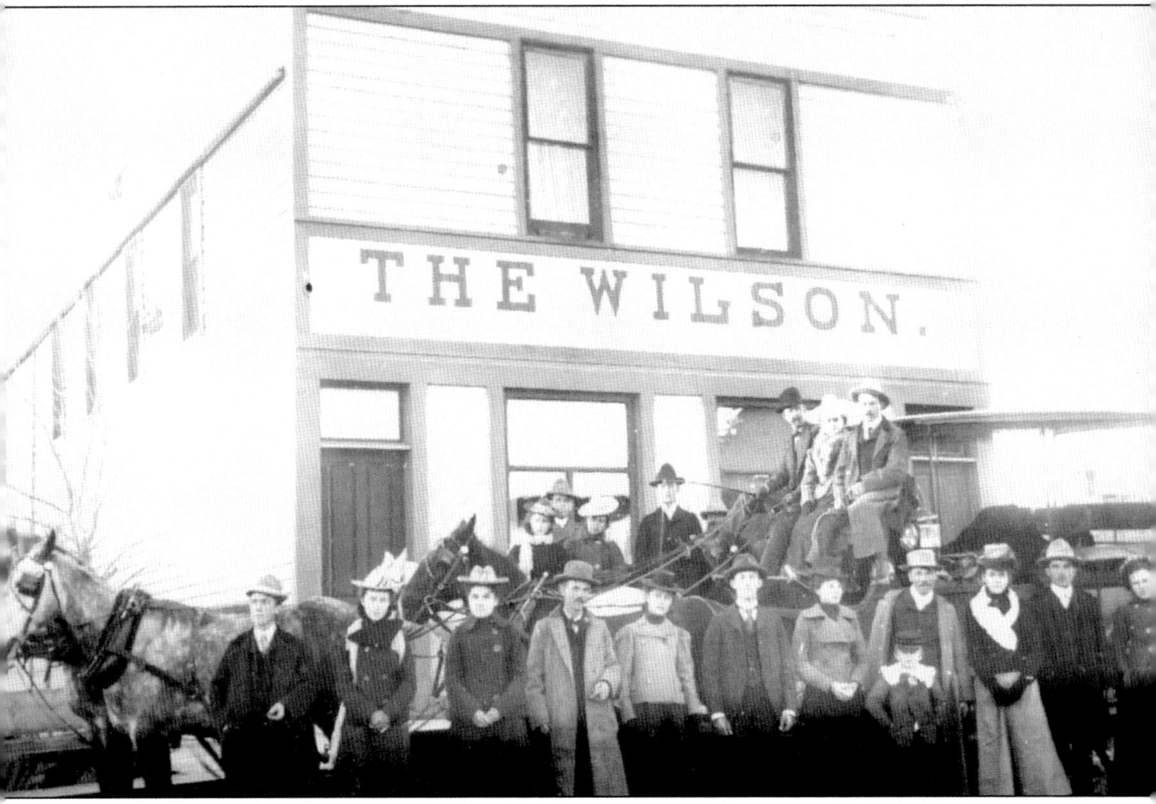

In 1901, the Wilson was one of 17 hotels and eating establishments in Buffalo Gap. The people shown in front of the hotel include Robert McNammee, Joe Bellemore, Alice Ennis and son Theo Shoemaker, Dora Tinsley (Levy), Scott Durst, and Grace Blockney, Margaret Bellemore (Finnerty), Tom Finnerty, Mildred Brooks (Miller), and Wes Bondurant. On the seat are Charles Crary (driver), Anna Tinsley, and Duane McVey. (Courtesy of Ed Streeter.)

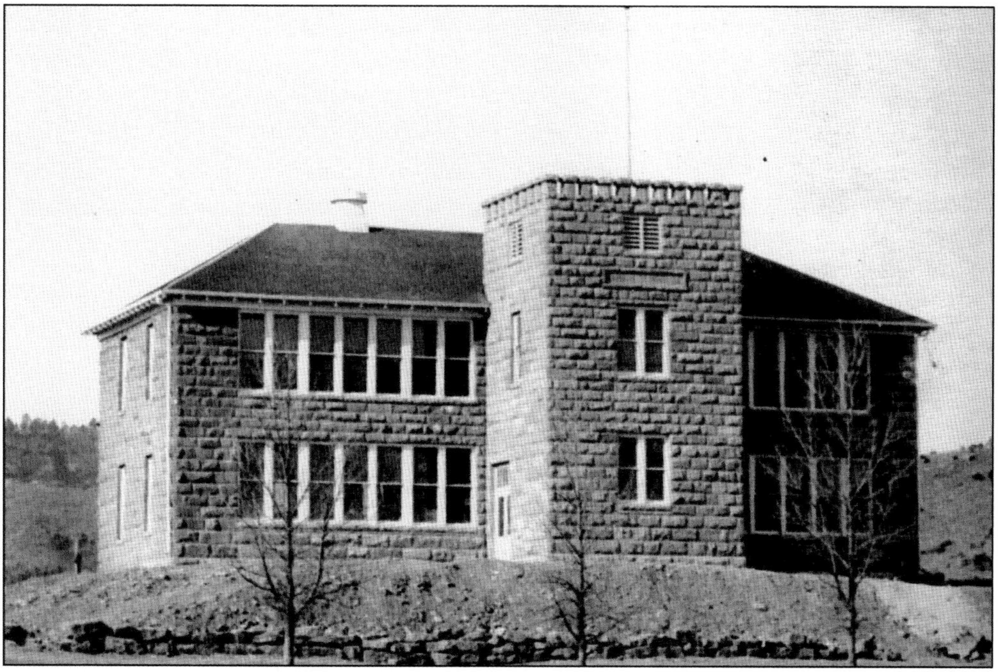

The sandstone school in Buffalo Gap was built in two parts. The south half was constructed around 1897, and the balance of the building was funded by a bond issue in 1923. W. A. Kepp Construction had the contract. Restrooms and showers were in the basement. (Courtesy of Pat Roseland.)

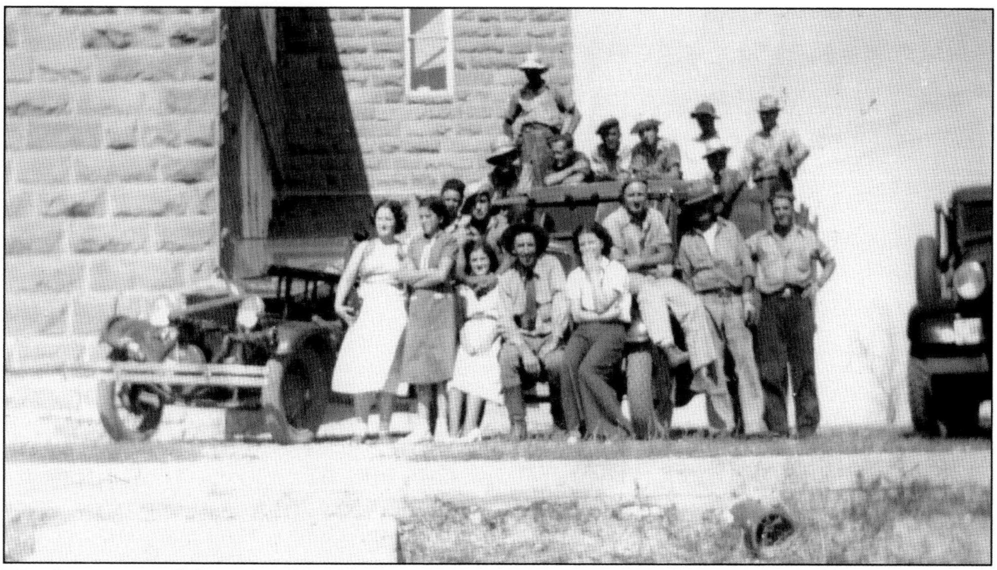

The basement of the school had a coal-fired furnace, at least during the years of 1937 to 1939. Roy Bledsoe, who was in the Civilian Conservation Corps at Wind Cave National Park during those years, tells this story: "The coal in the bin caught fire and they called the CCC boys to Buffalo Gap to pull out the coal in buckets and extinguish the fire, which we did." The people in this photograph include Viola Bondurant, Shortie Gallentine, Vivian Smith with her two sons, and Alice Lake. (Courtesy of Shortie Gallentine.)

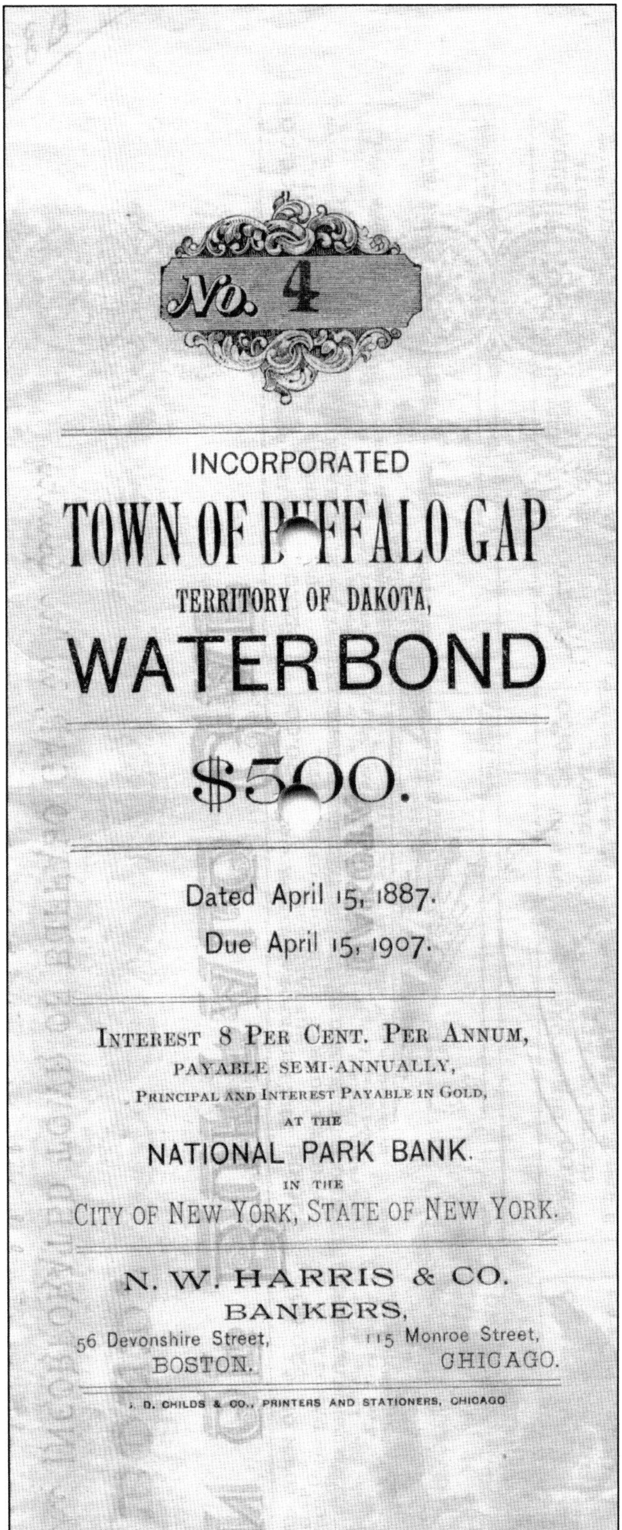

No. 4

INCORPORATED

TOWN OF BUFFALO GAP

TERRITORY OF DAKOTA,

WATER BOND

$500.

Dated April 15, 1887.

Due April 15, 1907.

INTEREST 8 PER CENT. PER ANNUM,

PAYABLE SEMI-ANNUALLY,

PRINCIPAL AND INTEREST PAYABLE IN GOLD,

AT THE

NATIONAL PARK BANK.

IN THE

CITY OF NEW YORK, STATE OF NEW YORK.

N. W. HARRIS & CO.

BANKERS,

56 Devonshire Street, BOSTON.

115 Monroe Street, CHICAGO.

J. D. CHILDS & CO., PRINTERS AND STATIONERS, CHICAGO

Even today, Buffalo Gap is still struggling with its water system. (Courtesy of Jim and Marlene Galloway.)

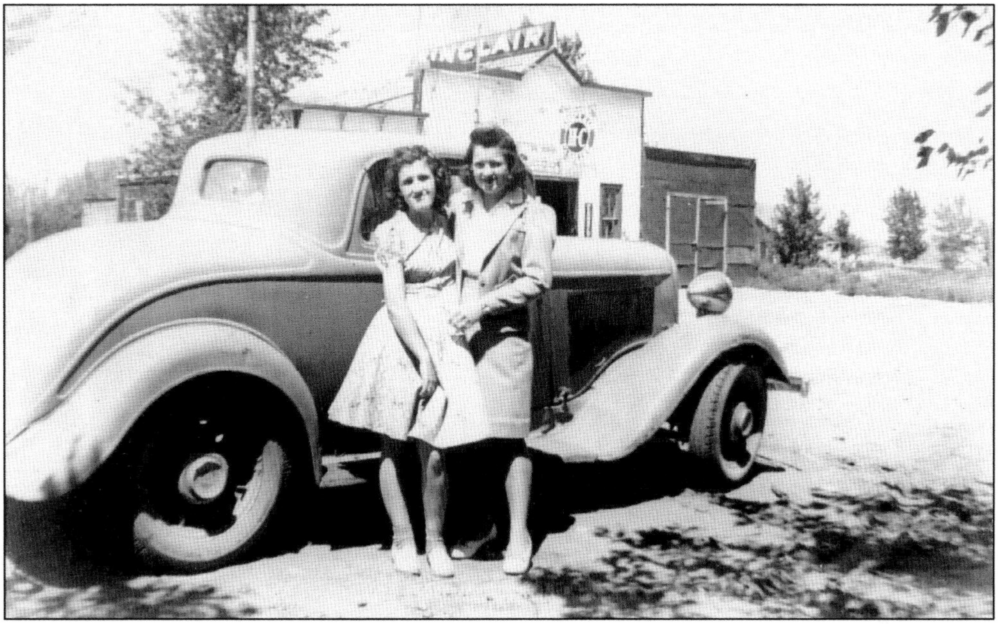

Shortie (Degnan) Gallentine traded in her Indian motorcycle for this car in 1940. Her sister Vivian (Degnan) Smith, on the left, stands with her in front of Buryl Degnan's service station in Buffalo Gap. Anita fixed tires there for 35¢ per tire, paying her brother Buryl 5¢ for each patch. Ed Snowden's blacksmith shop was next door. (Courtesy of Shortie Gallentine.)

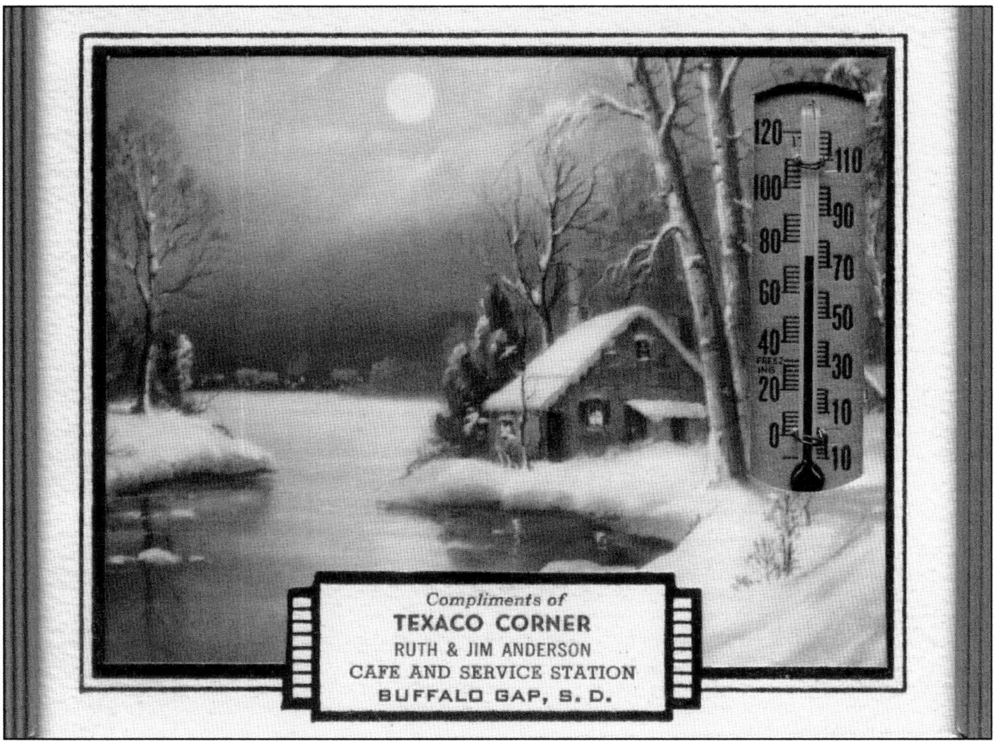

This 1951 calendar was a customer-appreciation gift from the Anderson family. (Courtesy of Wayne Anderson.)

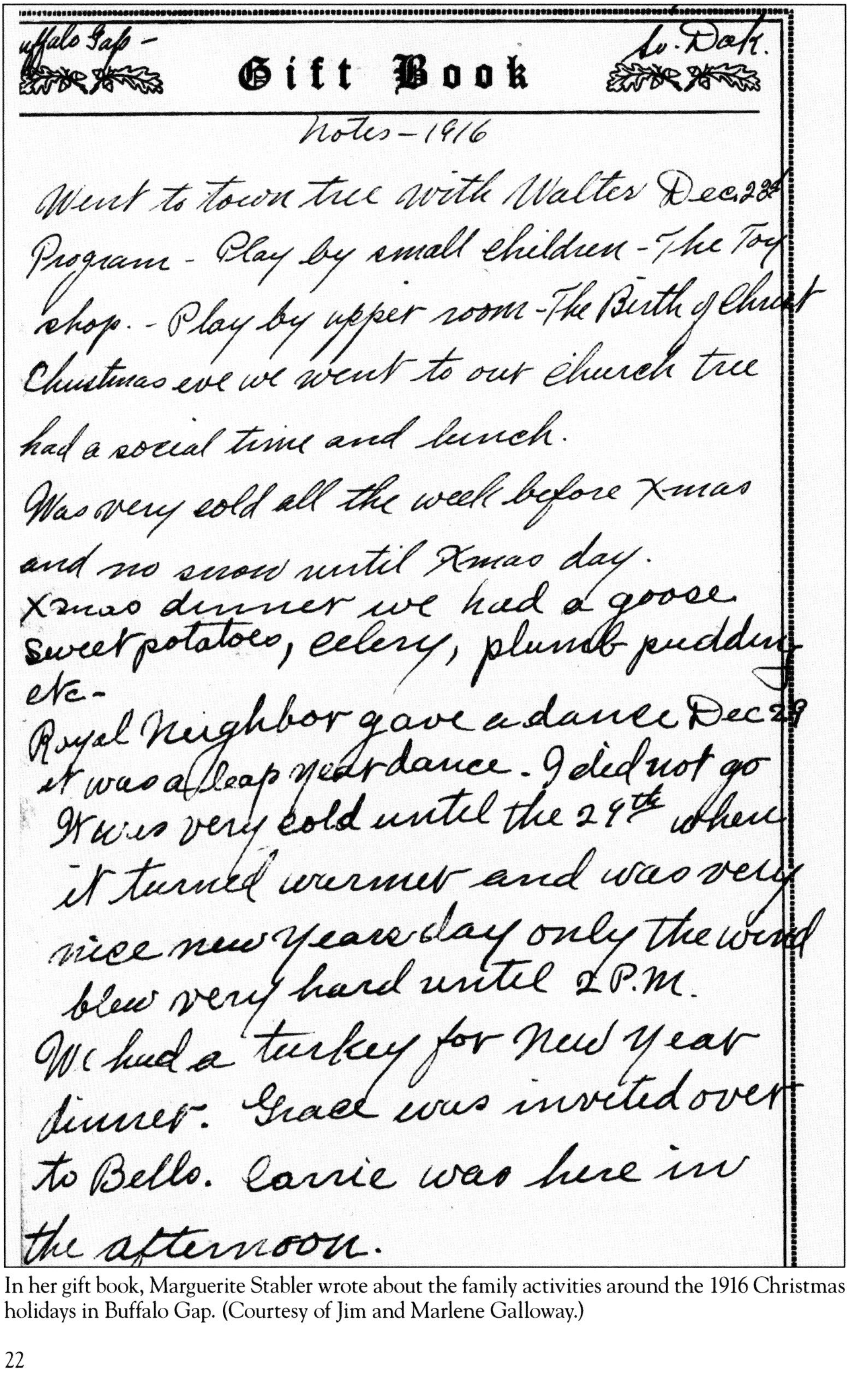

uffalo Gap - So. Dak.

Gift Book

Notes - 1916

Went to town tree with Walter Dec. 22nd
Program - Play by small children - The Toy
shop. - Play by upper room - The Birth of Christ
Christmas eve we went to our church tree
had a social time and lunch.
Was very cold all the week before Xmas
and no snow until Xmas day.
Xmas dinner we had a goose.
Sweet potatoes, celery, plumb pudding
etc -
Royal Neighbor gave a dance Dec 29
it was a leap year dance. I did not go
It was very cold until the 29th when
it turned warmer and was very
nice new years day only the wind
blew very hard until 2 P.M.
We had a turkey for New year
dinner. Grace was invited over
to Bells. Carrie was here in
the afternoon.

In her gift book, Marguerite Stabler wrote about the family activities around the 1916 Christmas holidays in Buffalo Gap. (Courtesy of Jim and Marlene Galloway.)

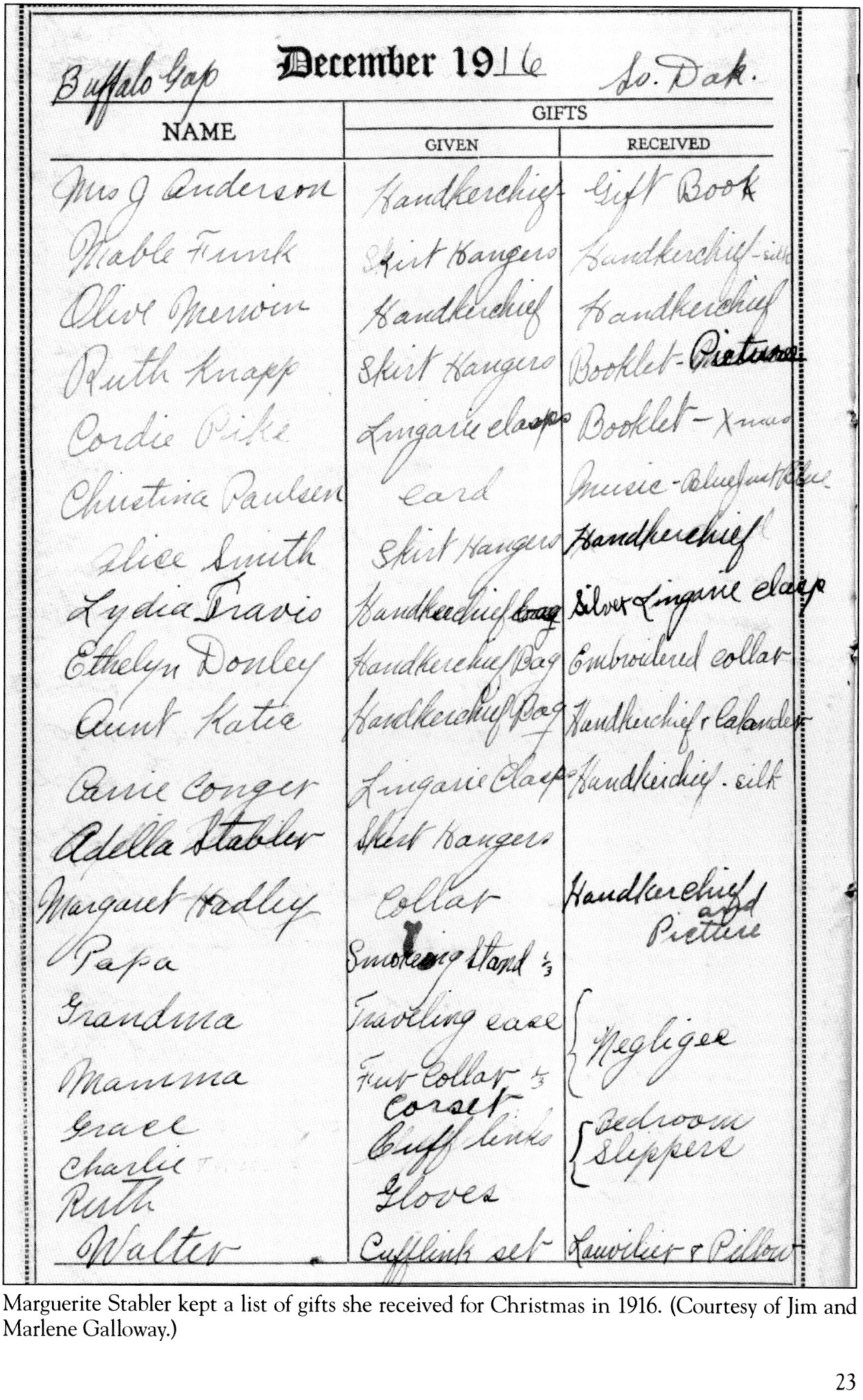

Buffalo Gap **December 1916** So. Dak.

NAME	GIFTS	
	GIVEN	RECEIVED
Mrs J Anderson	Handkerchief	Gift Book
Mable Funk	Skirt Hangers	Handkerchief - silk
Olive Merwin	Handkerchief	Handkerchief
Ruth Knapp	Skirt Hangers	Booklet - Picture
Cordie Pike	Lingarie clasps	Booklet - Xmas
Christina Paulsen	card	Music - Blue [illegible]
Alice Smith	Skirt Hangers	Handkerchief
Lydia Travis	Handkerchief bag	Silver Lingarie clasp
Ethelyn Donley	Handkerchief Bag	Embroidered collar
Aunt Katie	Handkerchief Bag	Handkerchief & Calander
Carrie Conger	Lingarie Clasp	Handkerchief - silk
Adella Stabler	Skirt Hangers	
Margaret Hadley	Collar	Handkerchief and Picture
Papa	Smoking Stand 1/3	
Grandma	Traveling case	Neglige
Mamma	Fur Collar 1/3	
Grace	Corset	Bedroom Slippers
Charlie	Cuff links	
Ruth	Gloves	
Walter	Cufflink set	Lavalier & Pillow

Marguerite Stabler kept a list of gifts she received for Christmas in 1916. (Courtesy of Jim and Marlene Galloway.)

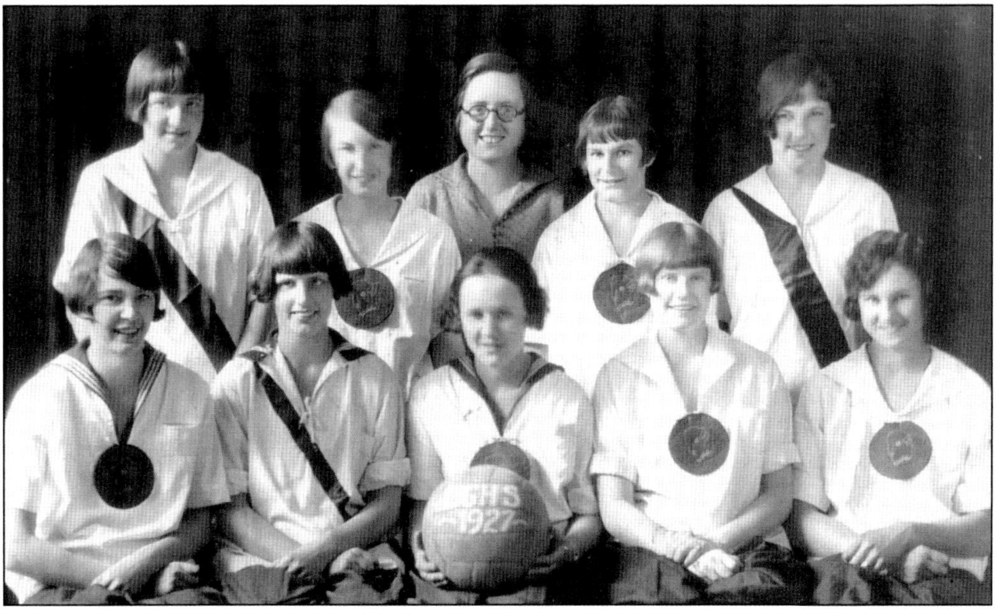

Different uniforms, some of the same team members as in the following photograph, and the date on the ball make it appear that this team was from the 1926–1927 school year. From left to right are (first row) Martha Korthaus, Nettie Sieger, Fern Snowden, Grace Kester, and Dorothy Snowden; (second row) Elma Morgareidge, Ruth Sewright, coach Adelaide Ward, Gladys Nehren, and Ione Howe. (Courtesy of Wade Fleming.)

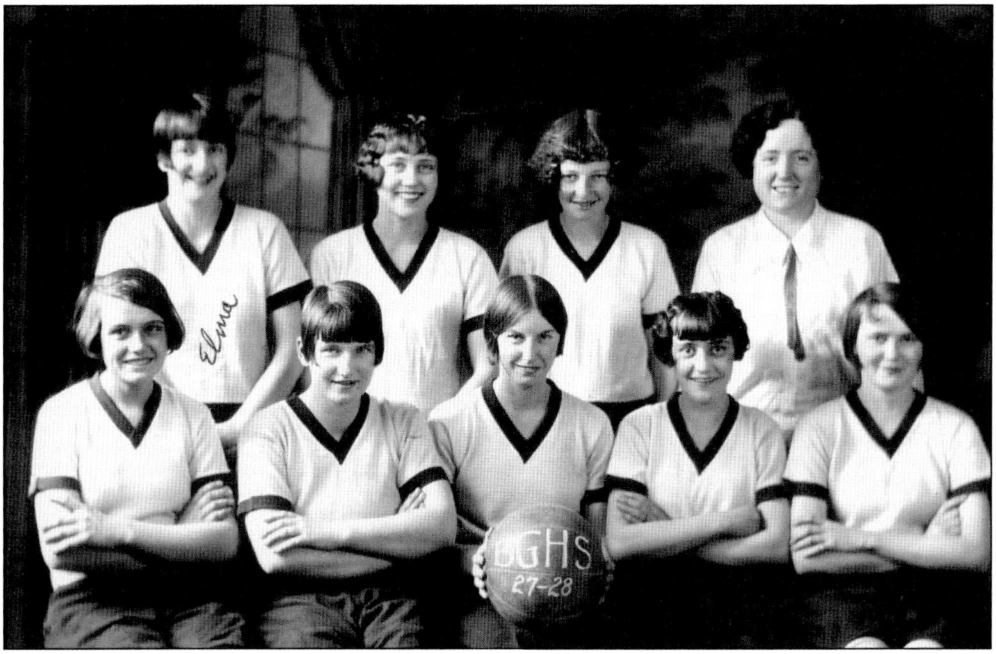

The Buffalo Gap girls basketball team for the 1927–1928 school year poses here. From left to right are (first row) Pansy Cooper, Opal Lake, Ruth Sewright, Thelma Grubbs, and Dorthea White; (second row) Elma Morgareidge, Sylvia Allen, Mildred Alkire, and coach Adelaide Ward. (Courtesy of Wade Fleming.)

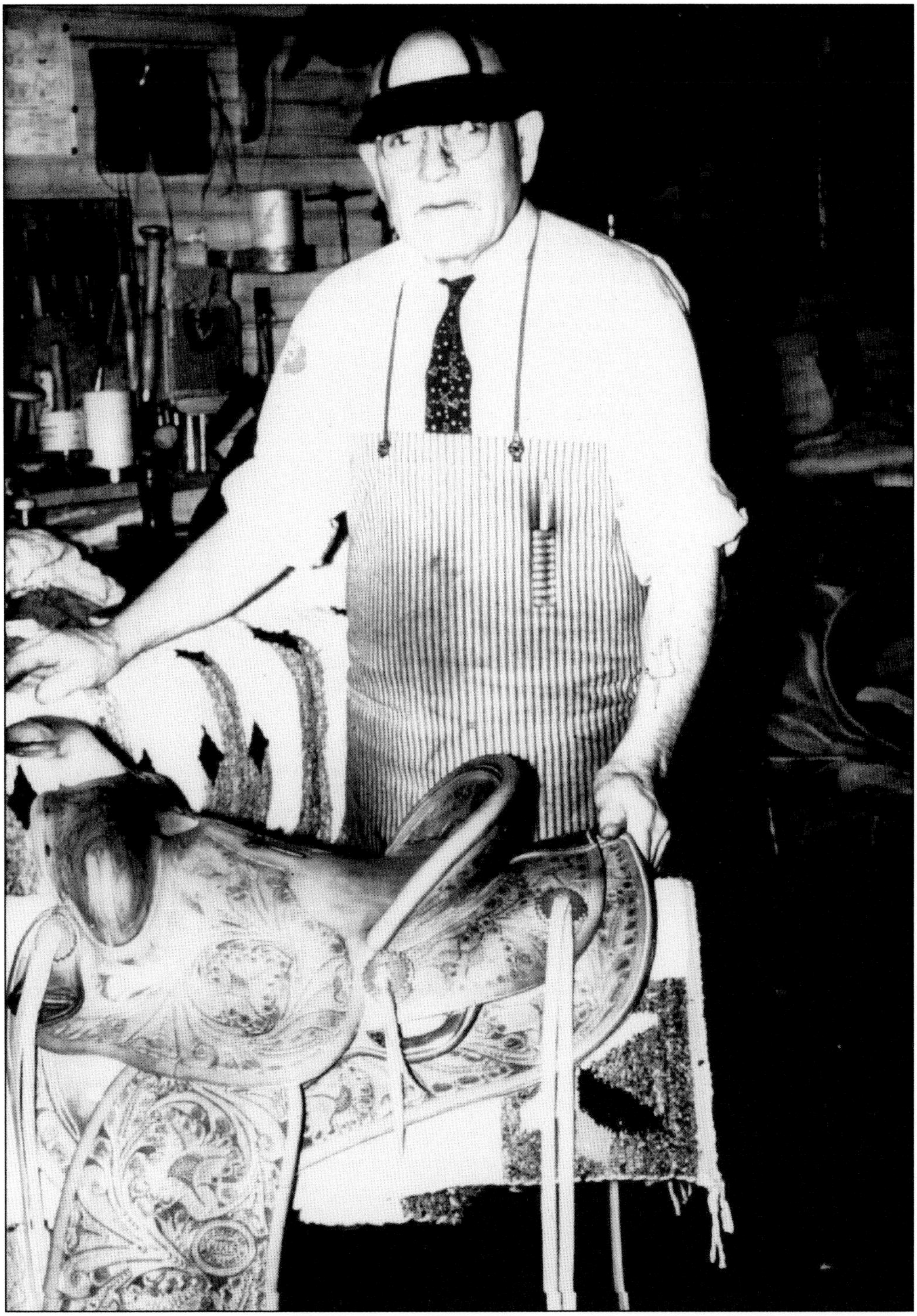

Charley Streeter was a self-taught saddle maker with extraordinary talent. Streeter owned and operated the C. G. Streeter Hardware and Saddle Shop, which he opened in 1919. Streeter Saddles, though not made after the late 1960s, are still a hallmark of quality in the saddle industry. (Courtesy of Ed Streeter.)

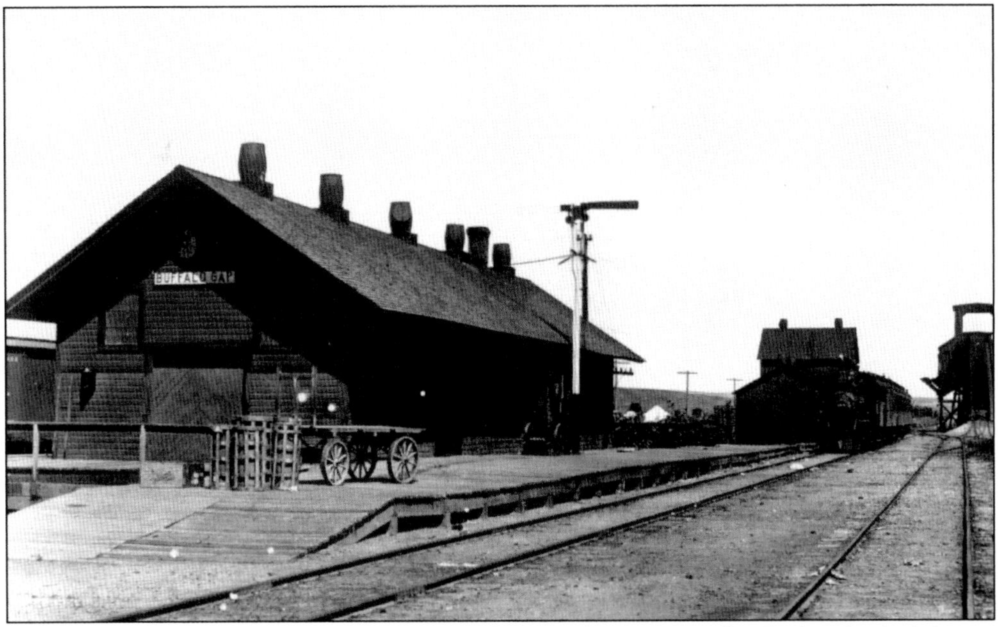

The depot served the needs of the Fremont, Elkhorn and Missouri Valley Railroad, which began service to Buffalo Gap from Chadron, Nebraska. In 1906, the railway was purchased by the Chicago and North Western Railroad. (Courtesy of Shortie Gallentine.)

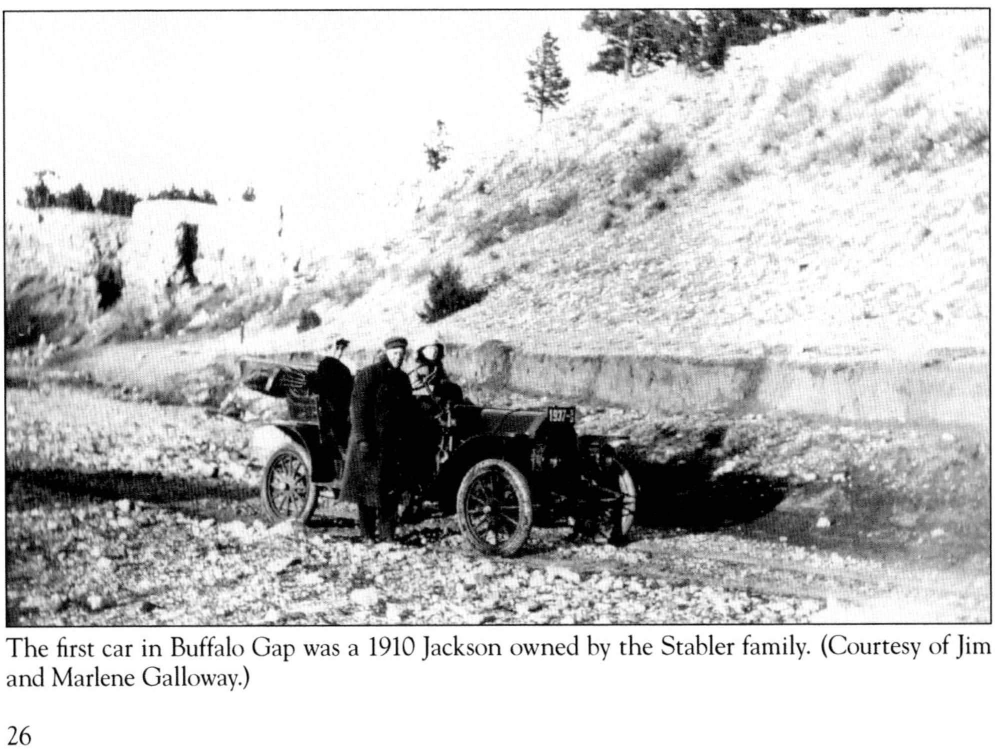

The first car in Buffalo Gap was a 1910 Jackson owned by the Stabler family. (Courtesy of Jim and Marlene Galloway.)

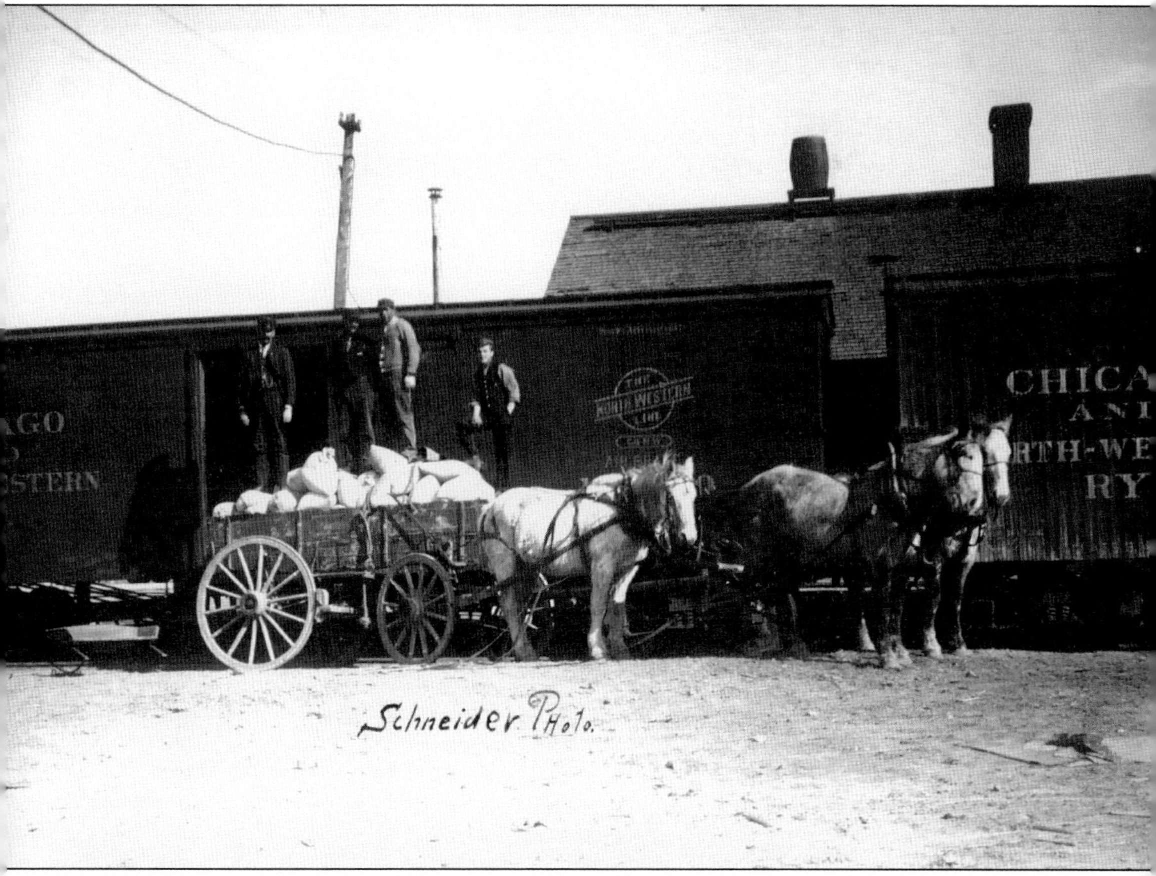

Alfalfa seed bound for Yankton, South Dakota, was loaded onto these railroad cars on March 2, 1911. The carload of seed sold to Gurney's Seed Company for $4,000. One seller of the $9-per-bushel seed was William Schneider. A Mr. Henne is on the back of the wagon, and Schneider is the driver as they prepare to take the load to the railway station. (Courtesy of Shortie Gallentine.)

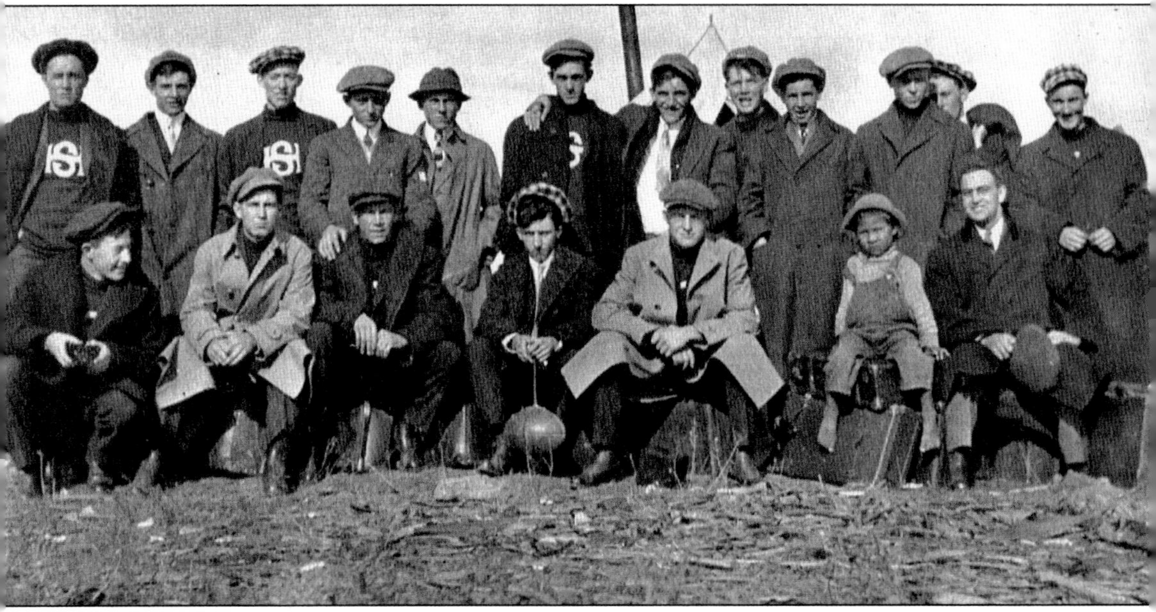

The 1914 Hot Springs football team waits for the train in Buffalo Gap. From left to right are (first row) Rupert Gillespie, Vern Scott, Harry Marty, Fulton Dudley, Leonard March, an unidentified child, and coach Fred Ingle; (second row) George Leach, Roy Williams, John Volin, Francis Case, Carl Hunter, Ross Magowan, George Miller, Herbert Kime, Dean Eastman, John Murry, and two unidentified players. (Courtesy of Fall River County Pioneer Museum.)

Sheep used to be sheared with hand clippers. The wool was bundled, sold, and eventually manufactured into clothing and blankets. (Courtesy of Don Sieger.)

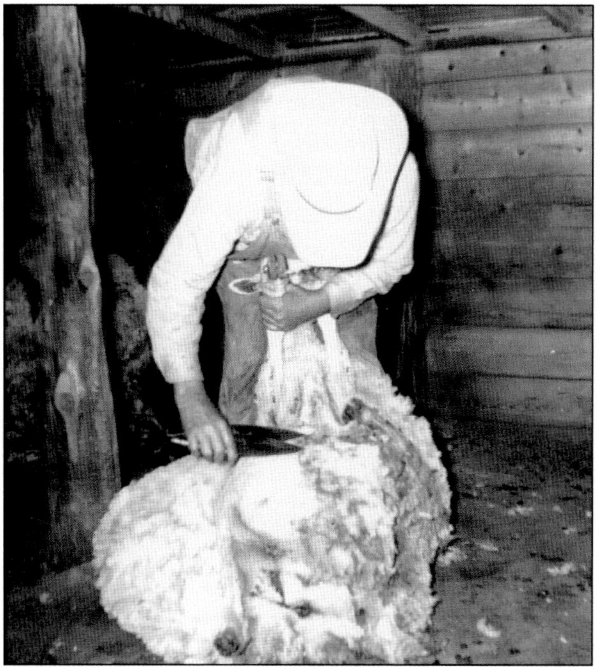

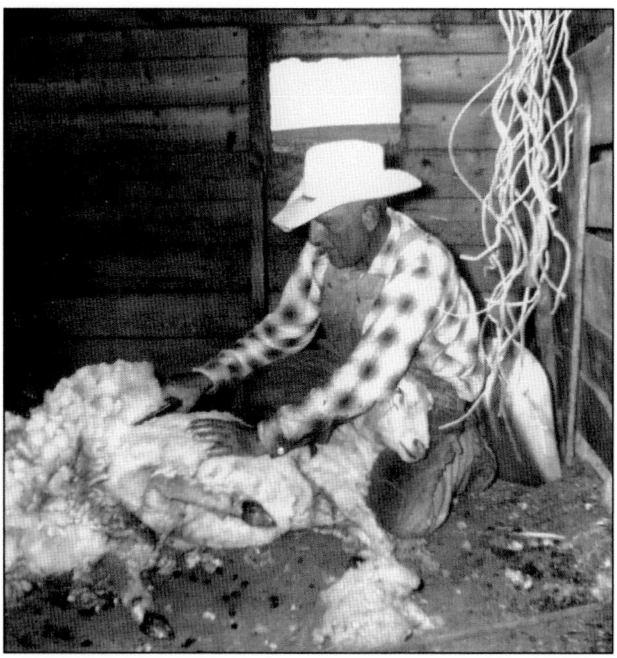

Leonard Sieger cradles the ewe's head in his lap as he completes the shearing job. (Courtesy of Don Sieger.)

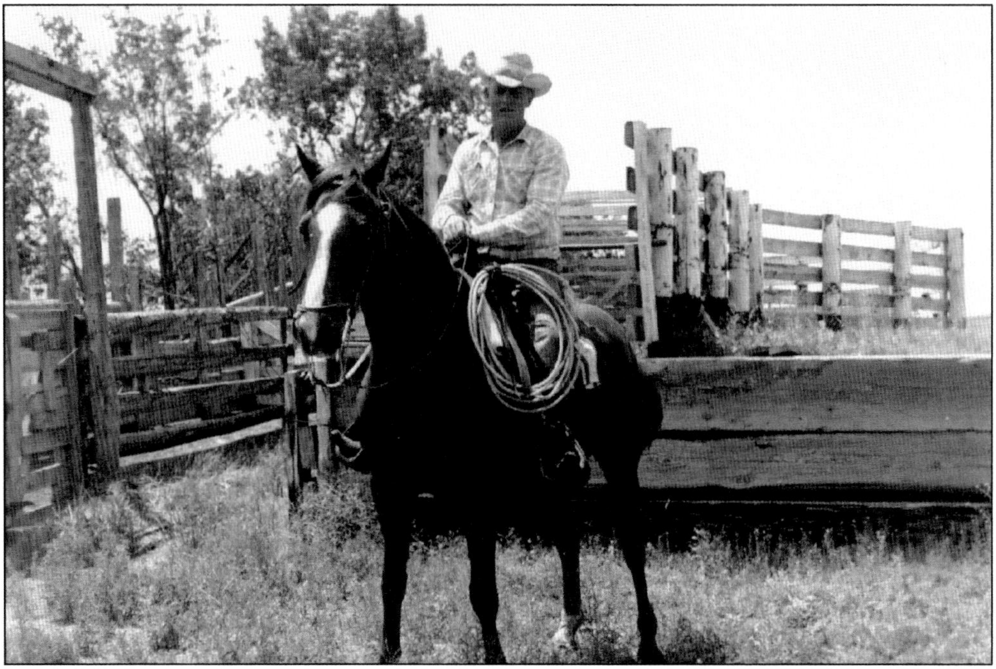

Charles Bondurant is getting ready to go to his office—the cow pasture—in this May 13, 1961, photograph. (Author's collection.)

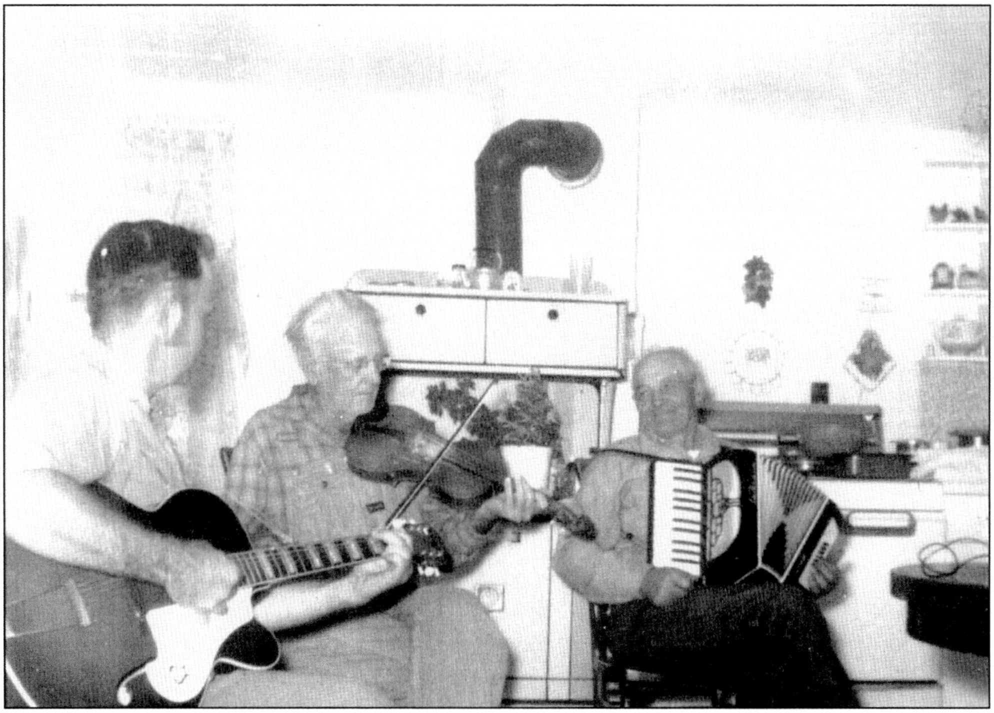

From left to right, Don and Leonard Sieger and Bill Walker play a jam session in the Sieger kitchen. (Courtesy of Don Sieger.)

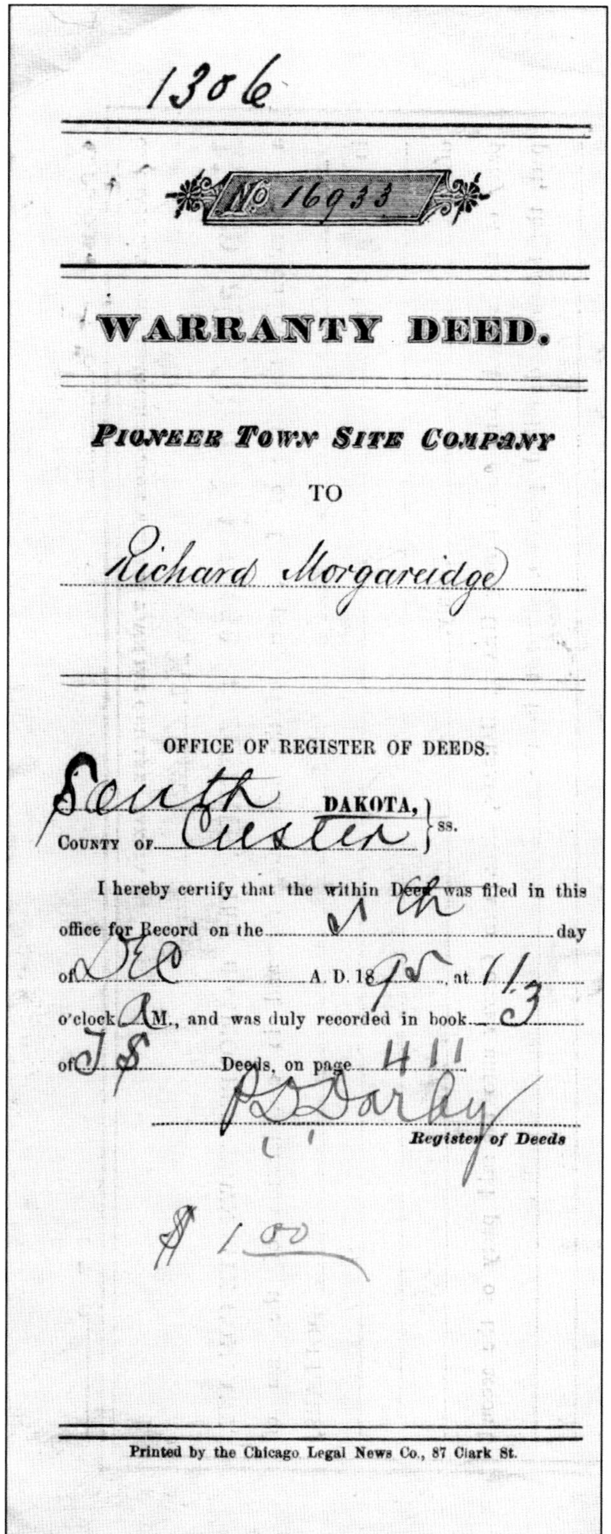

1306

No 16933

WARRANTY DEED.

PIONEER TOWN SITE COMPANY

TO

Richard Morgareidge

OFFICE OF REGISTER OF DEEDS.

South DAKOTA, } ss.
COUNTY OF Custer

I hereby certify that the within Deed was filed in this office for Record on the 1 th day of Dec A. D. 1895, at 11 o'clock A M., and was duly recorded in book 3 of TS Deeds, on page 411

P S Darley
Register of Deeds

$1.00

Printed by the Chicago Legal News Co., 87 Clark St.

The Pioneer Townsite Company was a subsidiary of the Fremont, Elkhorn and Missouri Valley Railroad. The company founded a number of towns in Nebraska and South Dakota. (Courtesy of Shortie Gallentine.)

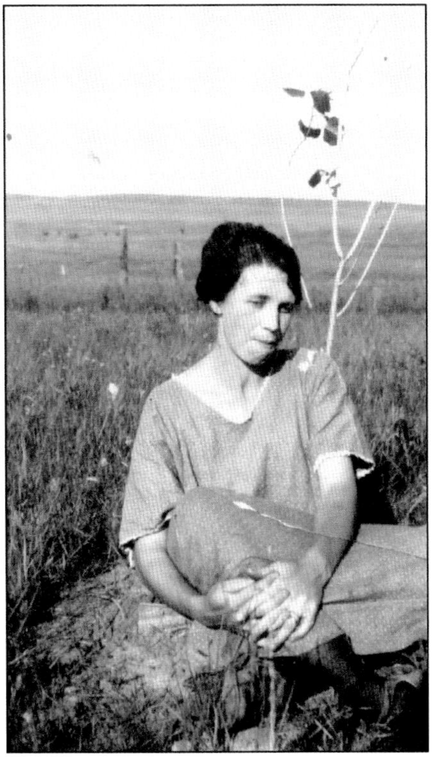

Gladys Degnan looks wistful as she sits near a newly planted tree. Could she be imagining the shade the tree will one day yield? Or is she dreaming of her daughter? (Courtesy of Shortie Gallentine.)

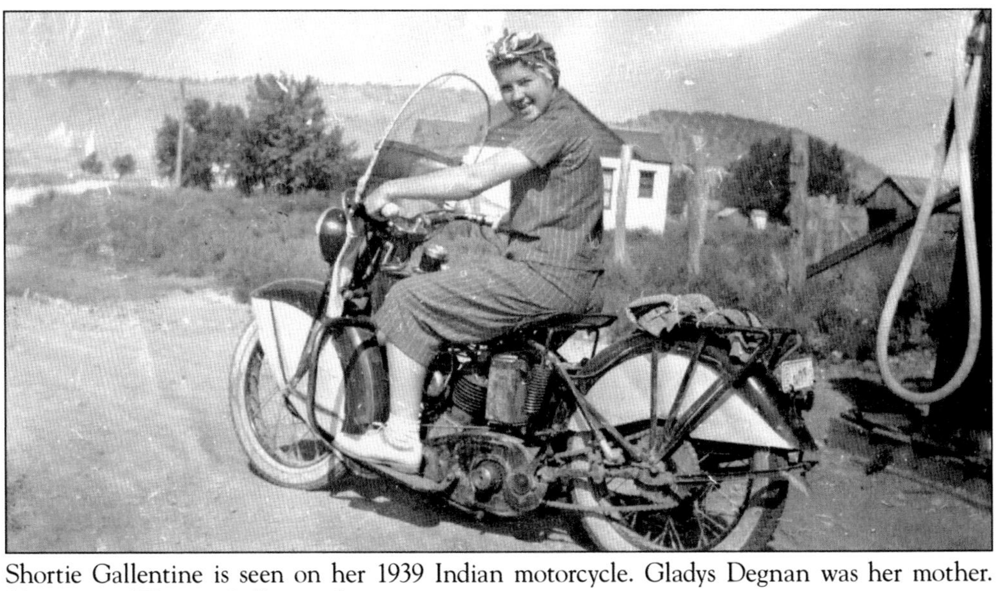

Shortie Gallentine is seen on her 1939 Indian motorcycle. Gladys Degnan was her mother. (Courtesy of Shortie Gallentine.)

Two

TOWN AND COUNTRY

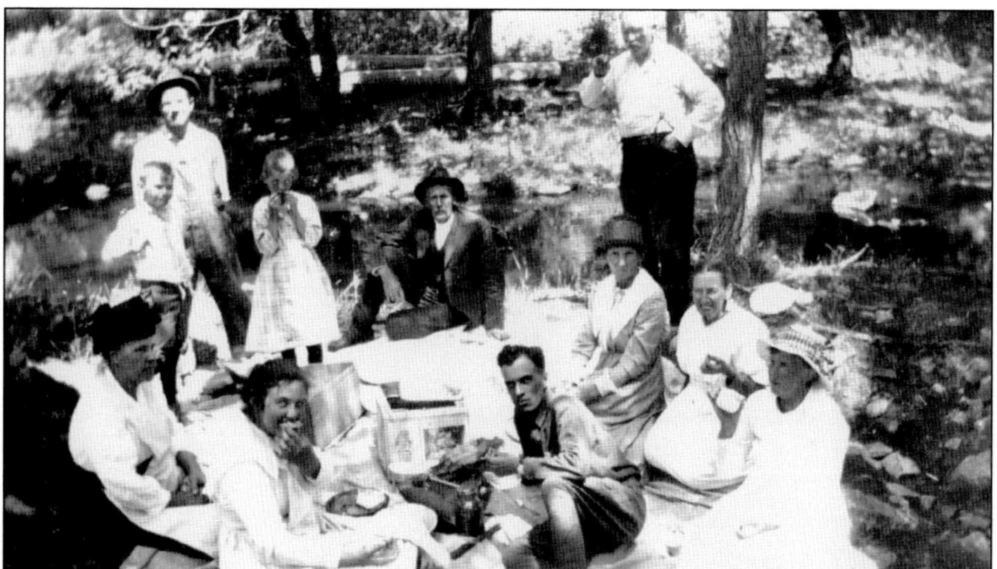

An extended Tillotson family picnic on Beaver Creek in 1919 includes, counterclockwise, (seated) an unidentified woman, Fern Tillotson, Lyston Wyatt, Hattie (Lindsay) Tillotson, Erepta (Lindsay) Parrish, and Electa (Lindsay) Crowley; (standing) Ira Tillotson; (seated) Al Lindsay, Erepta (who was called Rep), and Electa (or Lec). The other man and two children are unidentified. Ira Tillotson is the husband of Hattie and the father of Fern. Al Lindsay is the brother of Hattie. (Author's collection.)

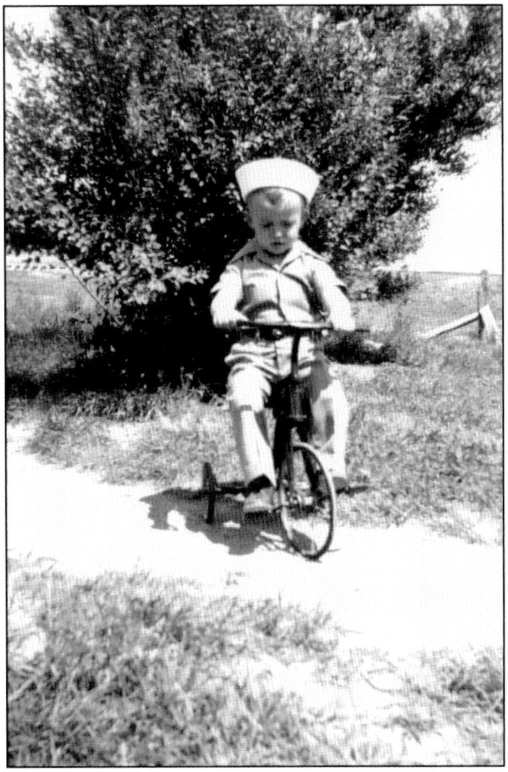

Donnie Sieger spent many hours riding his hard-wheeled tricycle. (Courtesy of Don Sieger.)

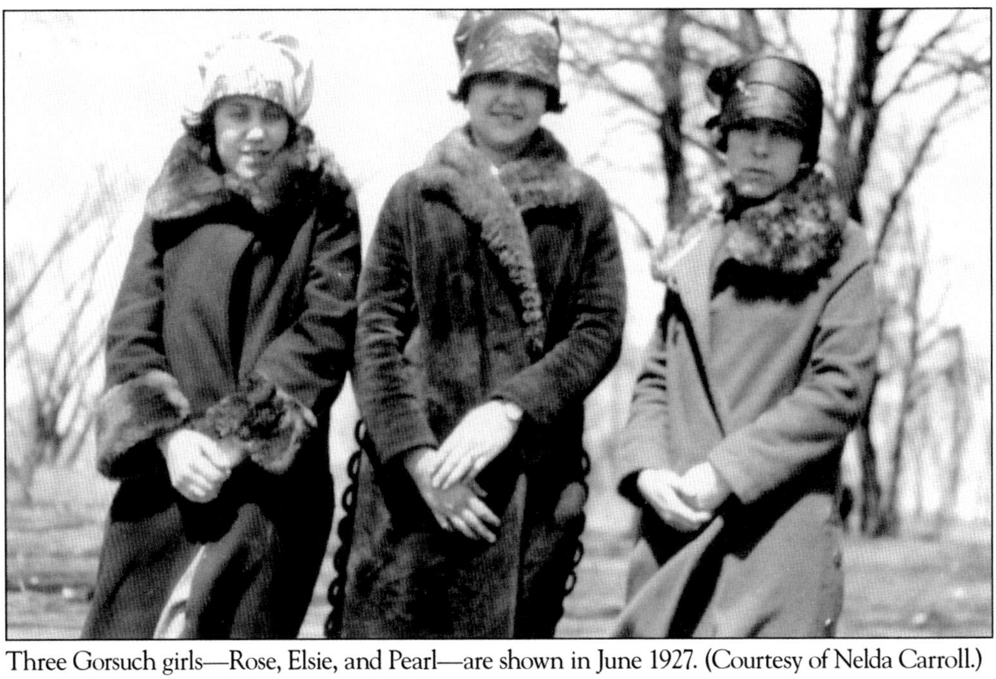

Three Gorsuch girls—Rose, Elsie, and Pearl—are shown in June 1927. (Courtesy of Nelda Carroll.)

Seen here are Miles and Faus Bodenner as little boys. In later years, Miles was a worker in the Civilian Conservation Corps (in Company 1793, Pine Creek) when the CCC built Horsethief Lake near Mount Rushmore. (Courtesy of Pat Roseland.)

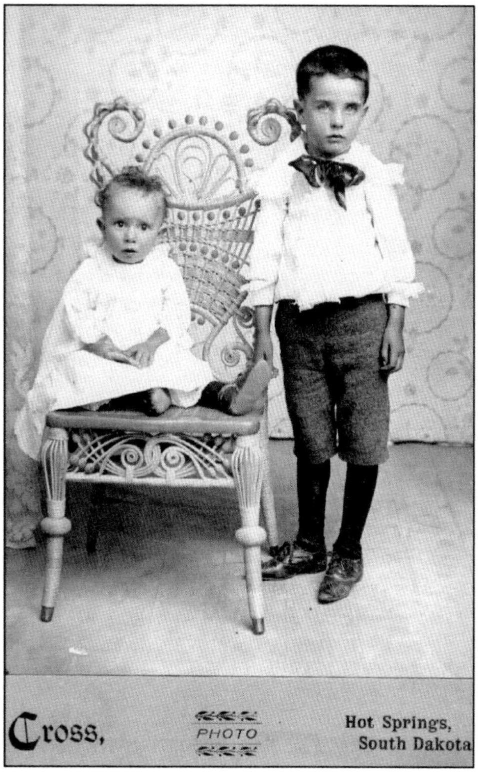

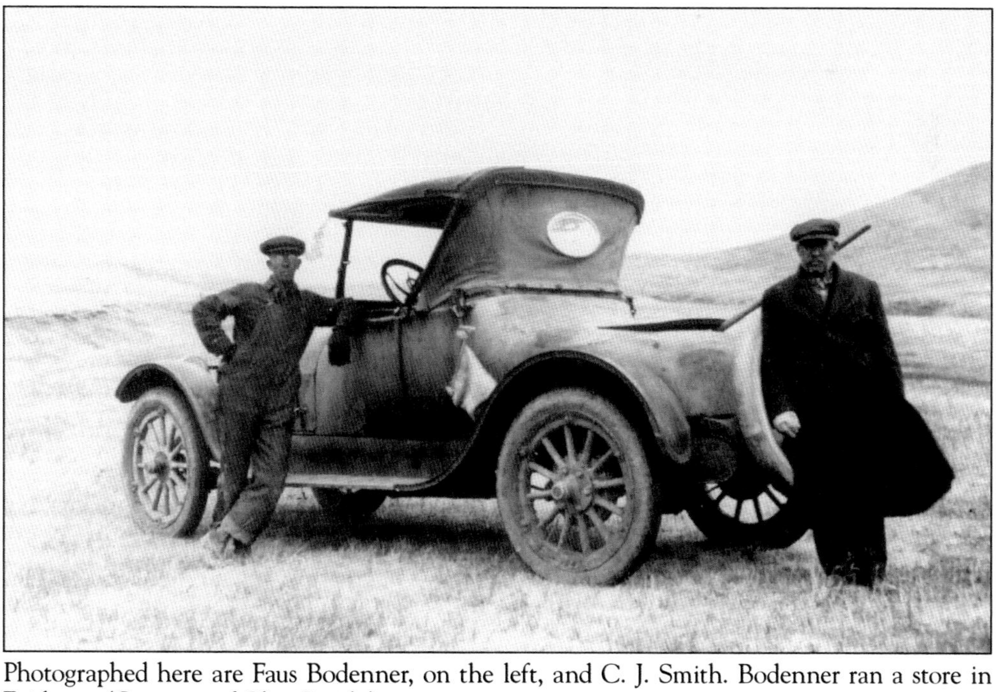

Photographed here are Faus Bodenner, on the left, and C. J. Smith. Bodenner ran a store in Fairburn. (Courtesy of Glen Smith.)

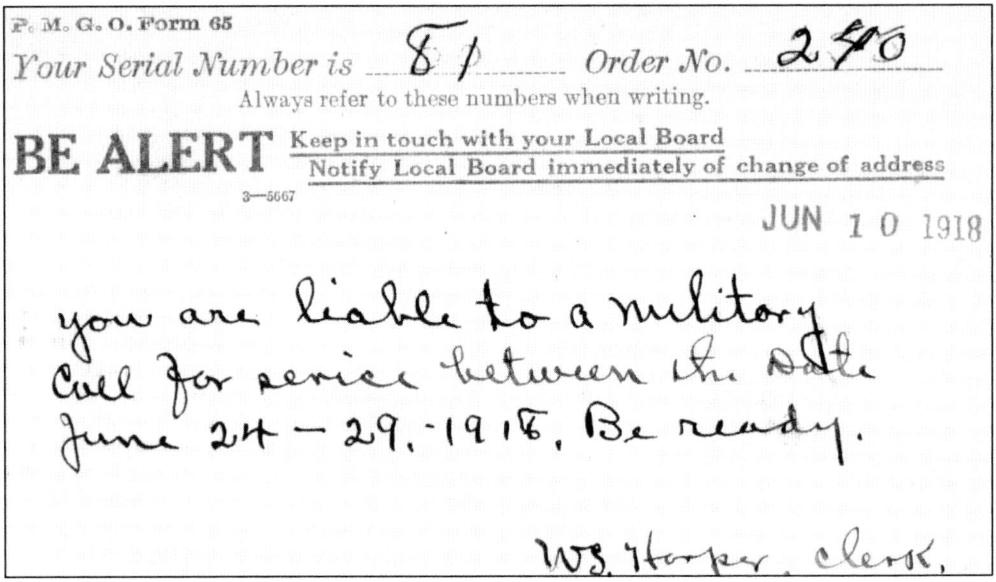

P. M. G. O. Form 65

Your Serial Number is 81 *Order No.* 240

Always refer to these numbers when writing.

BE ALERT Keep in touch with your Local Board
Notify Local Board immediately of change of address

3—5667

JUN 10 1918

you are liable to a military Call for serice between the date June 24 – 29. 1918. Be ready.

W.S. Harper, Clerk.

This notice was received by Furman Smith. (Courtesy of Glen Smith.)

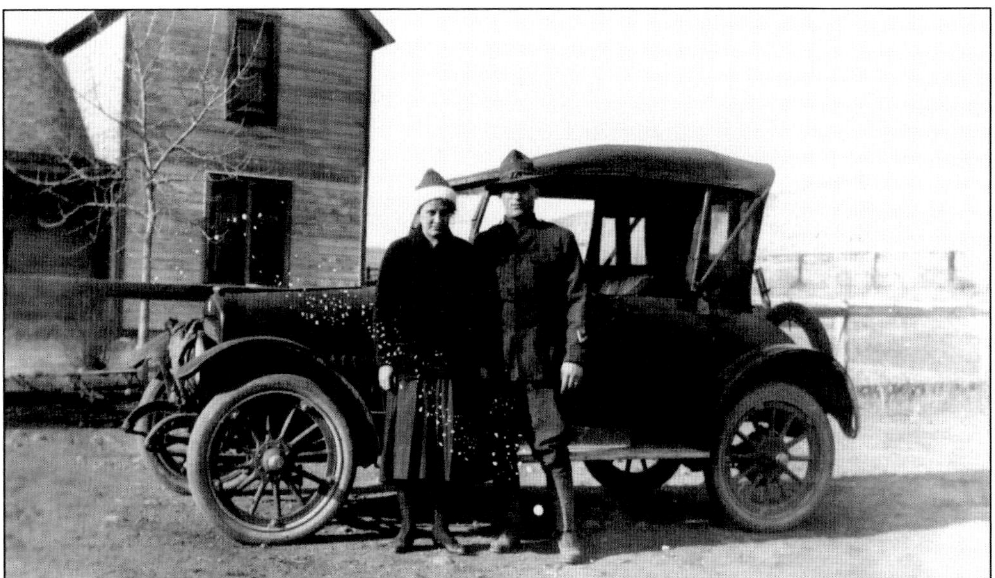

Merle and Furman Smith are standing next to their Dort car and their home in 1919. They were married on May 8, 1918. (Courtesy of Glen Smith.)

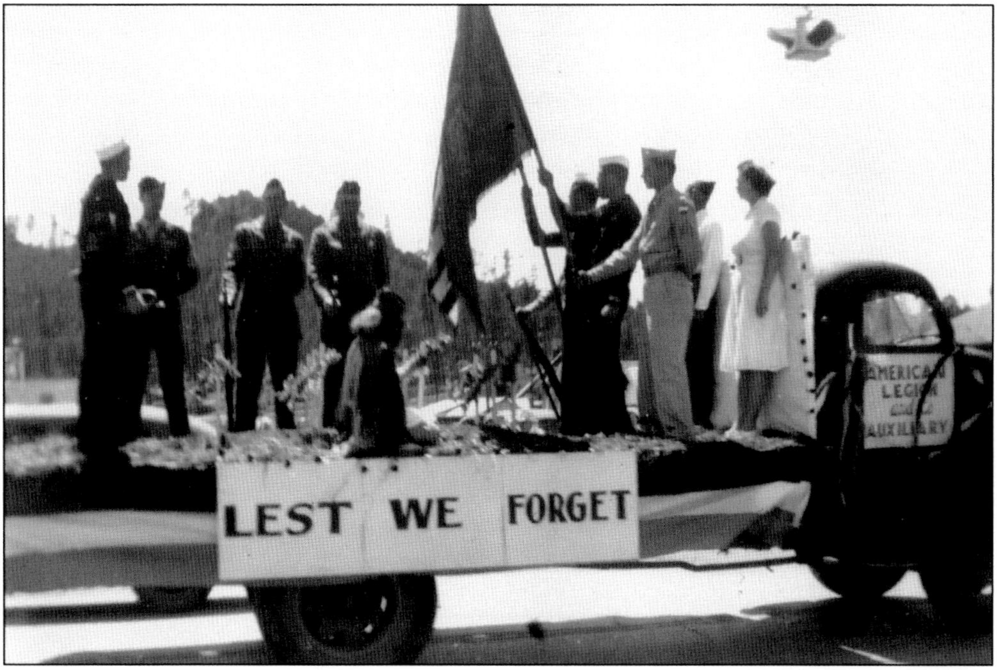

Gold Discovery Days was started in Custer in 1924. Over the years, there have been rodeos, pageants, parades, and other events associated with the event, held annually the fourth weekend in July. This American Legion patriotic float was part of the parade. (Courtesy of Russell Wyatt.)

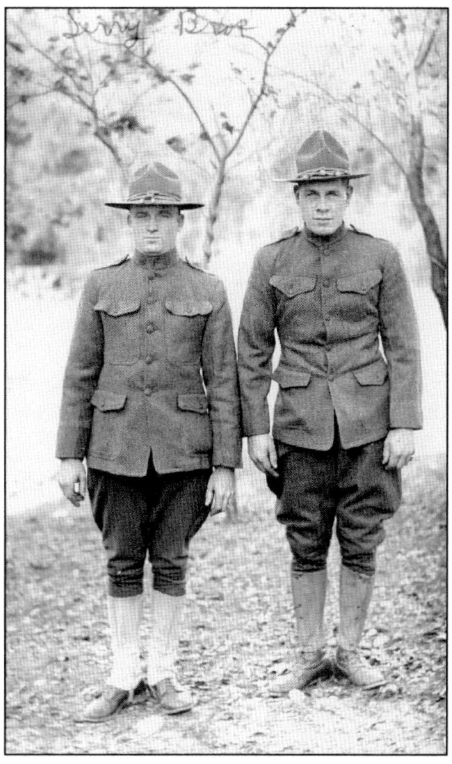

The Serry brothers from Argyle, South Dakota, served their country in World War I. (Courtesy of Wayne Kewley.)

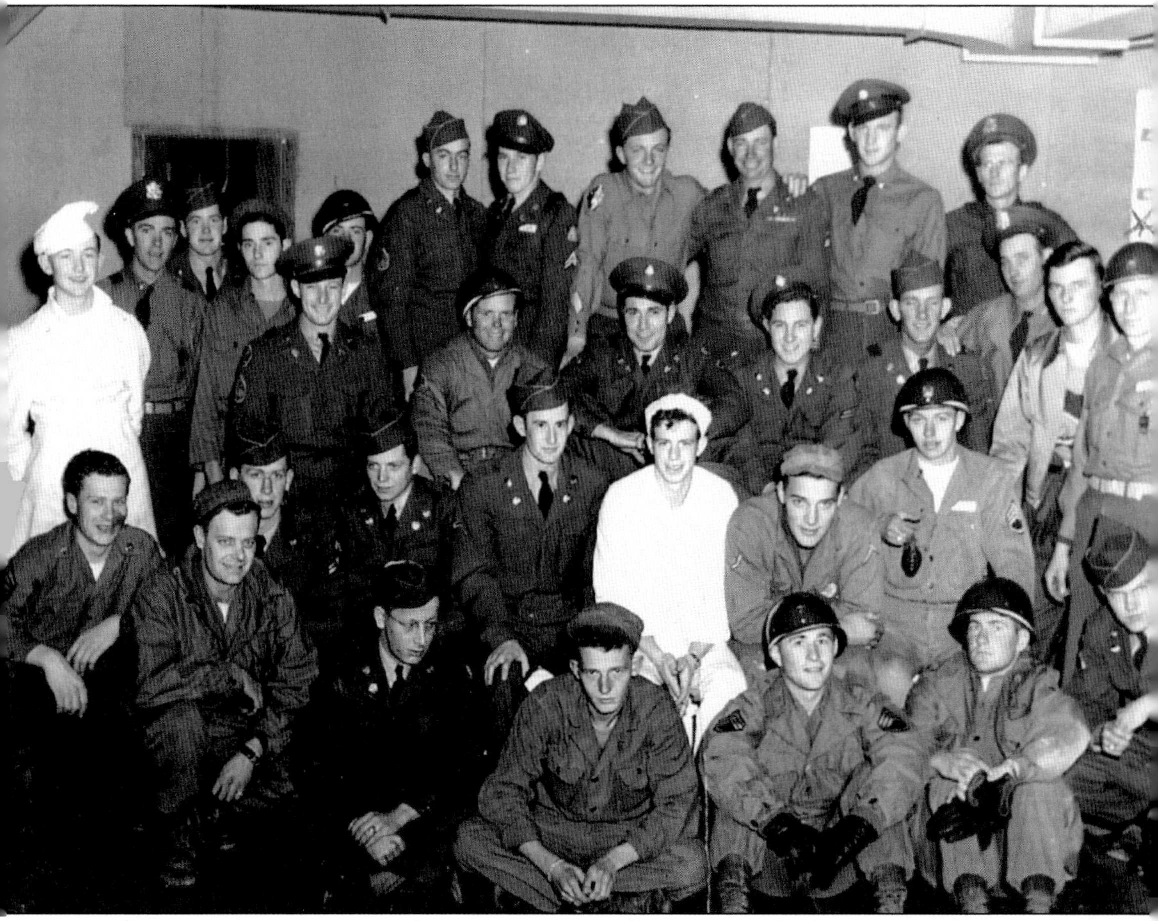

The 200th Engineering Combat Company out of Custer, attached to the 196th Regimental Combat Team of the South Dakota National Guard, was called to active duty on September 1, 1950. From left to right are the following: (first row) Sfc. Glen Harley, Corporal Lang, Private Willey, Pvt. Ed Turner, Sergeant Howes, Corporal Kendall, and Private First Class Olson; (second row) Corporal Garvey, Private Stratton, Private First Class Love, Private First Class Compton, Private First Class Nielsen, and Sergeant Landis; (third row) Sergeant First Class Slawson, Sergeant Kautzsch, Cpl. Bill Theison, Cpl. Don Theison, Pvt. Joe Hammer, Lieutenant Harbach (commanding officer), and Corporal Turner; (fourth row) Private Martin, Lieutenant Williams, Corporal Borgen, Private Crofutt, Sergeant Harris, Sergeant Best, Corporal Scott, Private Johnson, Corporal Leach, Pfc. Gene Hammer, and Lieutenant Barnes. (Identifications and photograph courtesy of M.Sgt. Carl E. Clements.)

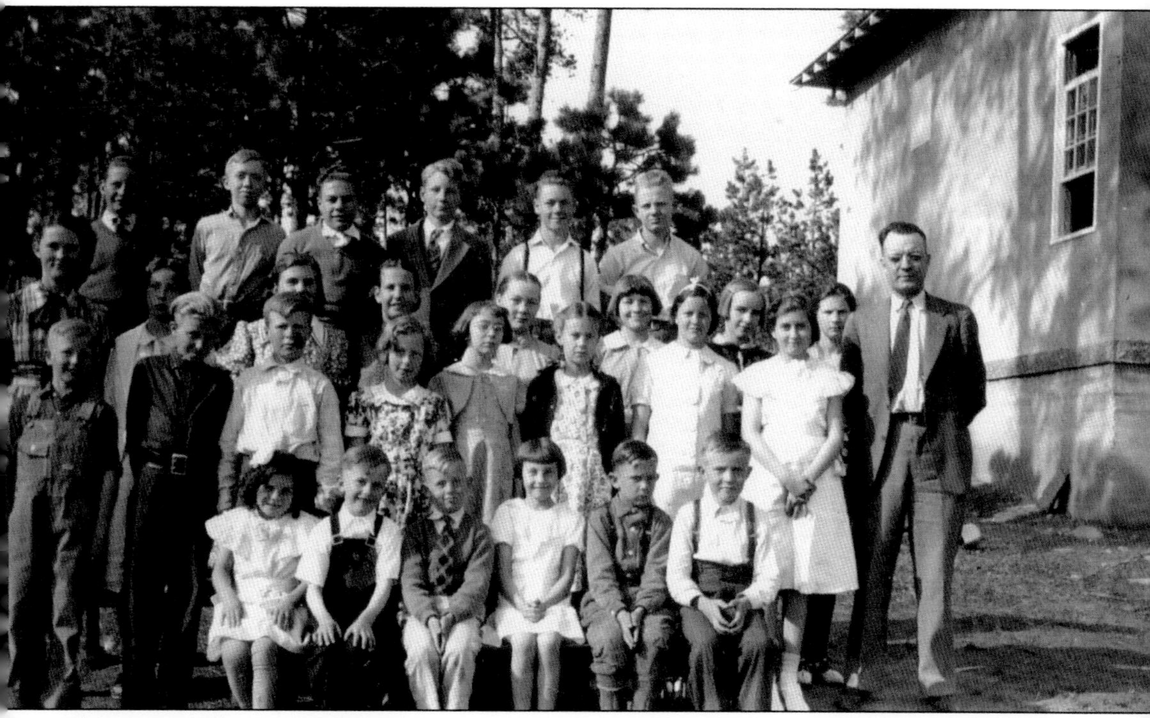

The Sanator Elementary School was attended by students who lived nearby. Only the Harley children are identified. Ann is on the left in the first row, and Glen is directly behind Ann. Oleta, in the flowered dress, is to the right of Glen. LeRoy is the tall young man in a suit standing in the back row. (Courtesy of Russell Wyatt.)

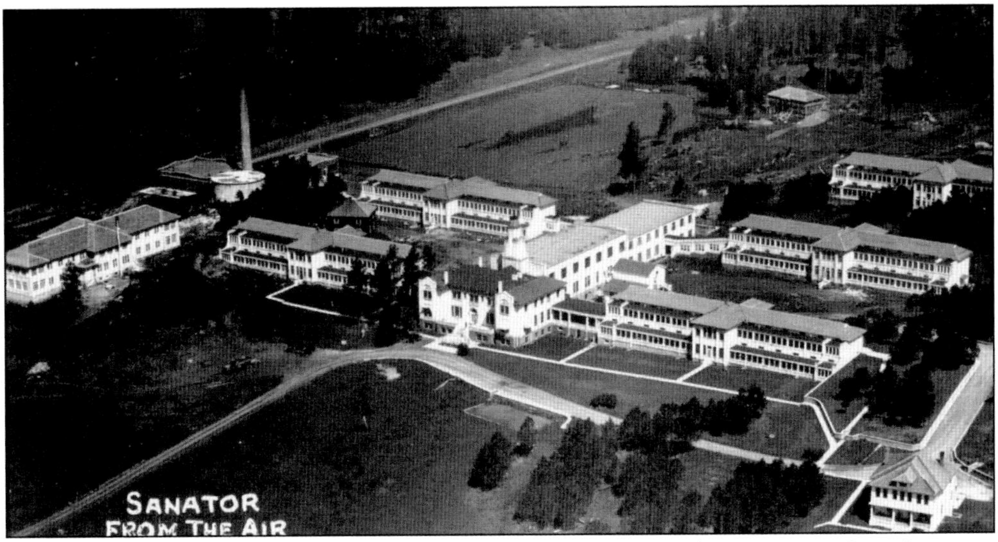

The South Dakota Sanatorium for Tuberculosis opened in 1911 with 14 patients. Over the years, additional buildings were constructed as the need arose and finances allowed. Sanator, as it is called, used milk from its own dairy herd. (Courtesy of Gladys Reed.)

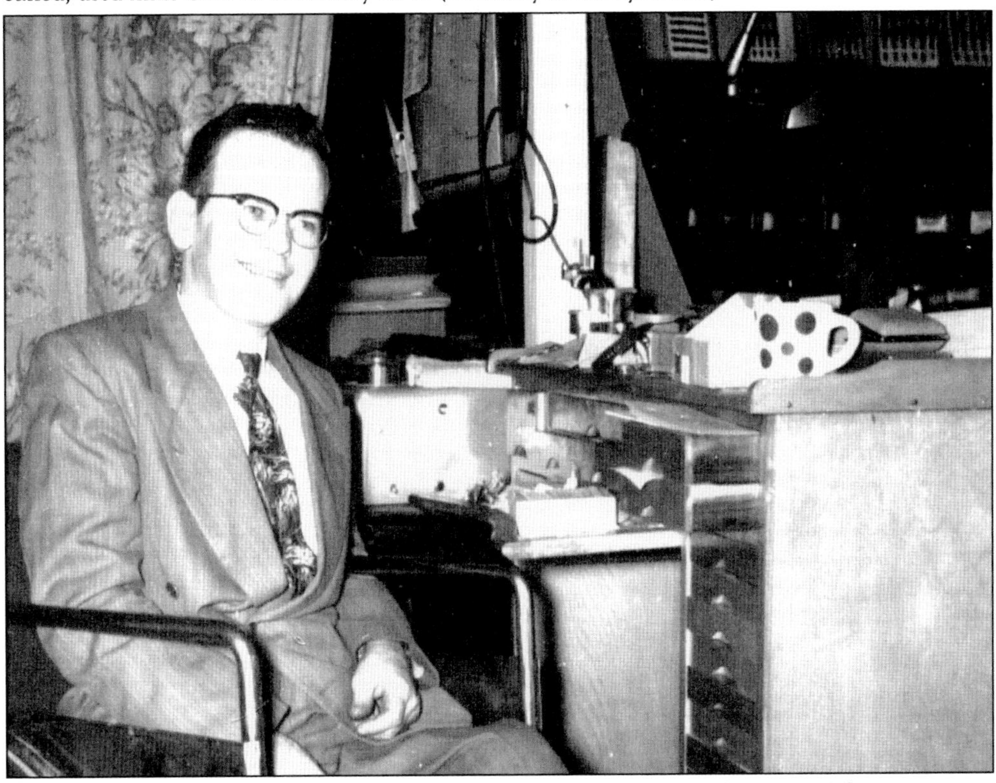
Jim Paulsen from Ardmore, South Dakota, contracted polio in November 1946. After treatments and rehabilitation, his legs remained paralyzed. In March 1953, Paulsen moved to Sanator, where he attended the Bulova School of Watchmaking. After he completed the course in July 1954, he worked for the Edgemont Drug and Jewelry Company and eventually had his own business. (Courtesy of Avelda Walker and Leona McMaster.)

Three

MAKING A LIVING

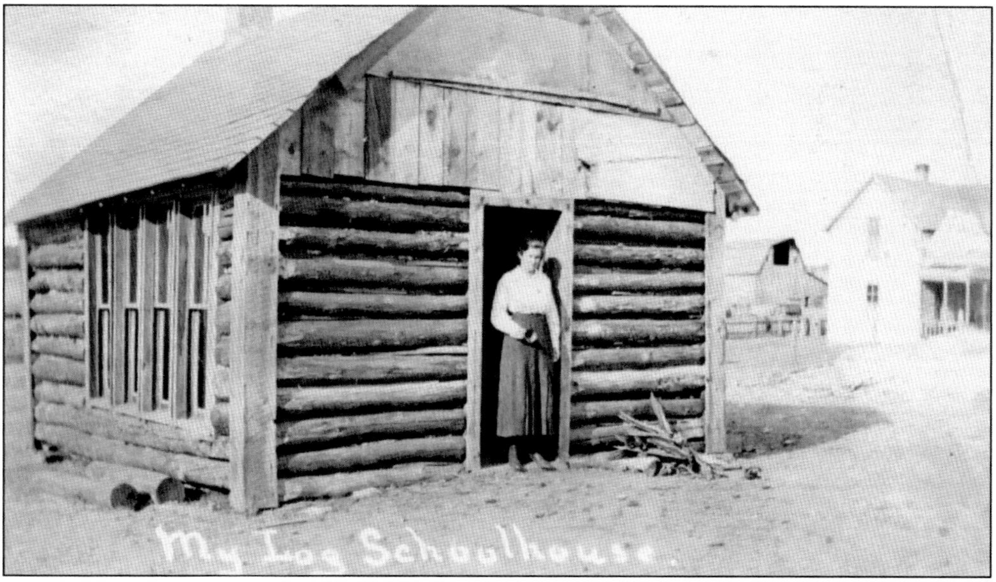

Fern Tillotson was born on June 11, 1900. As was common for teachers at the time, she began teaching school when she was 17 years old. She continued to teach, eventually went to college, and taught in many western South Dakota schools, including Harrison Flat, east of Buffalo Gap. (Author's collection.)

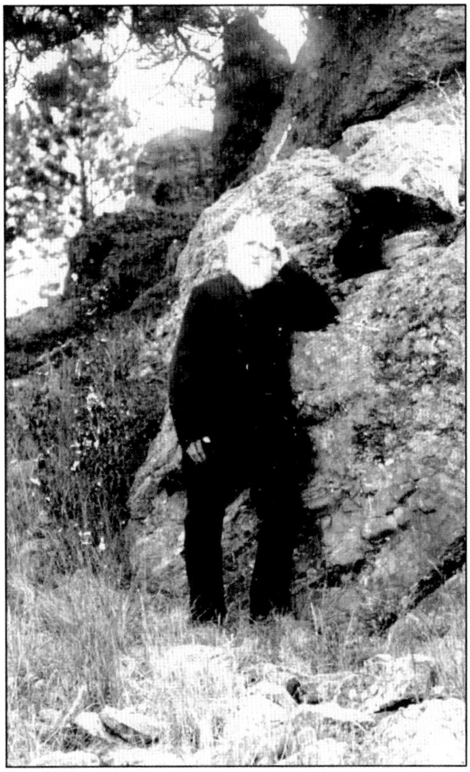

Peter Carr came from Ireland to Iowa in 1845. When Henry Pringle and his wife, Anna (Peter Carr's daughter), moved from Center Point, Iowa, to Point of Rocks in 1885, Peter came with them. (Courtesy of Leonard and Oonagh Wood.)

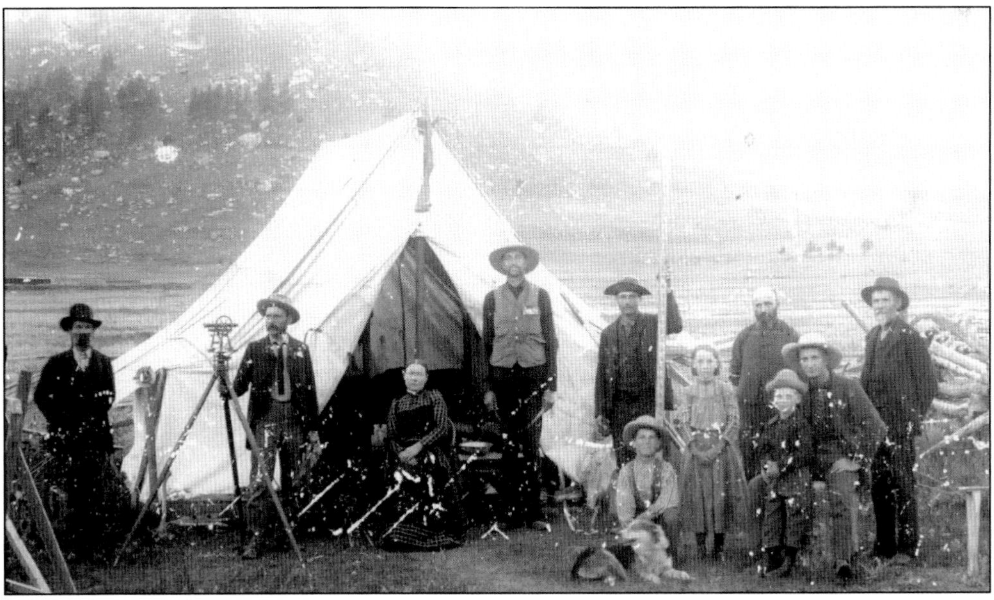

Railroad surveyors camped in their tents as they did their work at Point of Rocks. The Pringle family fed the surveyors, and the story goes that the surveyors named the town in their honor, changing the name from Point of Rocks to Pringle. (Courtesy of Leonard and Oonagh Wood.)

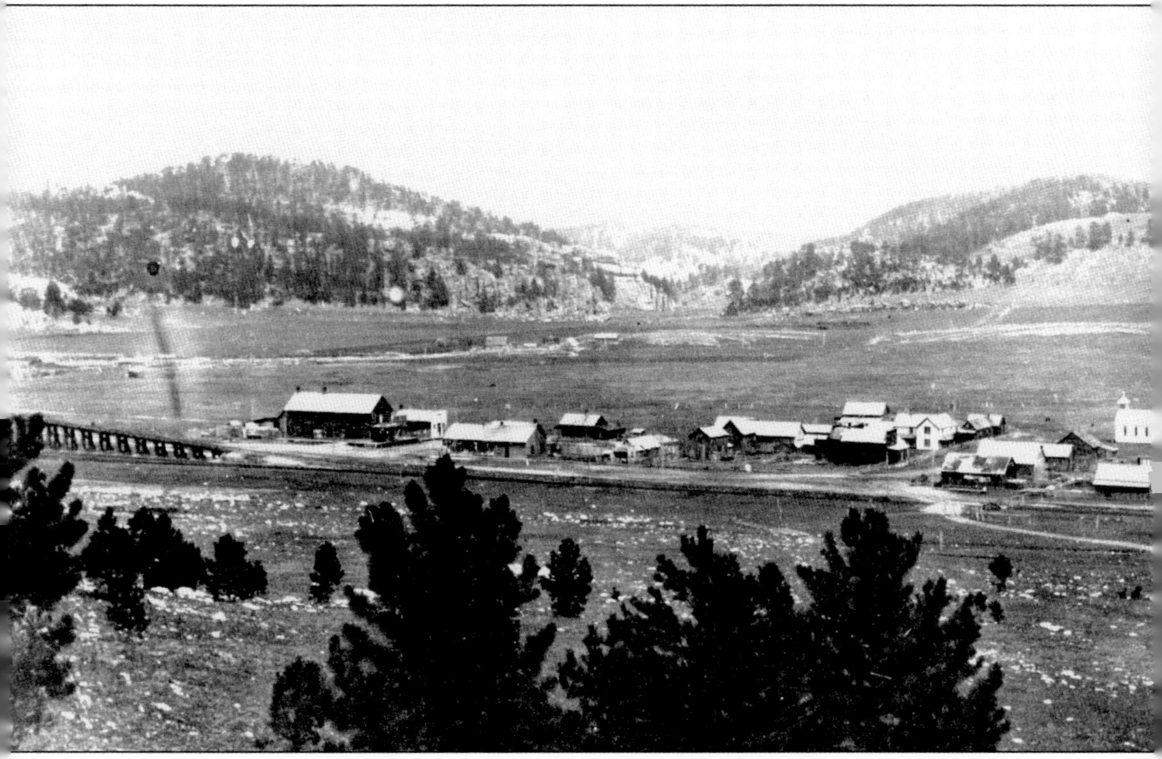

The early photograph of Pringle shows the coal chute, which along with a water tower, turned Pringle into a train re-coaling station on the Burlington and Missouri River Railroad (B&M). It later became the Chicago, Burlington and Quincy Railroad (CB&Q). (Courtesy of Leonard and Oonagh Wood.)

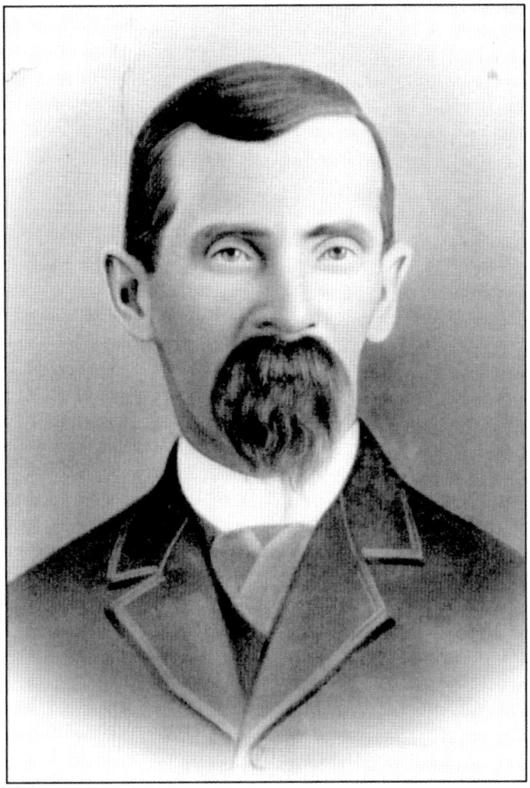

Henry Pringle, along with his family, ran the Point of Rocks stage stop. (Courtesy of Leonard and Oonagh Wood.)

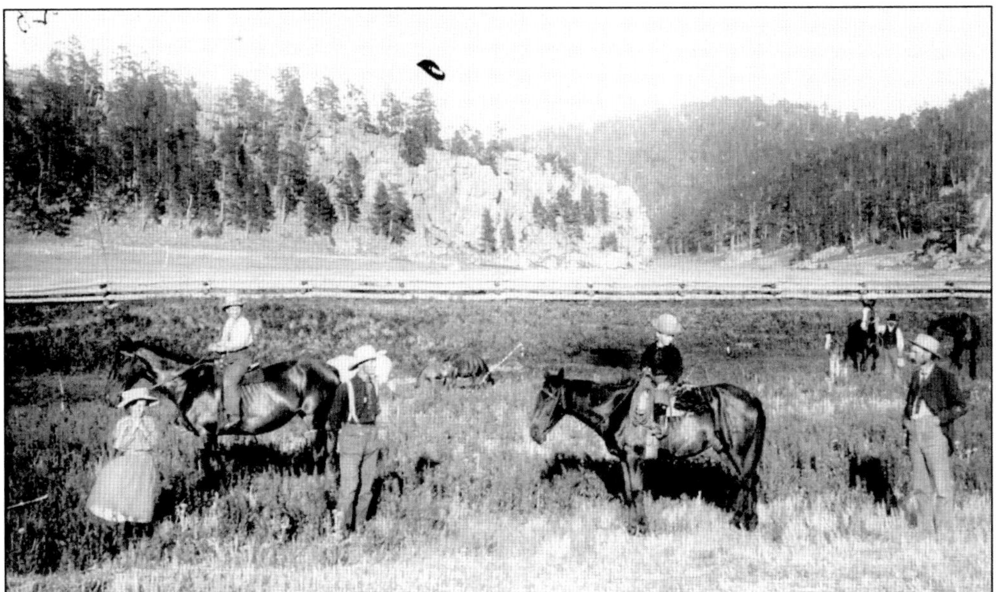

In 1887, near Pringle, the photograph shows Point of Rocks in the background. A note written (likely by Myrtle Pringle) on the back of the photograph reads, "My dad brought the horses from Center Point, Iowa in 1885." (Courtesy of Leonard and Oonagh Wood.)

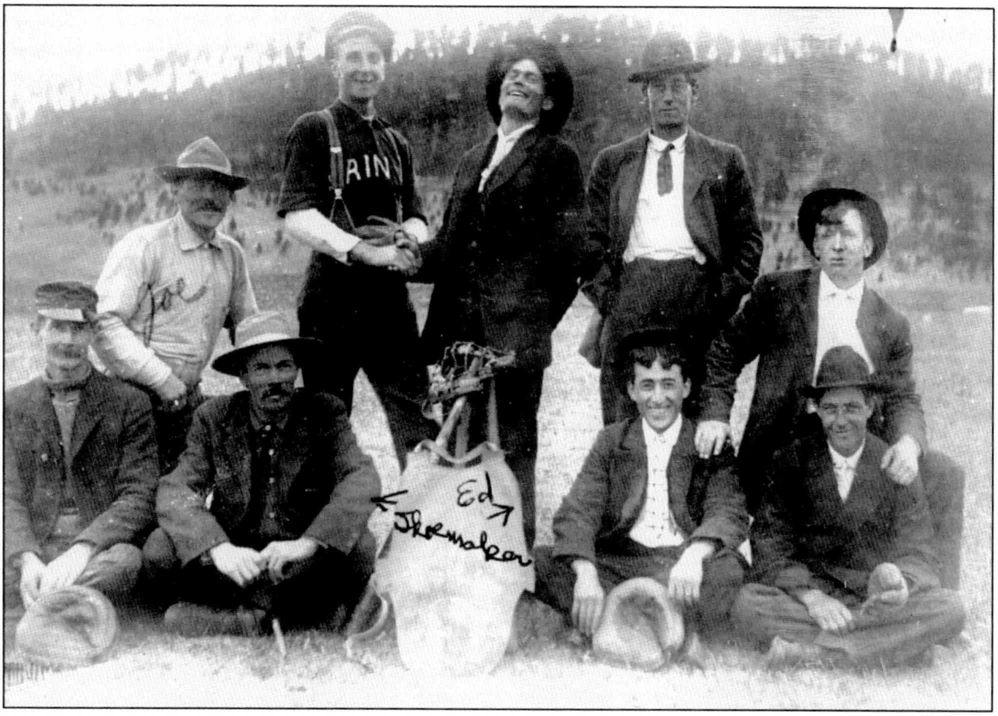

The Joe in this photograph is Joe Conlon. The other men on this Pringle baseball team who are identified are Theo Shoemaker and Ed Shalhoob. Bill Wolfe is named on the back of the photograph but not specifically identified. (Courtesy of Leonard and Oonagh Wood.)

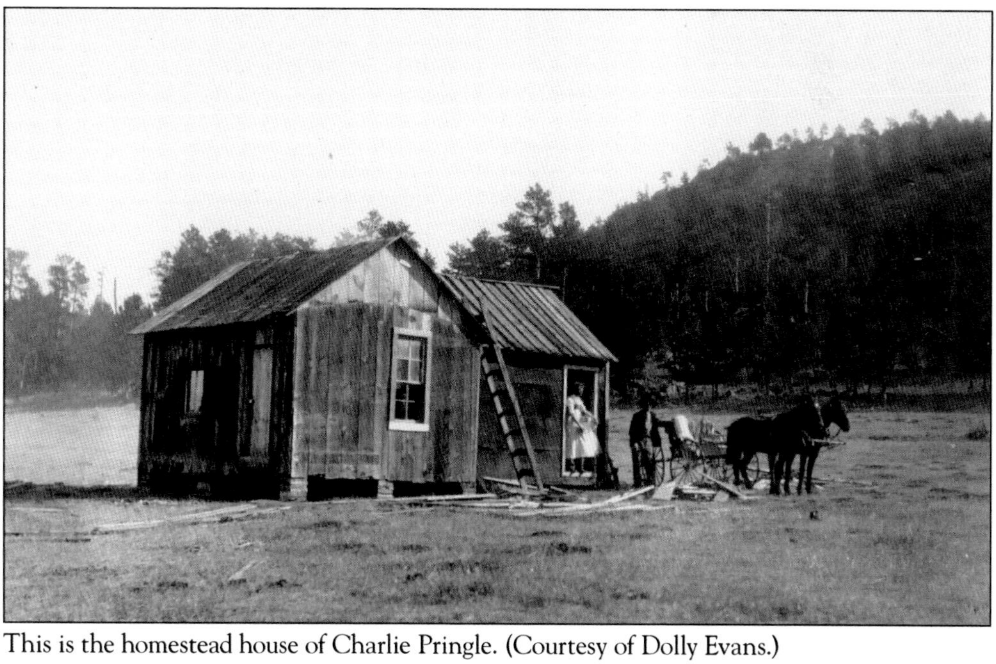

This is the homestead house of Charlie Pringle. (Courtesy of Dolly Evans.)

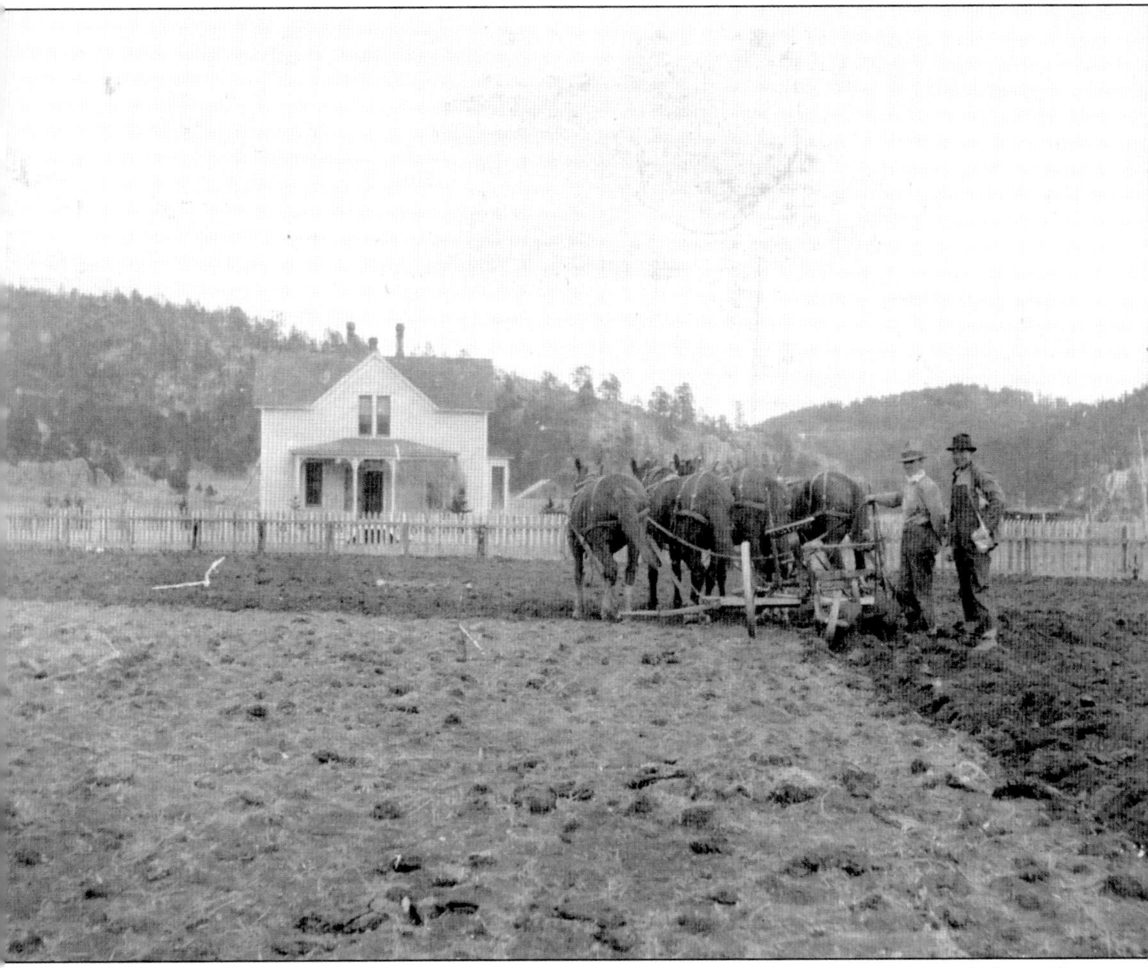

In 1890, this home had running water, glass windows, and an indoor bathroom. It belonged to Anna Agnes Carr Pringle Wolfe, who took in boarders. In this view, Charlie Pringle and John Wolfe are turning sod. (Courtesy of Dolly Evans.)

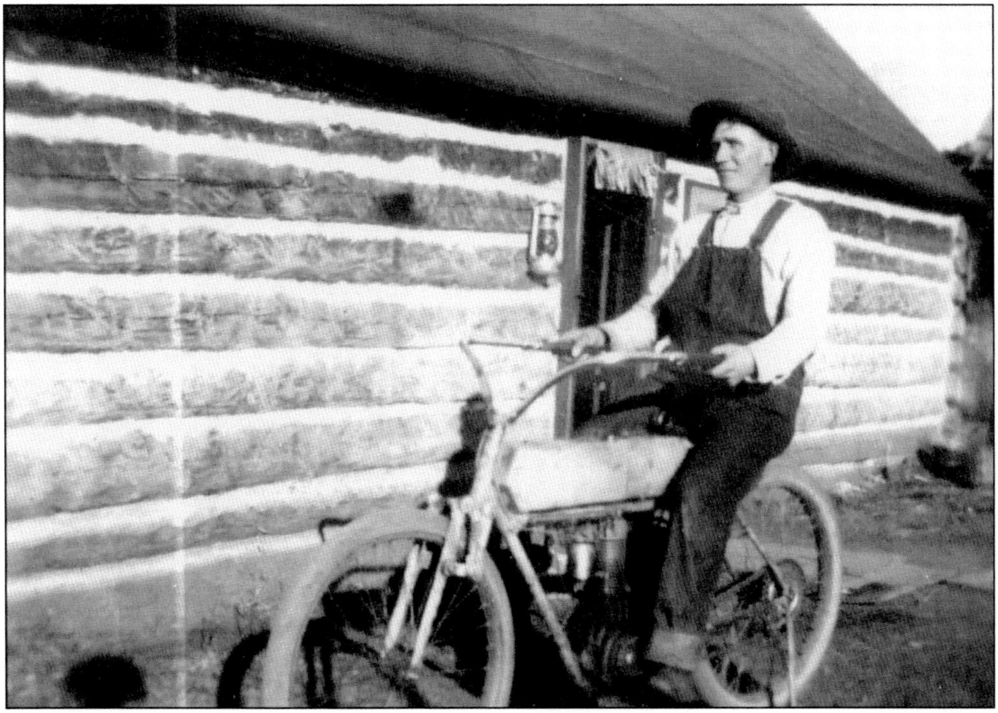

Seen here is Earl Tanner on an early motorcycle, possibly an Excelsior or a Norton. He lived in the Cold Springs area east of Pringle. (Courtesy of Dolly Evans.)

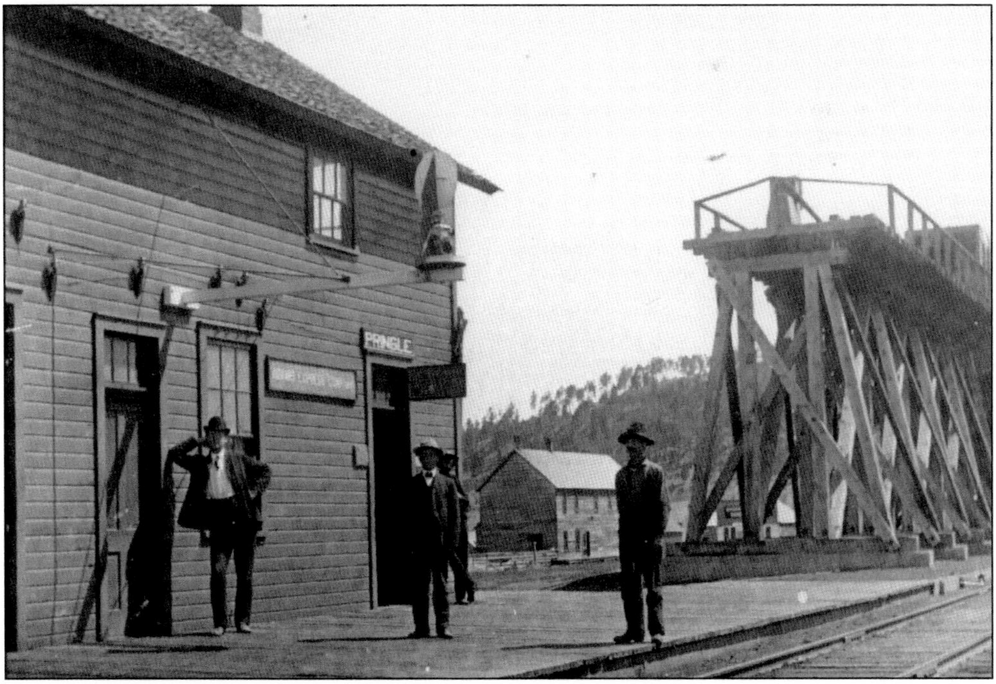

Three unidentified men are waiting for the train at the Pringle depot. (Courtesy of Dolly Evans.)

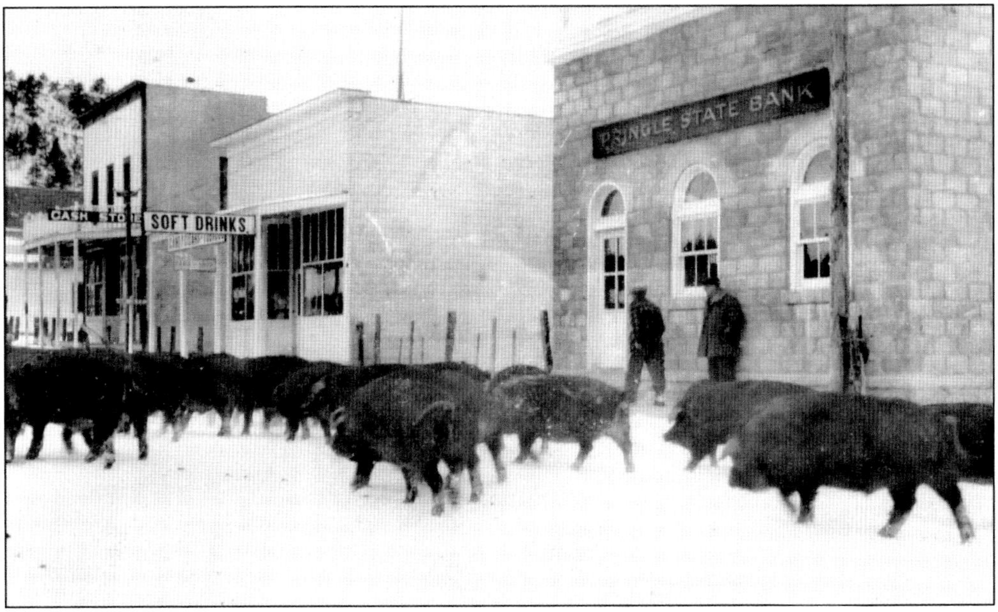

This series of photographs shows Charlie Pringle and his helpers herding pigs to the Pringle Stockyards west of Main Street, across the train tracks. The animals walked up a solid board incline from the stockyards to get onto the train for transport to market. (Courtesy of Dolly Evans.)

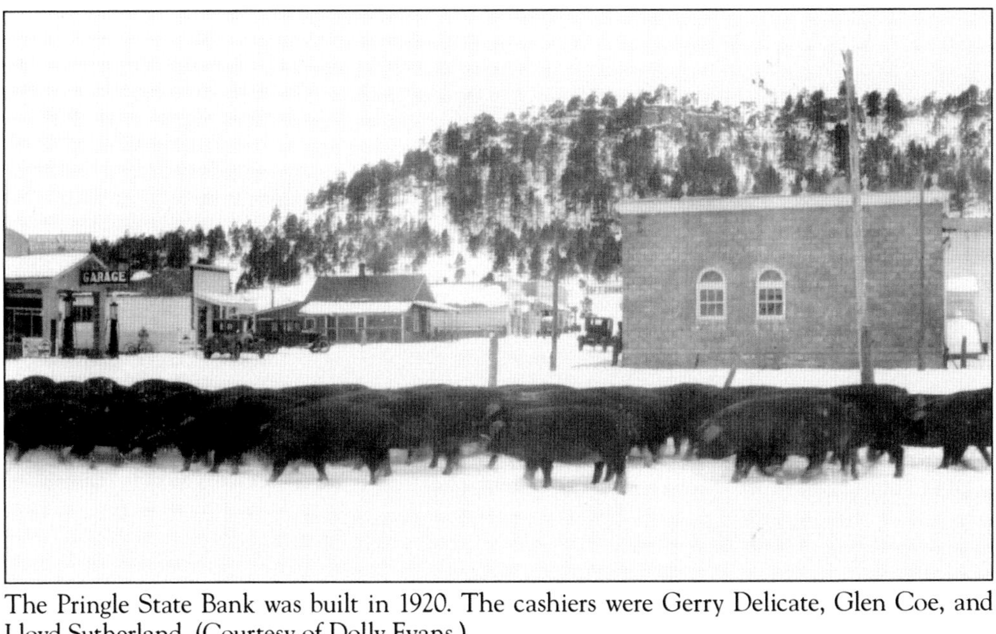

The Pringle State Bank was built in 1920. The cashiers were Gerry Delicate, Glen Coe, and Lloyd Sutherland. (Courtesy of Dolly Evans.)

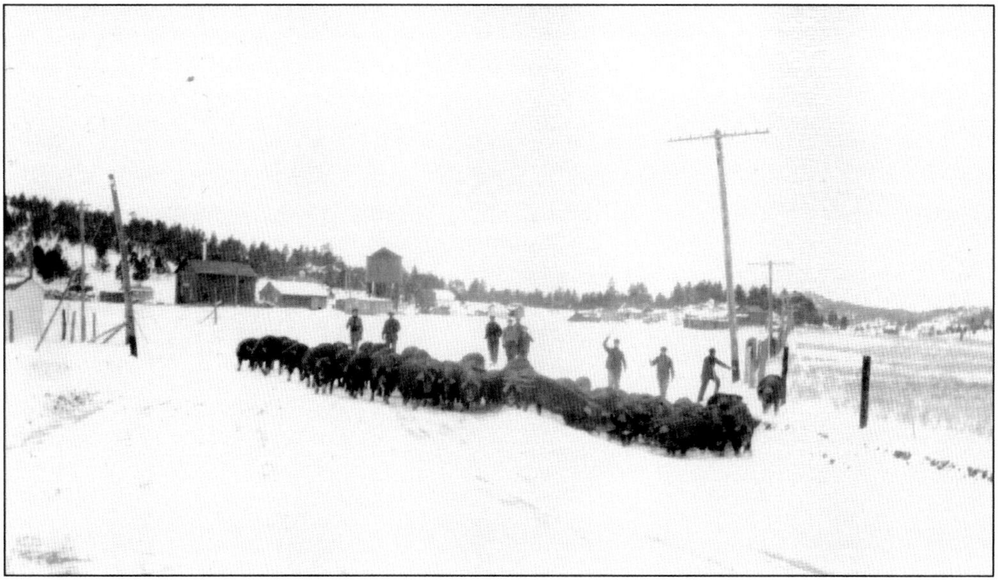

This photograph offers another view of Charlie Pringle's workers. (Courtesy of Dolly Evans.)

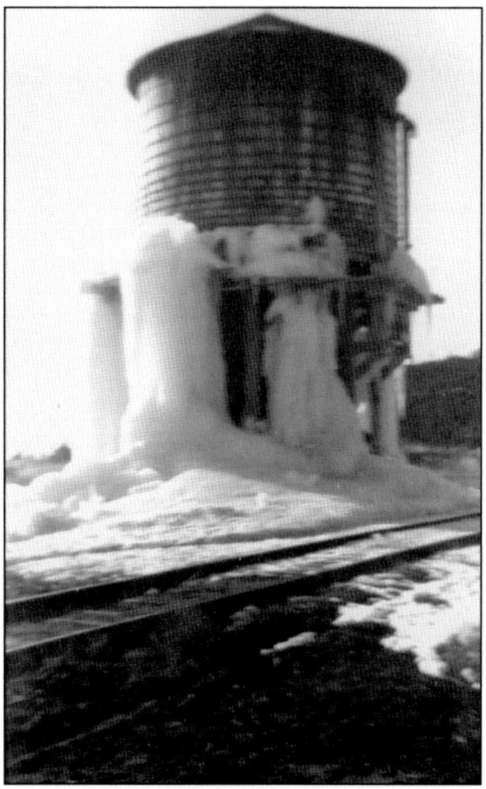

The frozen water tower at the Pringle depot was no longer in use by the railroad when this picture was taken. (Courtesy of Gladys Reed.)

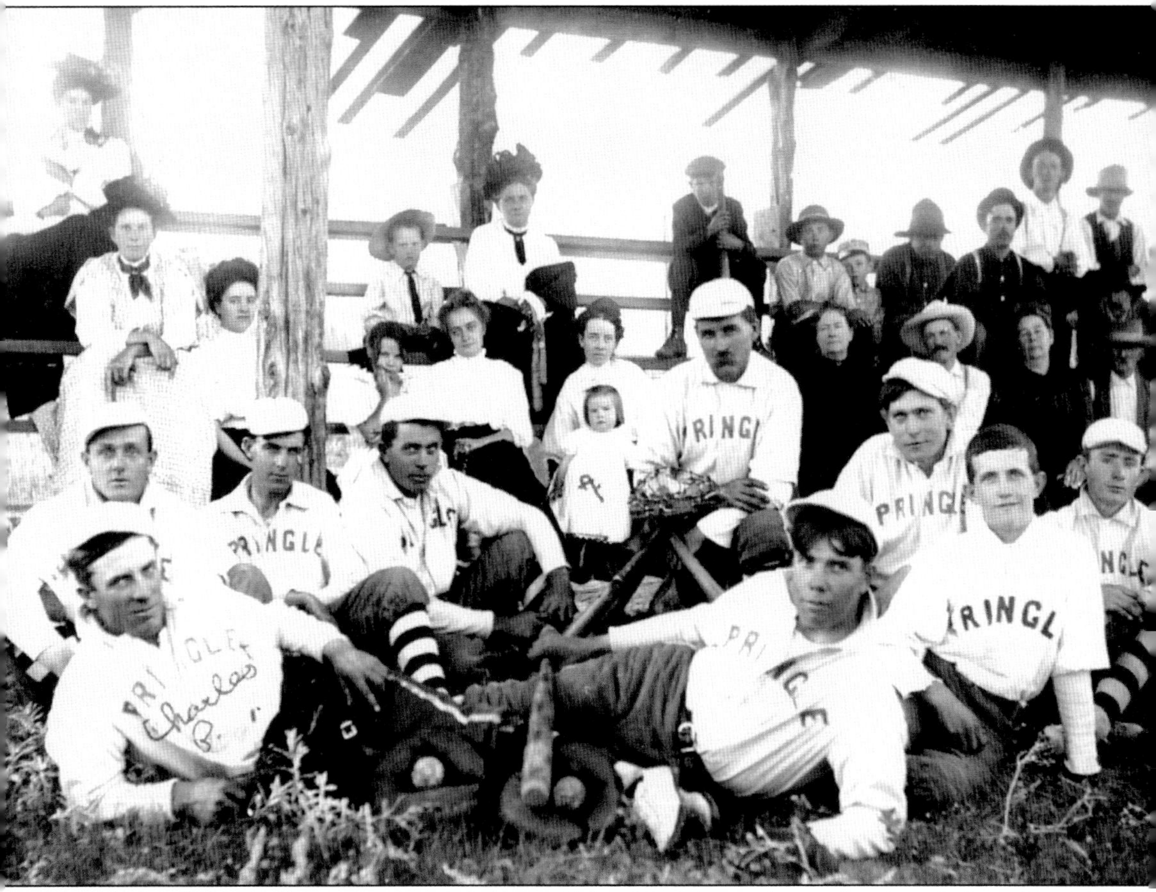

A Pringle baseball team poses with friends and families. Those who can be identified are Charlie Pringle (bottom left) and Victor Ross (bottom right). The infant in the center is Anna Marie Conlon, and her mother, Myrtle Conlon, is directly behind her. In the center, the man with the black mustache is Miles Raver. Anna Agnes Wolfe is the first woman to their right, wearing a black dress. Seated next to her is Joe Conlon. Next are Mary and Billy Fenwick. The woman in center back, sitting up high, is Mrs. Stanton. (Courtesy of Leonard and Oonagh Wood.)

Charlie Pringle created a potato-based feed for his hogs. He used two parts of wheat, two parts of barley, and one part of oats (ground up together) with four to eight bushels of chopped up potatoes, which he cooked all together in vats. Pringle did this because to have corn shipped in would have cost him $1.10 per bushel, and he had plenty of potatoes. On one of his sales, he marketed 87 head of 295-pound Duroc hogs at the day's top price of $10. (Courtesy of Dolly Evans.)

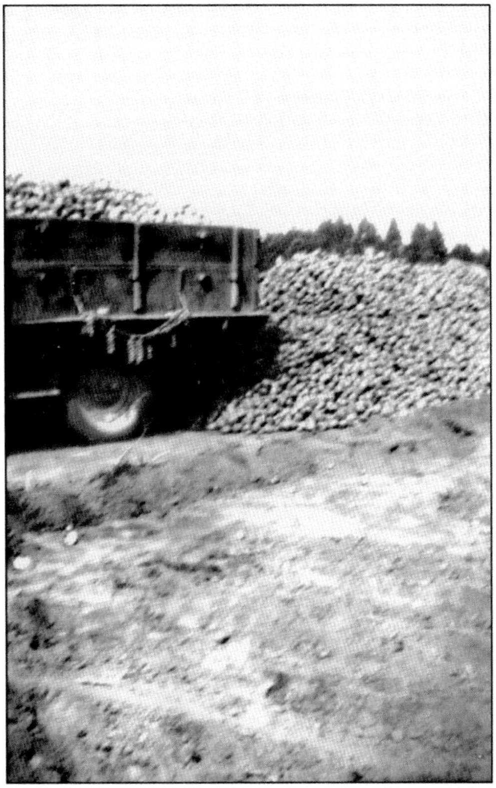

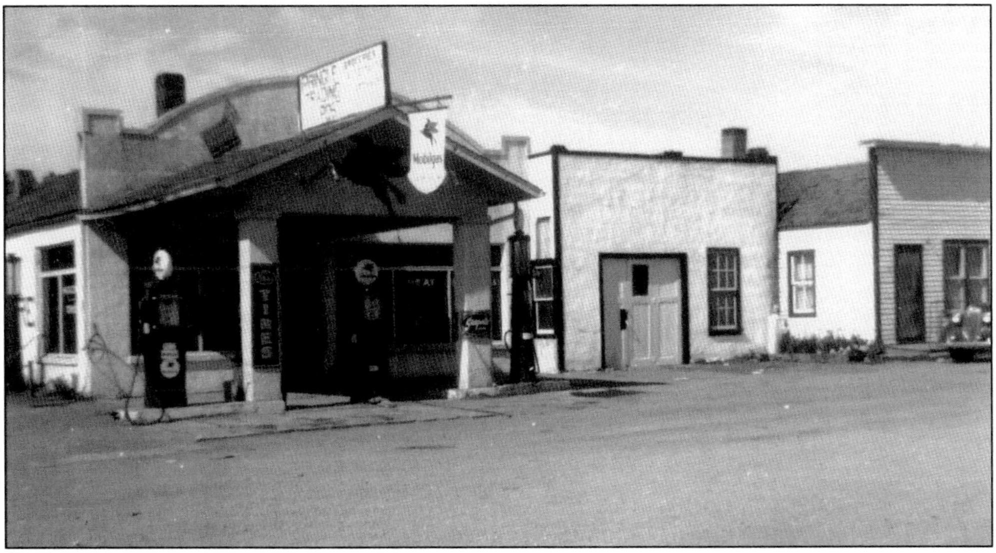

The Pringle Trading Post is now called Elk Junction. (Courtesy of Gladys Reed.)

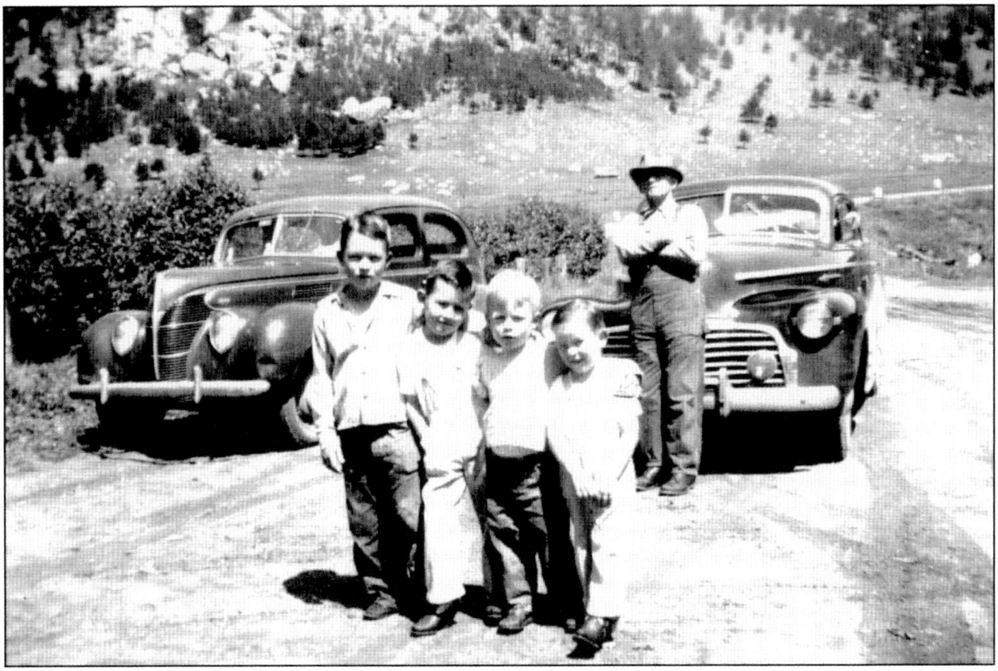

Four grandsons of Joe Conlon are, from left to right, Leonard Joe Wood, Joe Francis Conlon, Robert Eugene Wood, and Thomas Boyd Conlon. Grandfather Joe Conlon stands behind the boys in this June 1947 photograph. (Courtesy of Leonard and Oonagh Wood.)

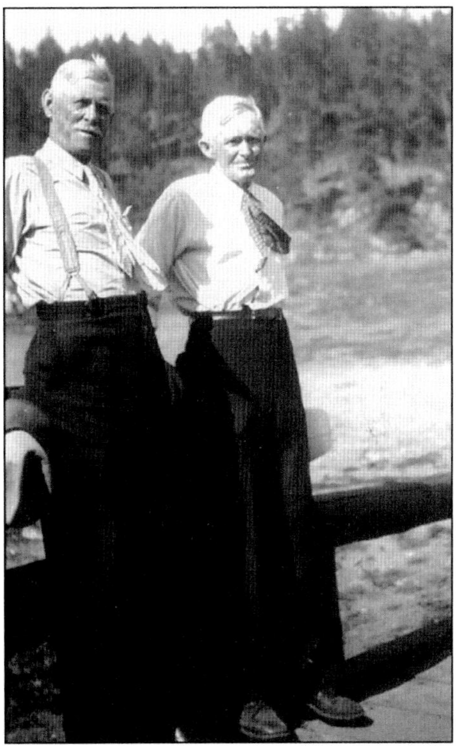

Brothers Joseph Conlon and Martin Conlon are seen on an afternoon outing. (Courtesy of Dolly Evans.)

Shown here are Anna Marie Wood, on the left, and Myrtle Pringle Conlon. The little girl is Dolly Wood. (Courtesy of Dolly Evans.)

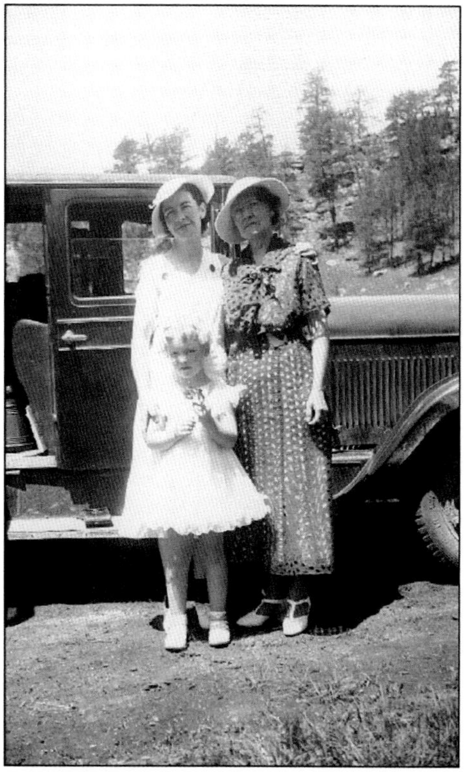

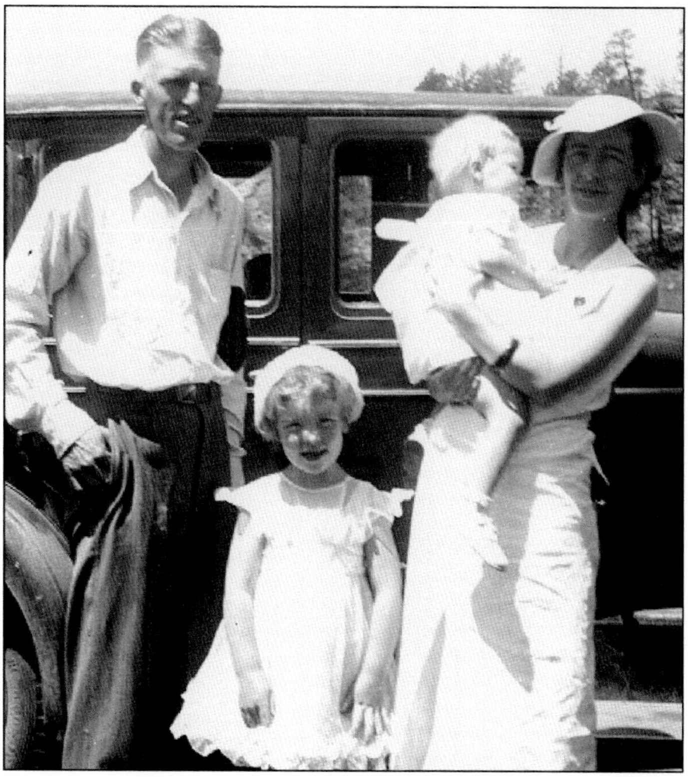

Leonard E. Wood and Anna Marie Wood are shown with daughters Dolly, standing, and Colleen. (Courtesy of Dolly Evans.)

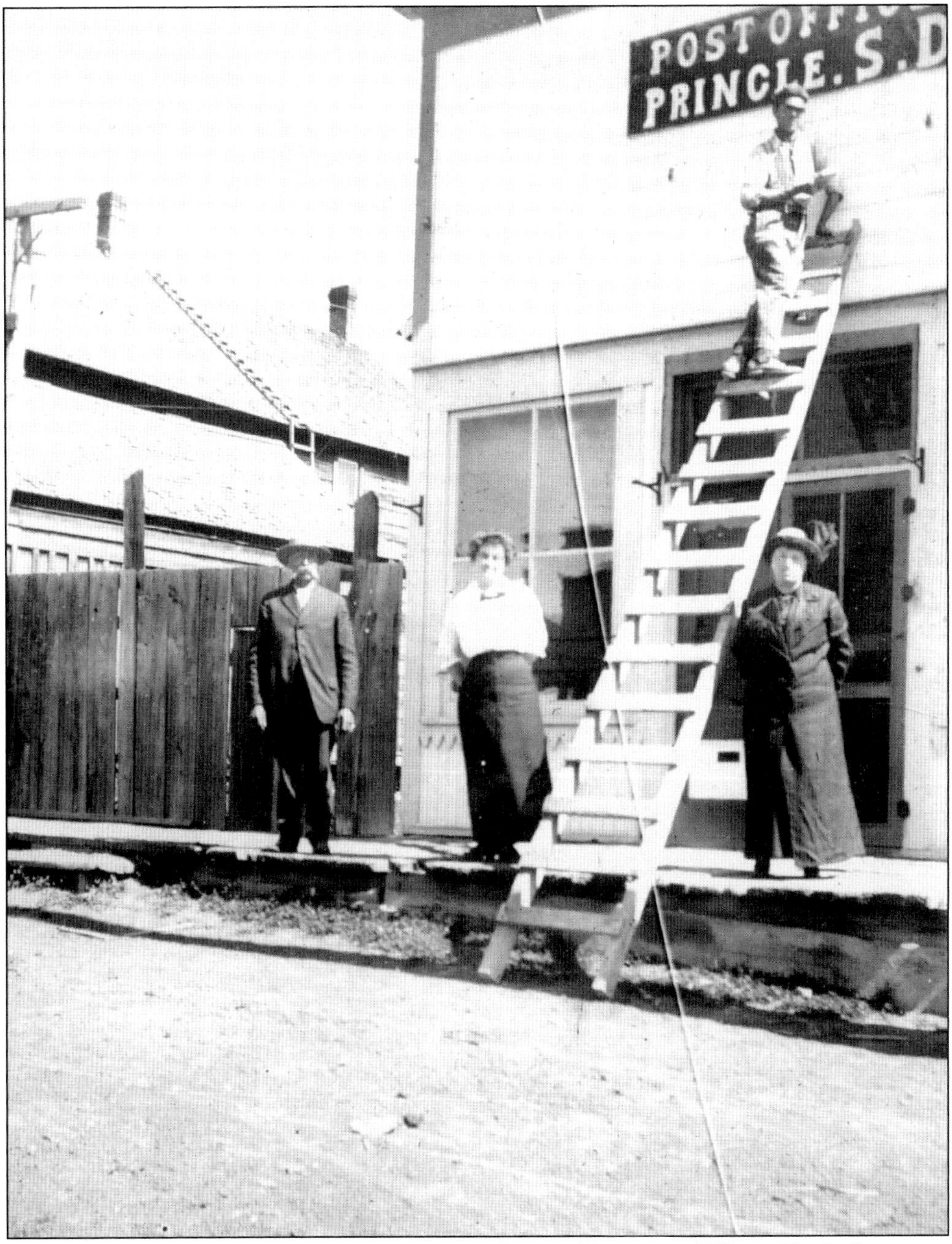

The Pringle Post Office sign receives a new coat of paint. (Courtesy of Wayne Kewley.)

Four

Families Are Forever

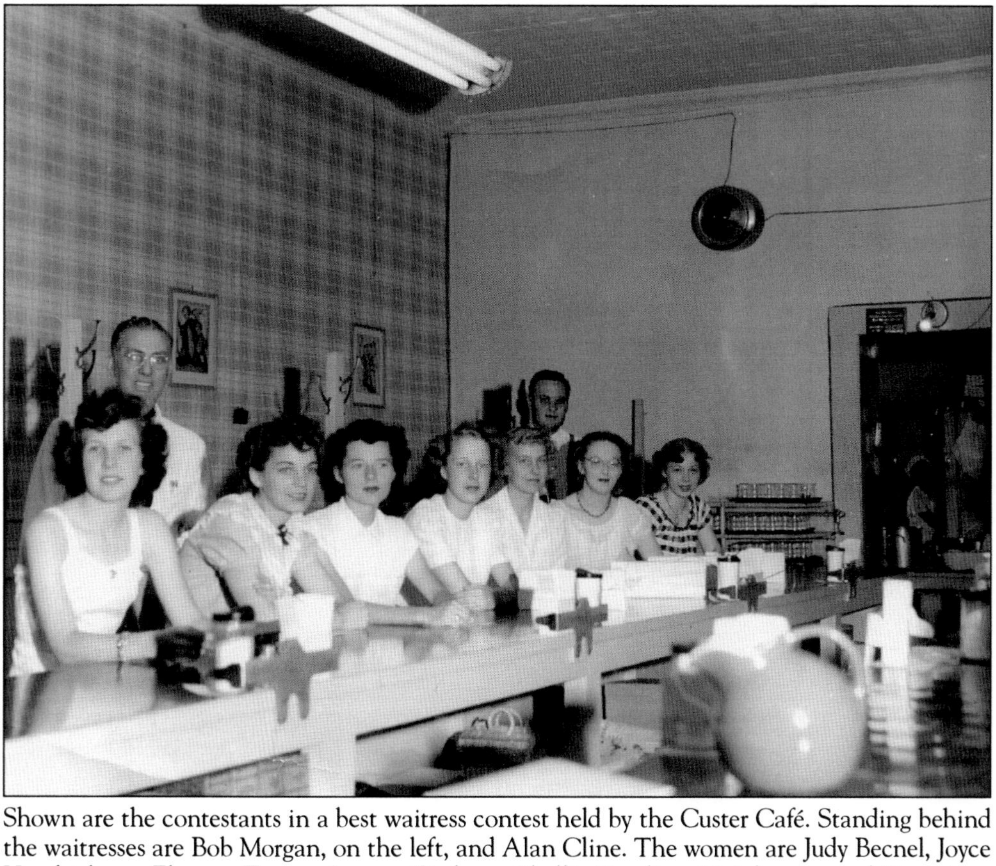

Shown are the contestants in a best waitress contest held by the Custer Café. Standing behind the waitresses are Bob Morgan, on the left, and Alan Cline. The women are Judy Becnel, Joyce Hendrickson, Eleanor Turner, Joanne Graham, Phyllis Ventling, V. Johnson, and Terry Van Overshield. Joyce Hendrickson was the winner. (Courtesy of Joyce Phillips.)

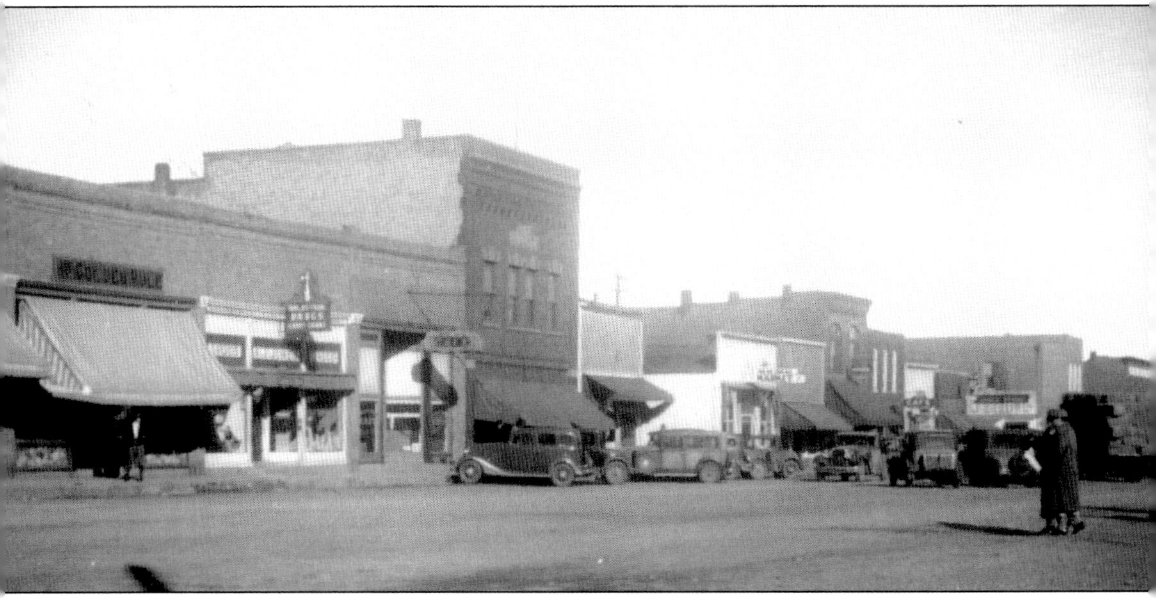

This is a 1934 view of downtown Custer in which you see the Golden Rule store, A. J. Jones Drugstore, and the Horseshoe Café. (Courtesy of Barbara [Dobesh] Robinson.)

A waitress at the Black Hills Café does double duty. (Courtesy of Susan Davis.)

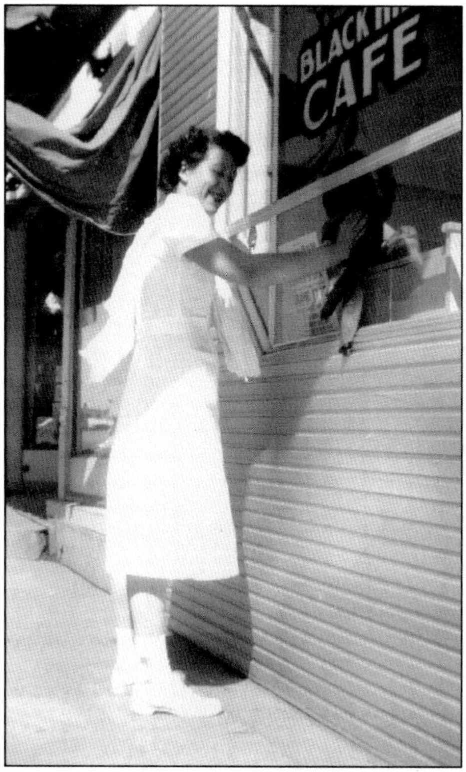

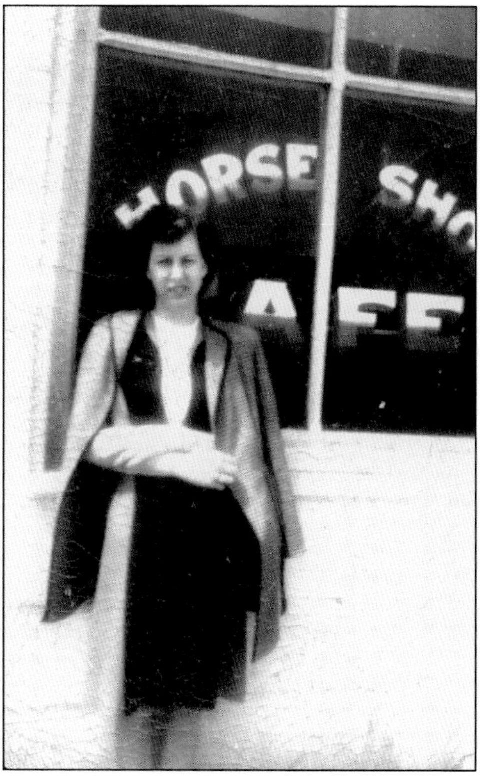

An unidentified woman waits in front of the Horseshoe Café, a popular eating spot. (Courtesy of Susan Davis.)

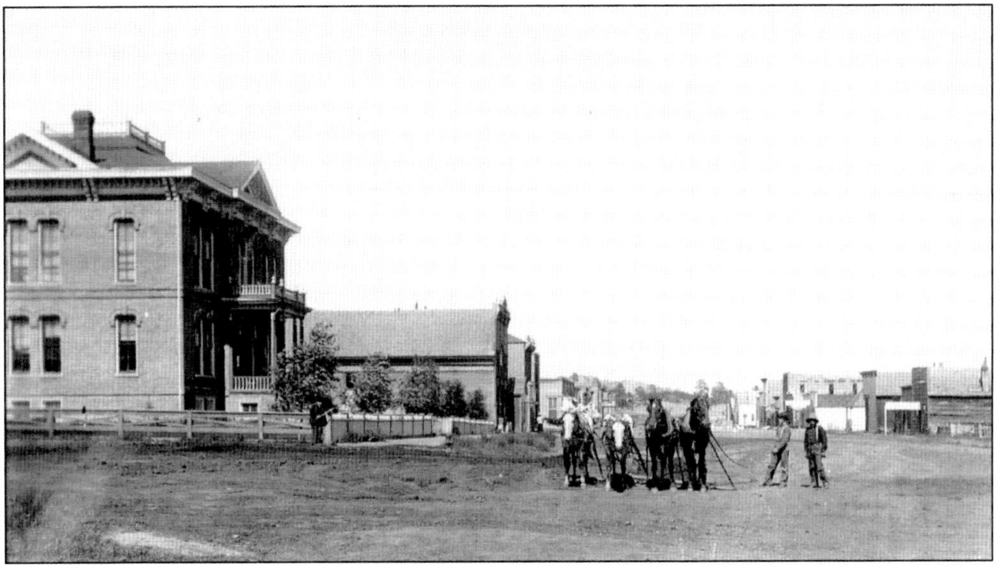

Looking east, this view shows the courthouse, now the Custer County 1881 Courthouse Museum. (Courtesy of Ed Streeter.)

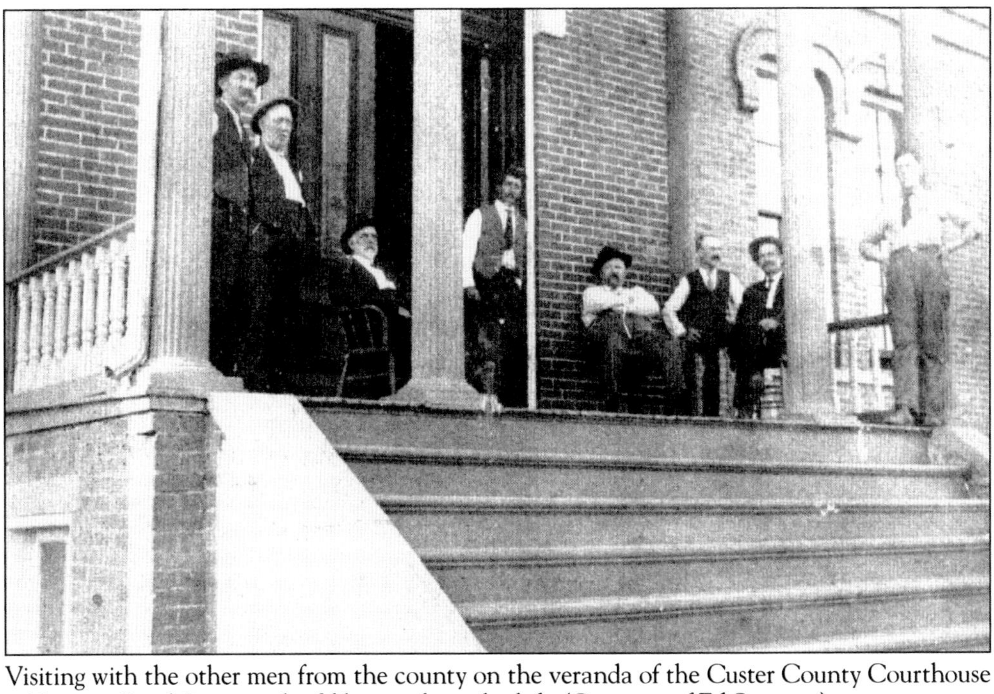

Visiting with the other men from the county on the veranda of the Custer County Courthouse is Norman Bazel Streeter, the fifth man from the left. (Courtesy of Ed Streeter.)

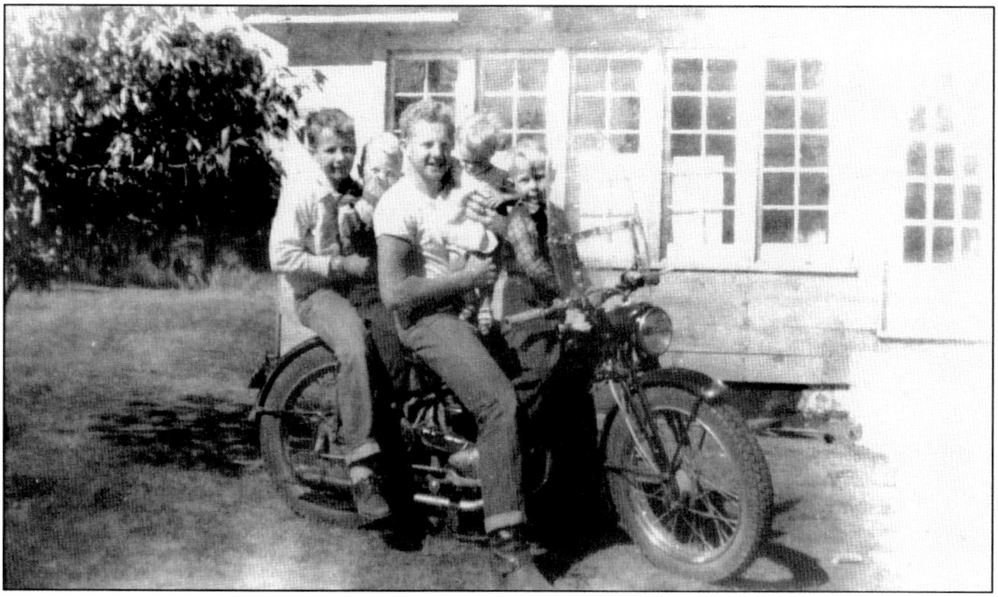

Enjoying a sunny afternoon in Custer are, from left to right, Larry Harley, Jerry Wyatt, Bob Harley, Peggy Wyatt, and Ray Harley. (Author's collection.)

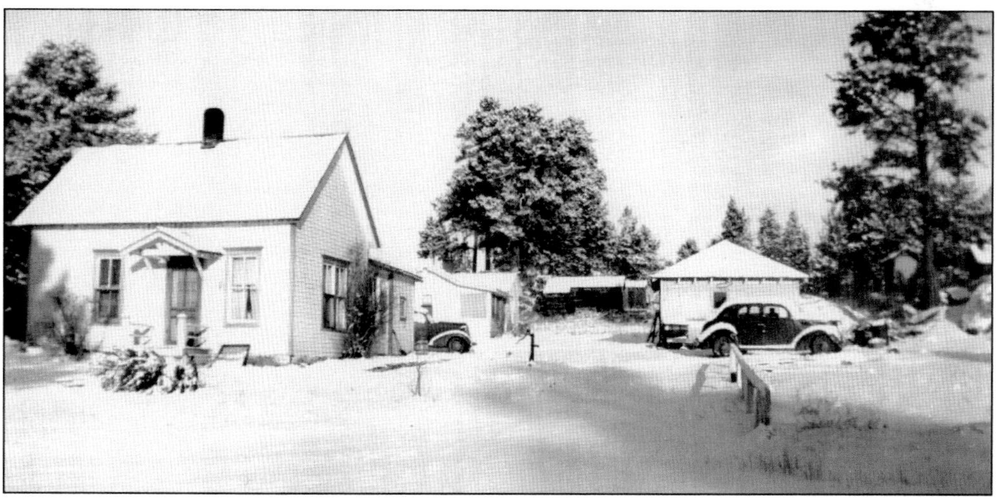

The home of George (Rob) and Bessie (Pearl) Harley was at 333 Lincoln Street in Custer. (Courtesy of Susan Davis.)

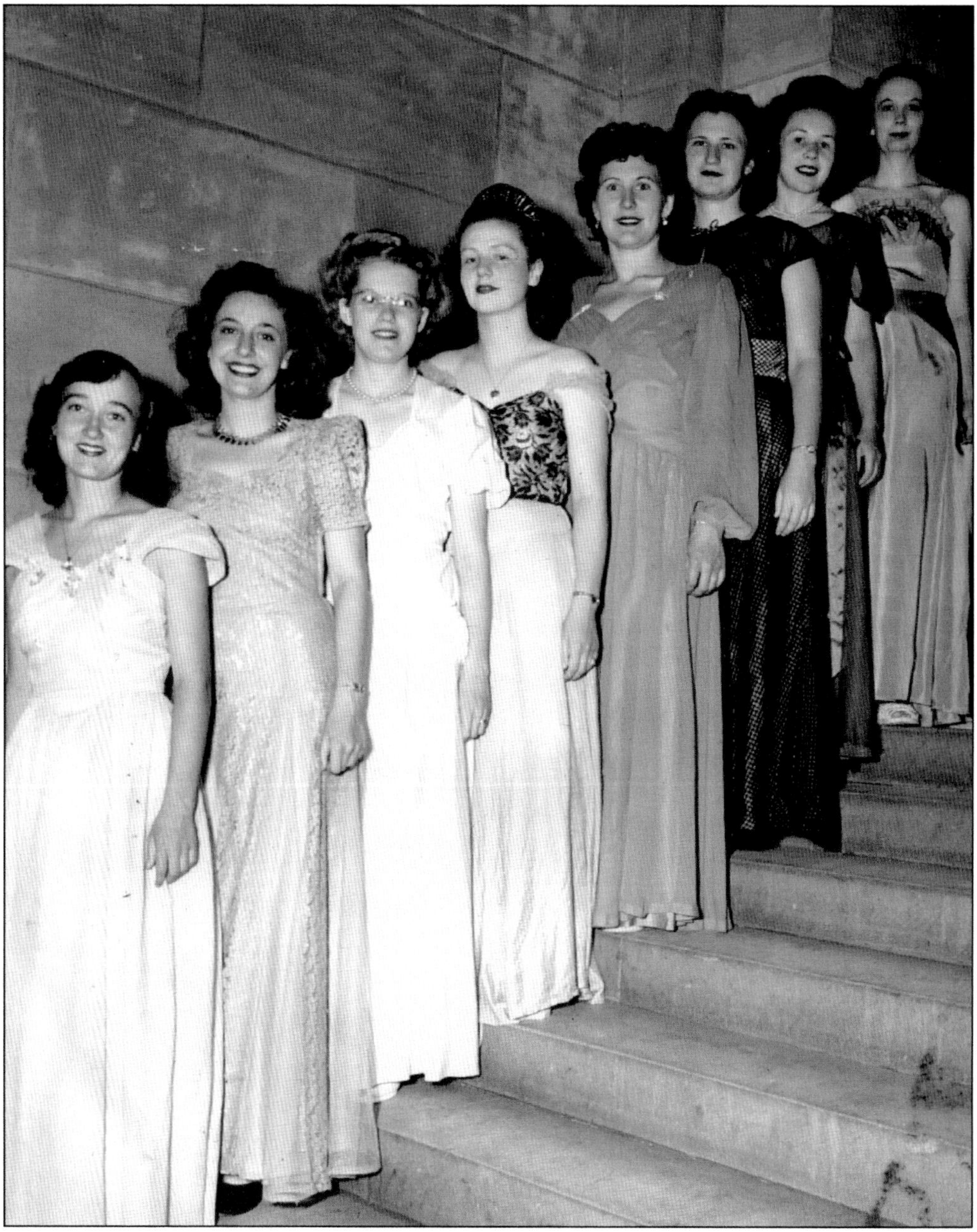

These eight lovely young women were employee contestants in 1947 for Miss Battle Mountain Sanitarium. The photograph was taken on the steps leading into the rotunda of the administration building. The Hot Springs sanitarium later became the Veterans Administration hospital. From left to right are Edna Young, Mary Lou Wasserberger, Hazel Trosper, Oleta Harley, unidentified, unidentified, Ann Harley (sister to Oleta), and unidentified. The Harley sisters were from Custer. (Author's collection.)

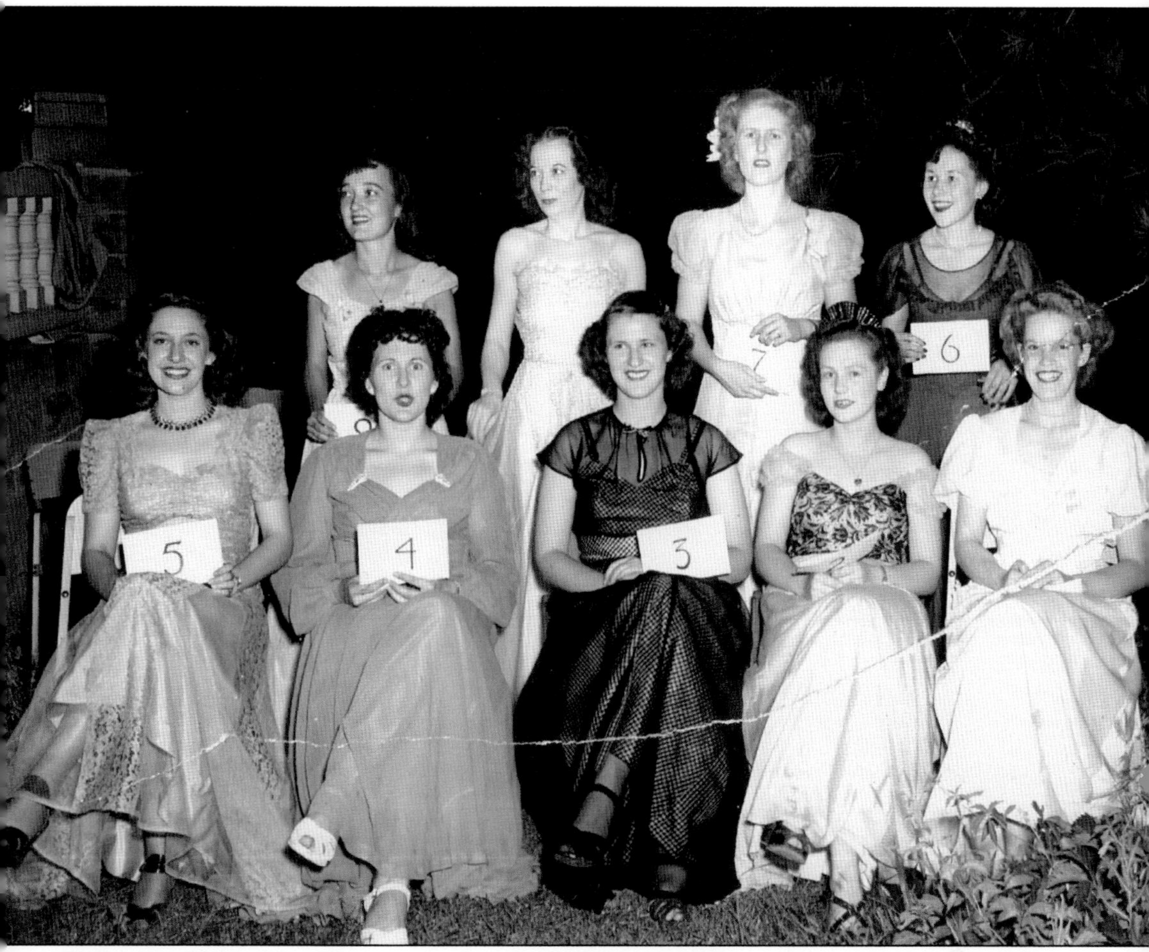

This view of the Miss Battle Mountain Sanitarium contestants shows nine women. From left to right are (first row) Mary Lou Wasserberger, unidentified, unidentified, Oleta Harley, and Hazel Trosper; (second row) Edna Young, unidentified, unidentified, and Ann Harley. (Author's collection.)

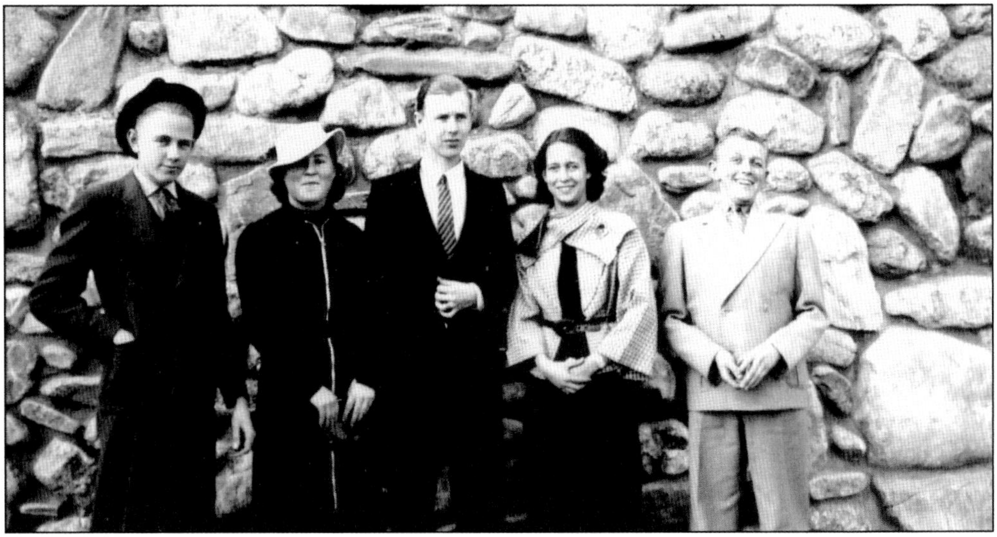

The cast members of a one-act play at Custer High School pose here. From left to right are Tom Marking, Lillian Broyles, Paul Anderson, Mary Louise Foltz, and Bob Gira. (Courtesy of Mary Brady, Custer High School graduate in 1939.)

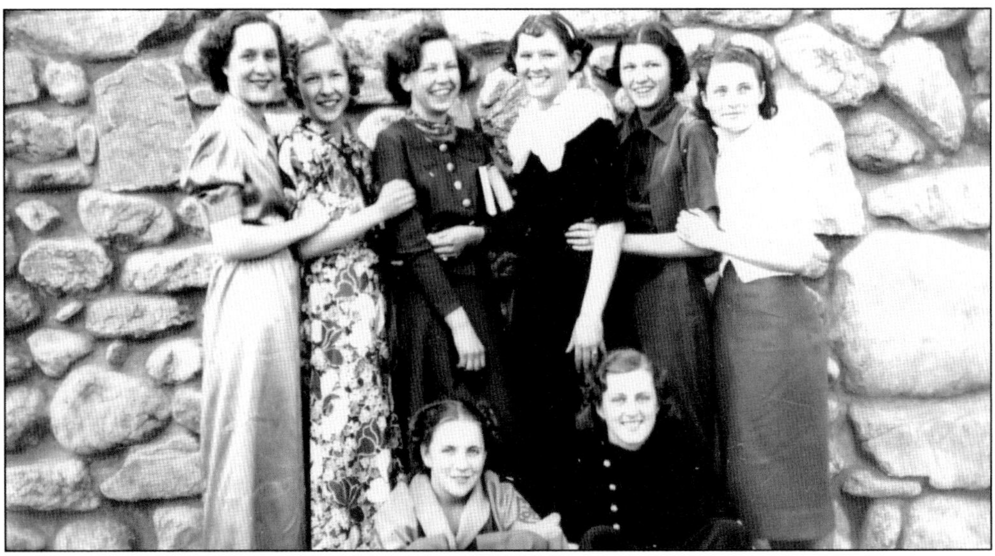

These Custer High School actors include Lucille Byers, Beverly Pitts, Gloria Rose, Laura Gano, Willa Jean Coats, Mary K. Bristol, Alice Roseberry, and Agnes Morgan. (Courtesy of Mary Brady.)

Custer High School students Jerome Heye (left), Alice Nystrom (center), and Paul Anderson perform in a one-act play. (Courtesy of Mary Brady.)

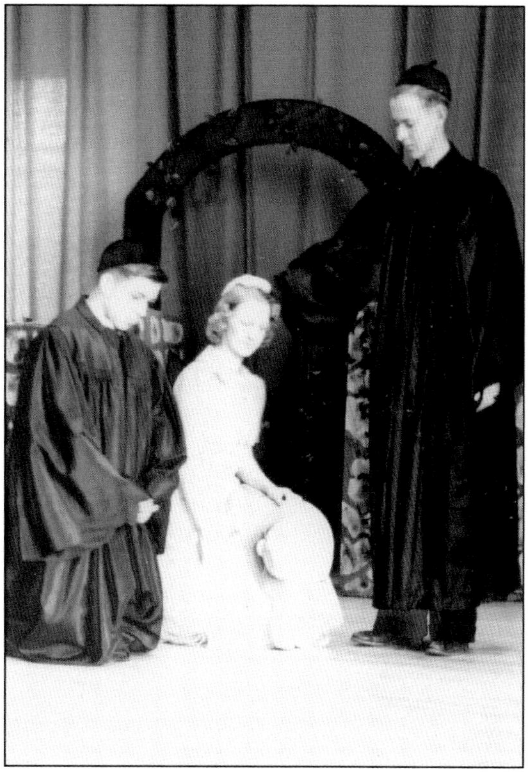

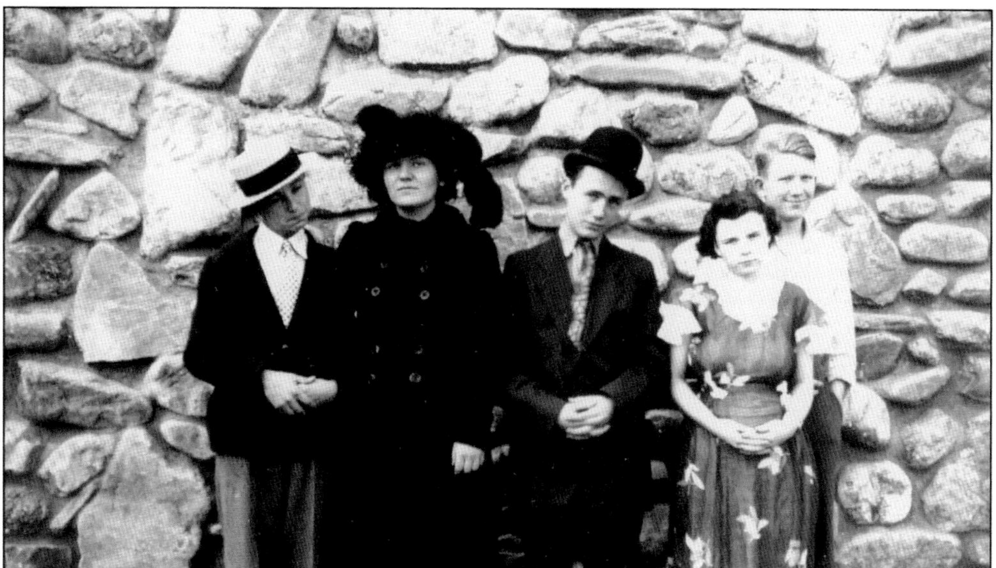

In character for this one-act play at Custer High School are, from left to right, Don Hassett, Florence Kidwell, James Parsons, Doris Greener, and Elton Geist. (Courtesy of Mary Brady.)

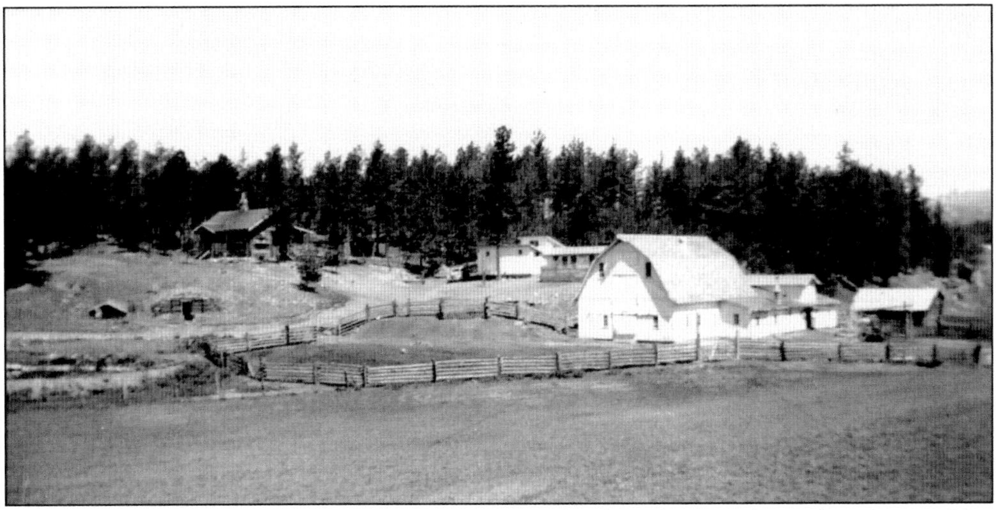

The big barn was called the Trocadero, and it was on the dairy farm run by Paul Paulson and his family. The Butts family ran the Outlaw Store nearby. Now owned by the Lutheran church and called the Outlaw Ranch, the land is an outdoor camp primarily for youth. (Courtesy of Mary Brady.)

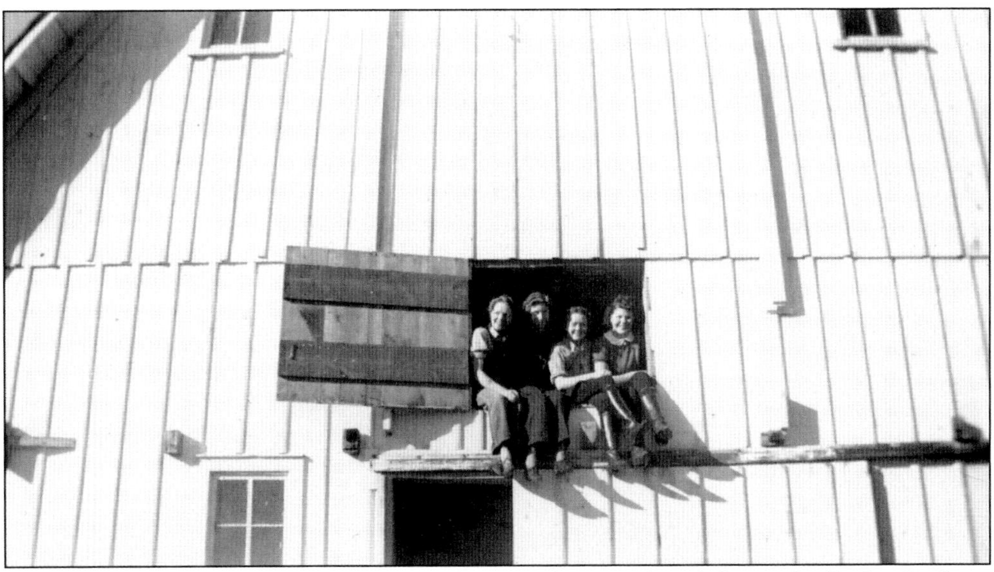

Sitting with their feet out of the hayloft in the Tracadero are, from left to right, Evelyn Paulson, Mary Retzhoff, Margit Paulson, and Dorothy Middleton. (Courtesy of Mary Brady.)

Violet Willy shows off the rumble seat in her car. Ira and Beulah Willa, Violet's aunt and uncle, operated the Star Camp, a motel in Custer. (Courtesy of Mary Brady.)

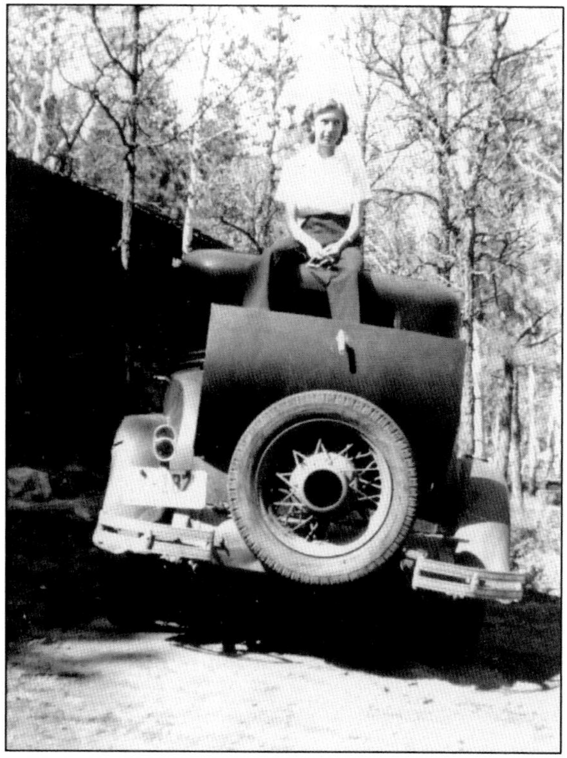

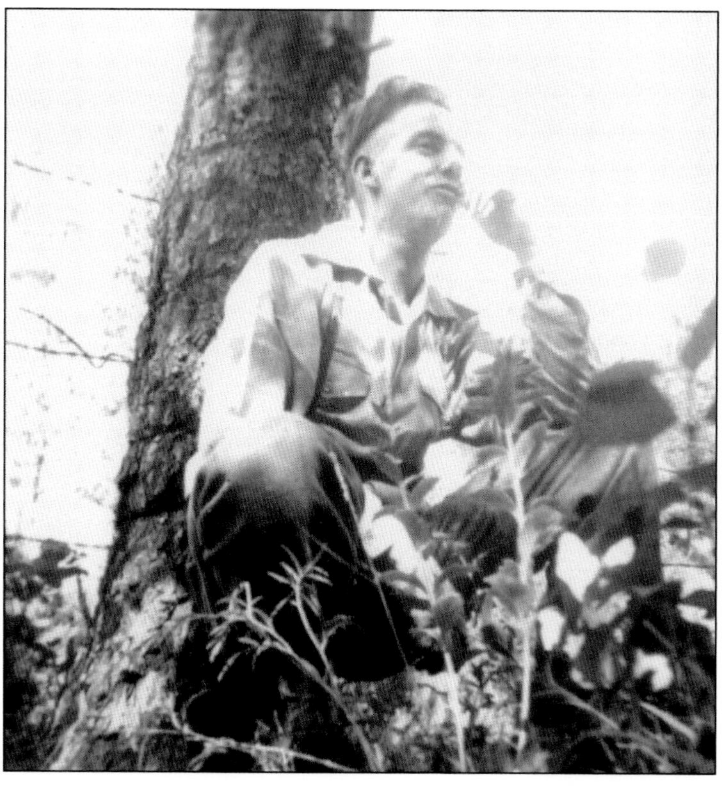

Shirley McClure is seen in a moment of contemplation. (Courtesy of Mary Brady.)

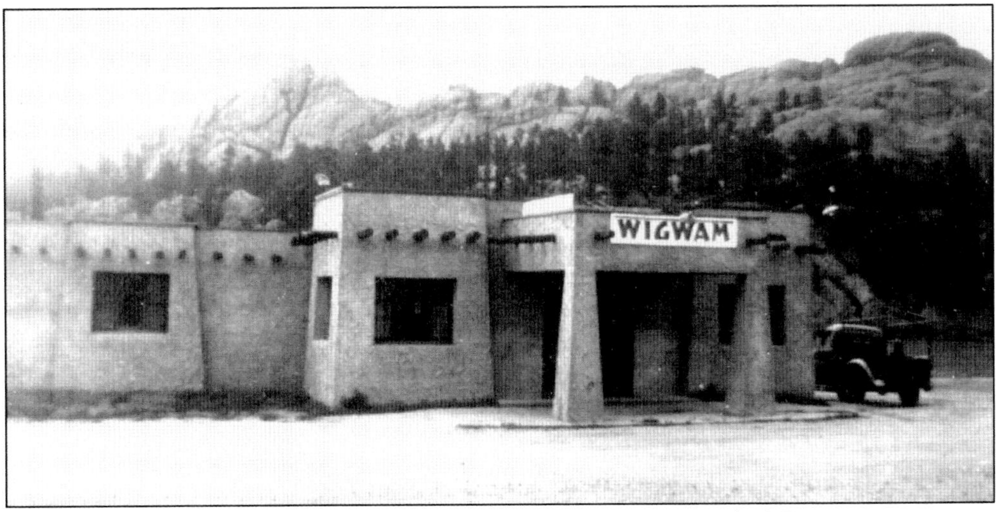

The Wigwam (A Famous Nite Club)

There was once a famous nite club just east
Of Custer town,
Everyone went out there.
It was known for miles around.

The miners, the loggers, they all went
To that old place.
Even the airmen came from the
Local air force base.

On the back wall was a jukebox
The prettiest thing you'd ever seen
The bubbling lights, the shining chrome
And the beautiful mahogany.

Many times I've walked across the floor
Of that old pub
Put a nickel in that jukebox to hear the latest
Hit by Ernest Tubb.

The Wigwam was a popular nightspot for many years. Donald Doughty's poem describes it well. (Courtesy of Roy and Hazel Doughty.)

They waltzed and did the two step
They really cut a rug
They even did the new dance
The famous jitterbug.

The laughter of the crowd could be
Heard through out the nite
But before they closed those swinging doors
There would always be a fight.

The fire whistle blow one nite in old Custer town,
Every body passed the word the old club
Was burning down.

Nothing marks the spot today, no sign
Or monument
Nothing but a rusty pipe and an old slab of cement.

I stopped by this place one nite just as the
Sun went down
Just to reminisce a bit
On my way into town

I closed my eyes for just a moment and let
My memory stray
I could hear the laughter of the crowd
I could hear the jukebox play

But then I realized it was just the wind in the trees
And the old club was just another page
In my book of memories.

Donald E. Doughty
(used with permission)

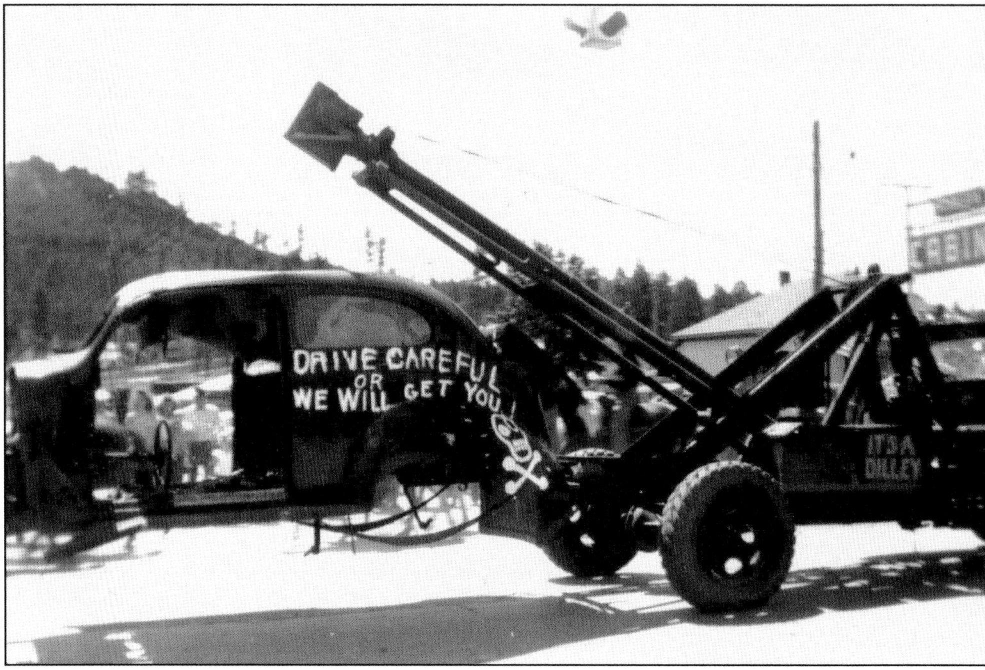

The Gold Discovery Days parade is a mile long. (Courtesy of Russell Wyatt.)

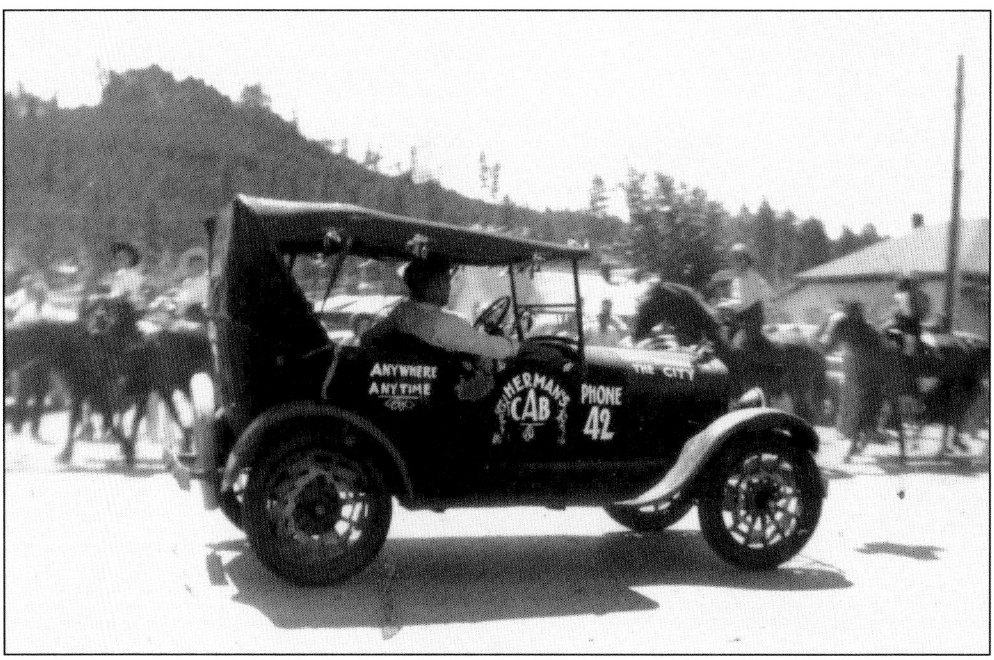

Pictured is another participant in the parade held during Gold Discovery Days. (Courtesy of Russell Wyatt.)

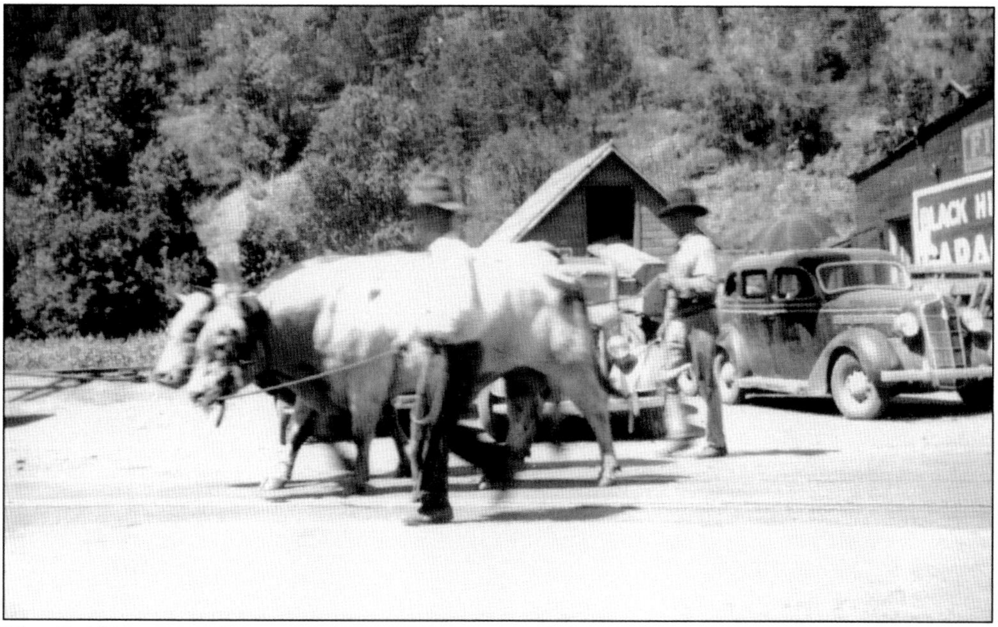

The Gold Discovery Days parade is just a portion of the festivities held to honor the history of the Custer gold rush. (Courtesy of Russell Wyatt.)

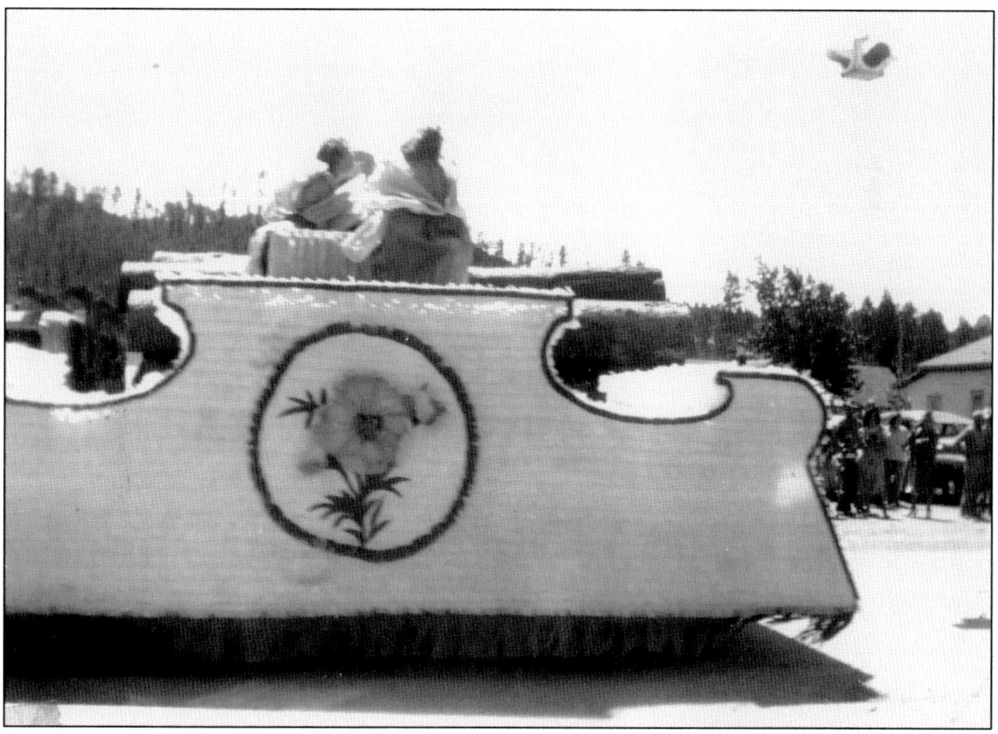

Another Gold Discovery Days float appears here. (Courtesy of Russell Wyatt.)

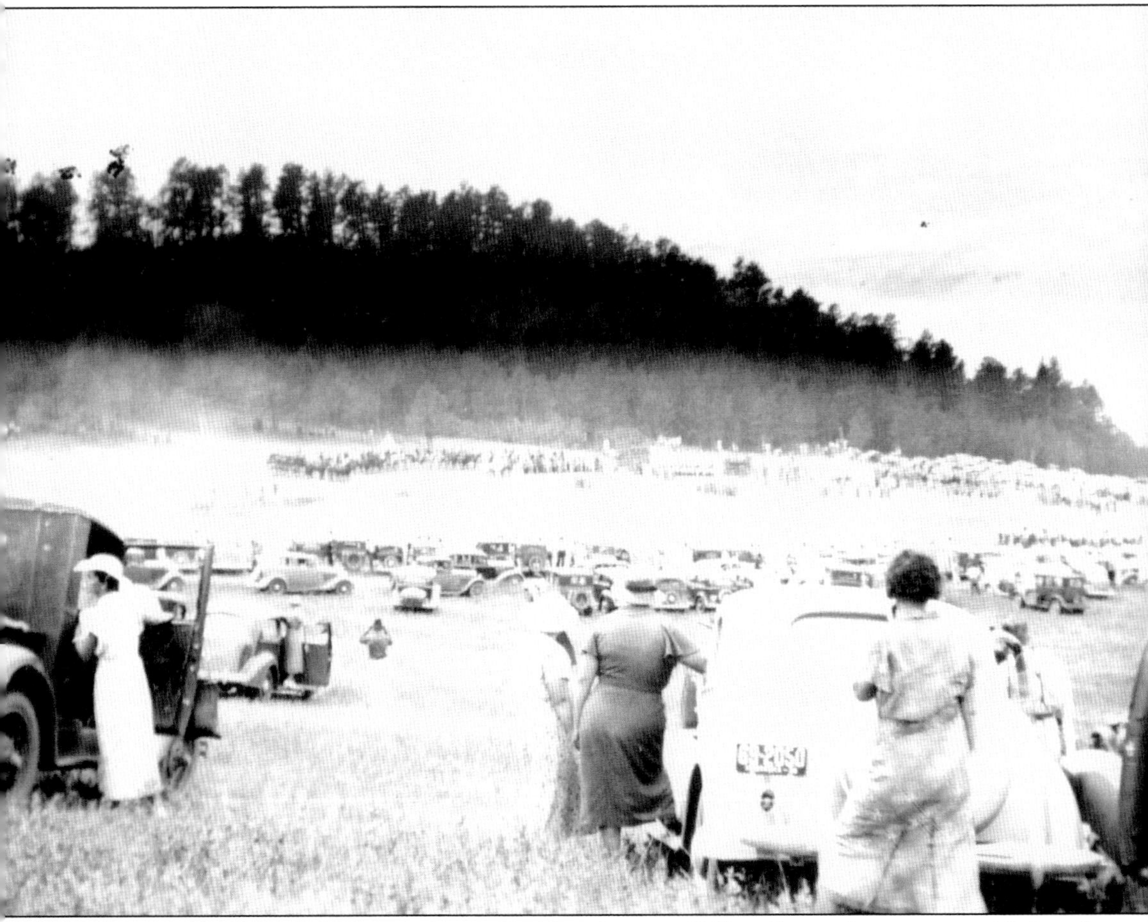

The Gold Discovery Days pageant was held on Pageant Hill in Custer, beginning in 1924, and it continued through 2001. On June 27, 1927, Pres. Calvin Coolidge and his wife, Grace, were among the spectators. Millie Heidepriem, a native of Custer, wrote the script for the pageant. (Courtesy of Russell Wyatt.)

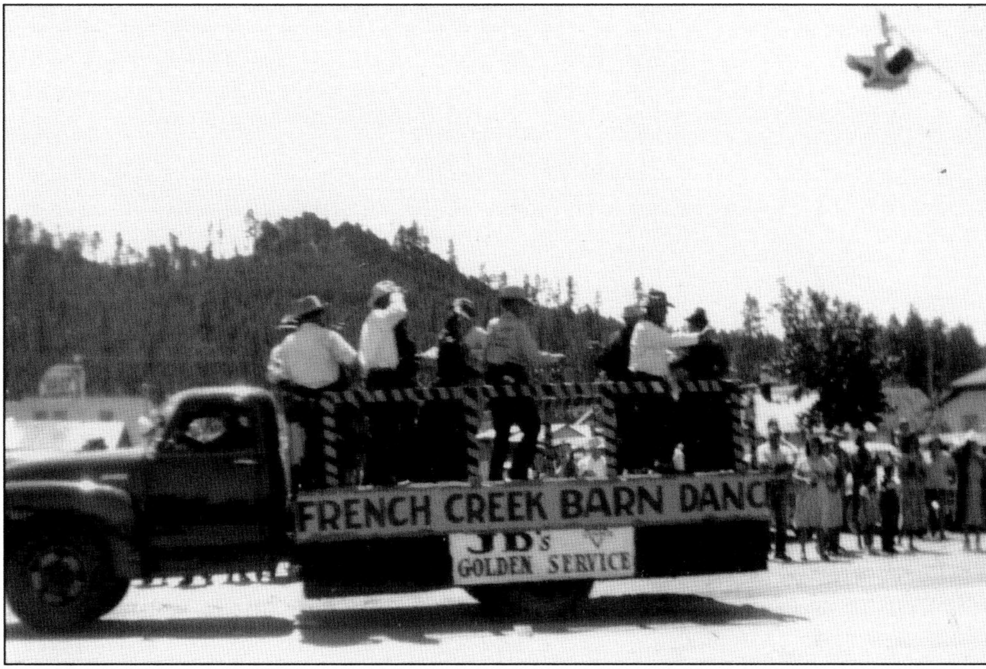

Residents of Custer are all involved in some aspect of Gold Discovery Days. Businesses, service organizations, churches all enter the best floats they can create. (Courtesy of Russell Wyatt.)

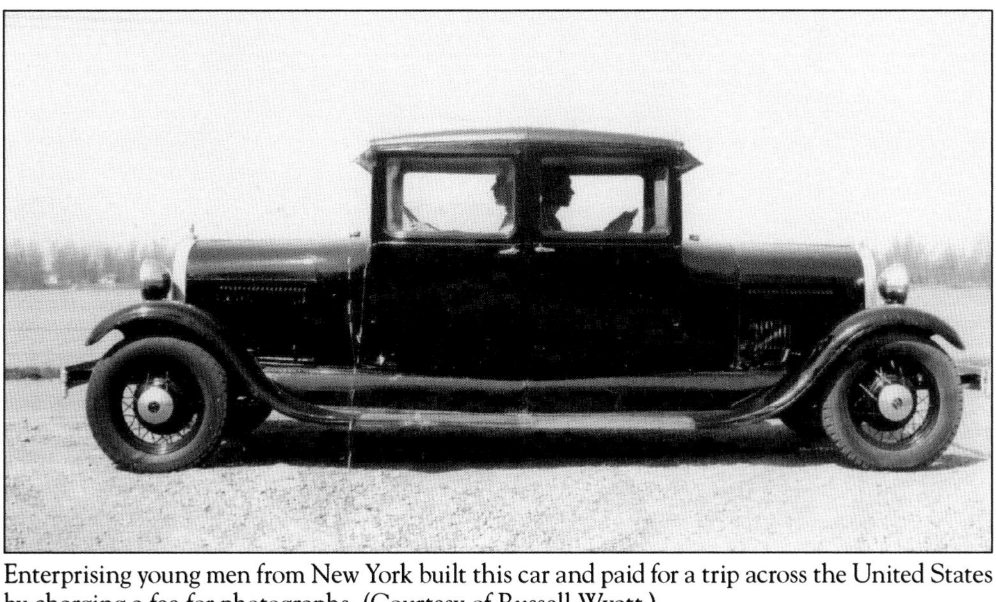

Enterprising young men from New York built this car and paid for a trip across the United States by charging a fee for photographs. (Courtesy of Russell Wyatt.)

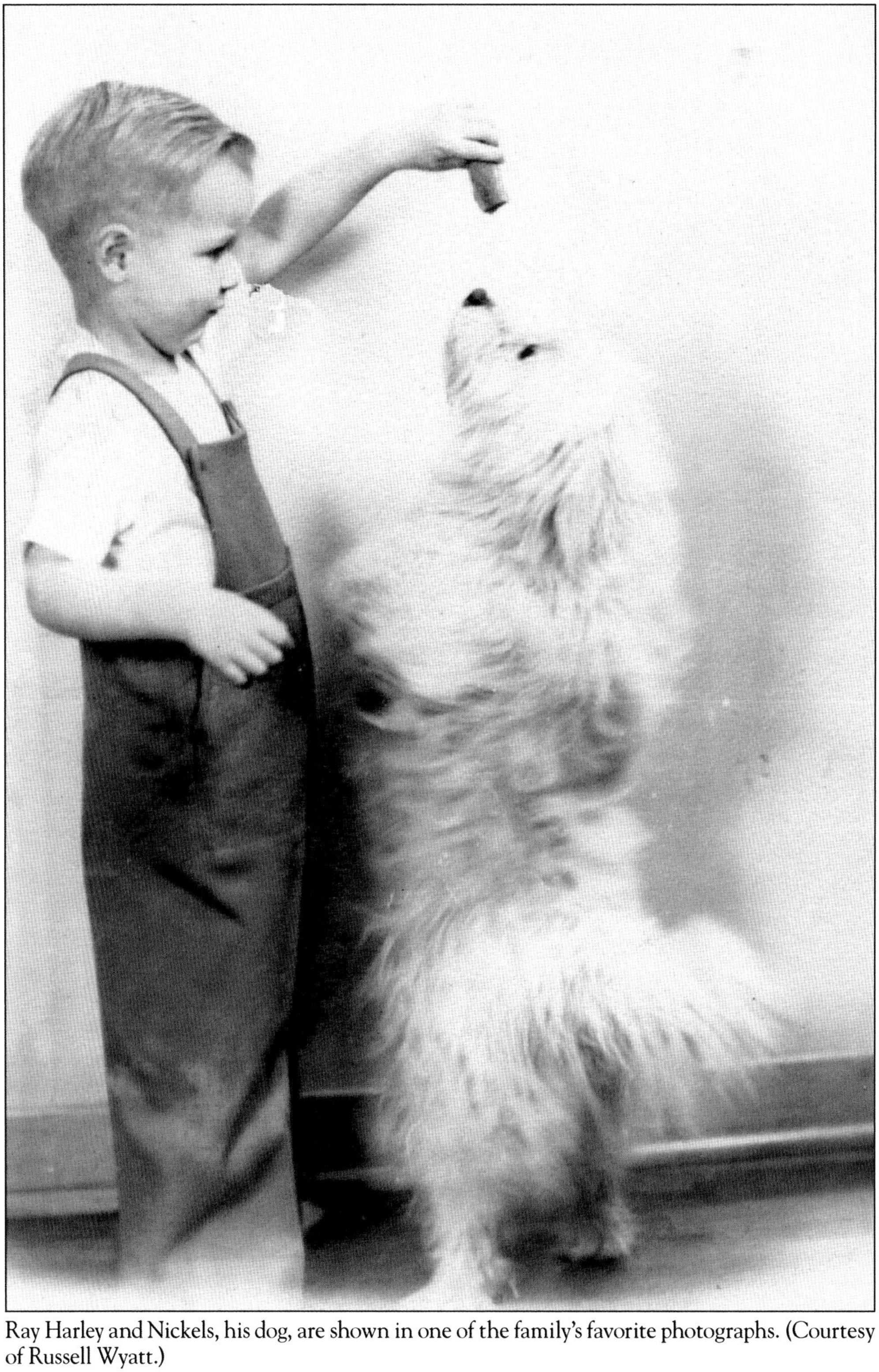

Ray Harley and Nickels, his dog, are shown in one of the family's favorite photographs. (Courtesy of Russell Wyatt.)

Five

Daily Lives

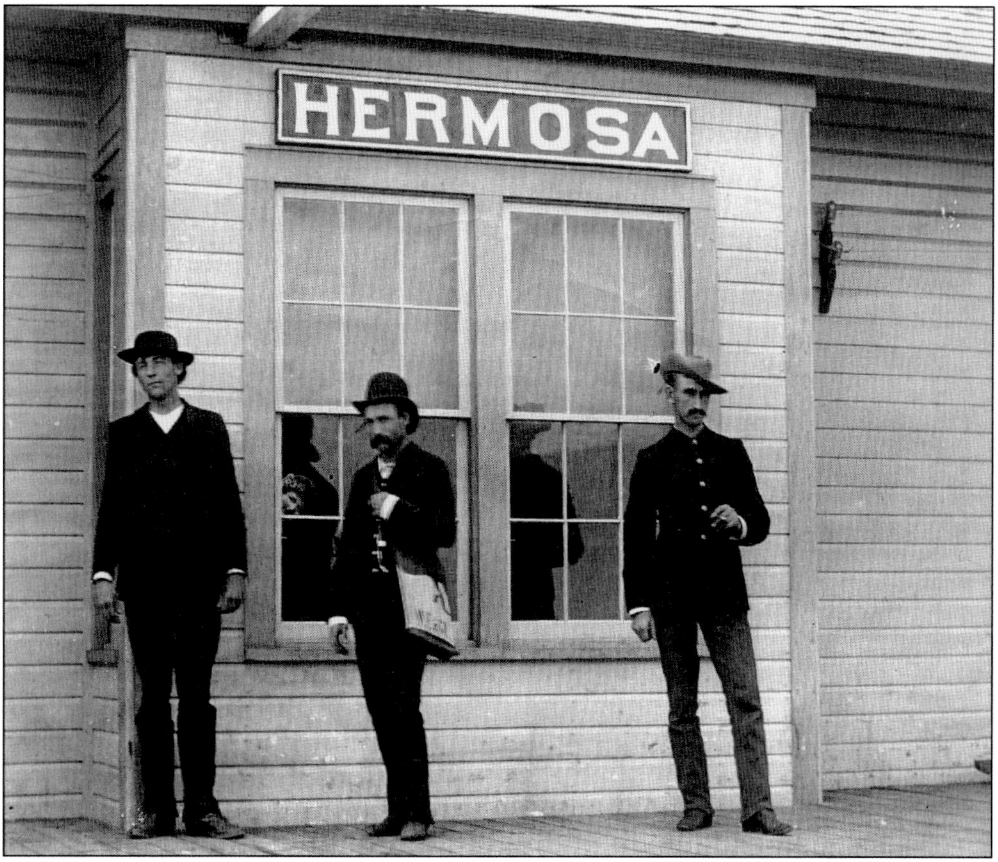

A woman peeks out the window at these dandies in Hermosa. (Courtesy of the Hermosa Arts and History Association.)

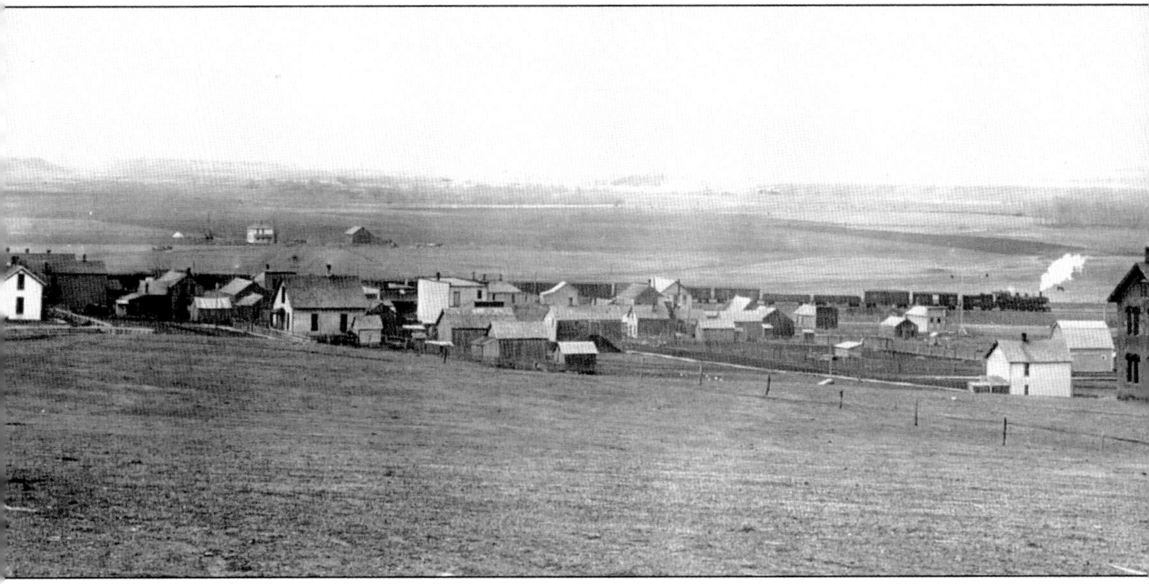

A steam engine pulling a long train travels along the edge of Hermosa. (Courtesy of Rick Mills.)

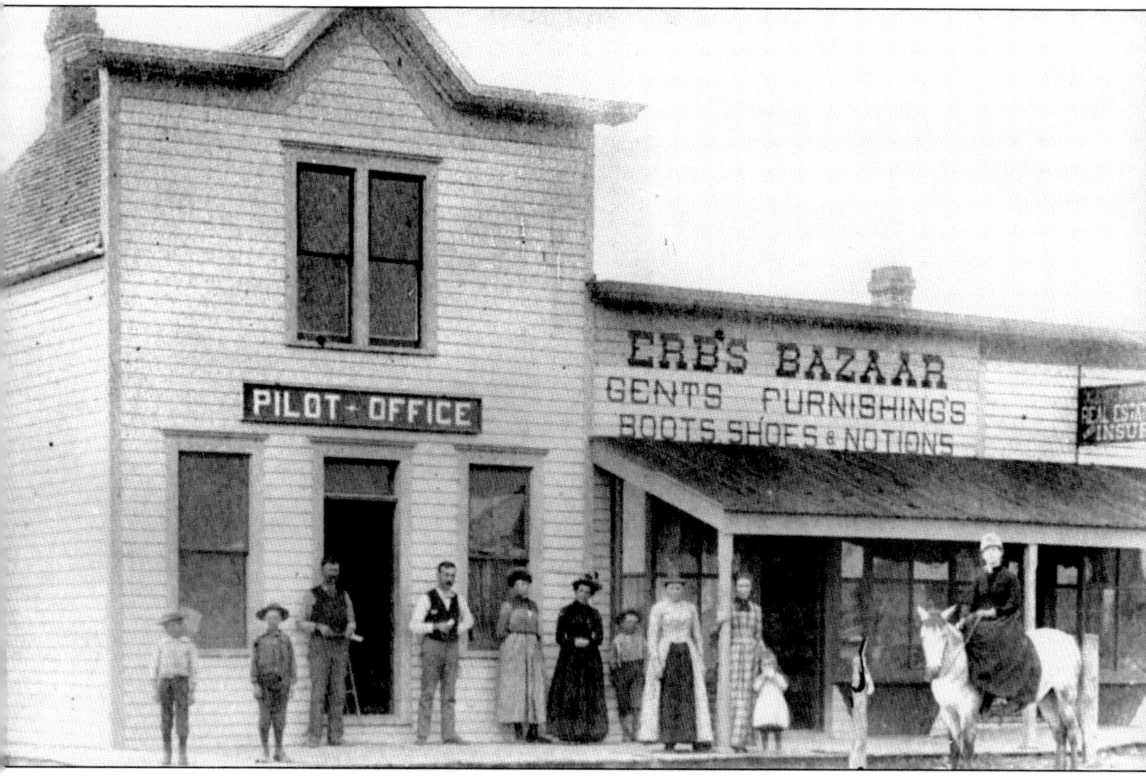

The *Hermosa Pilot* newspaper was owned and operated by John Stanley for about 10 years beginning in 1886. Erb's Bazaar, a general merchandise store, was owned by Emery Erb in the late 1800s. (Courtesy of the Hermosa Arts and History Association.)

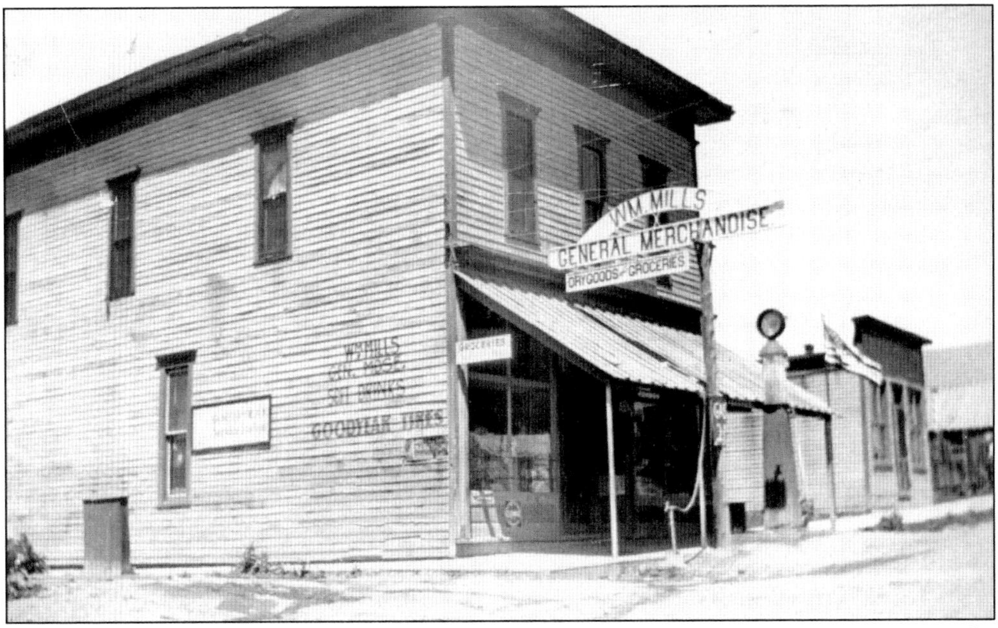

Seen here is the William Mills store in Hermosa. William was a brother of Jesse L. Mills. (Courtesy of Rick Mills.)

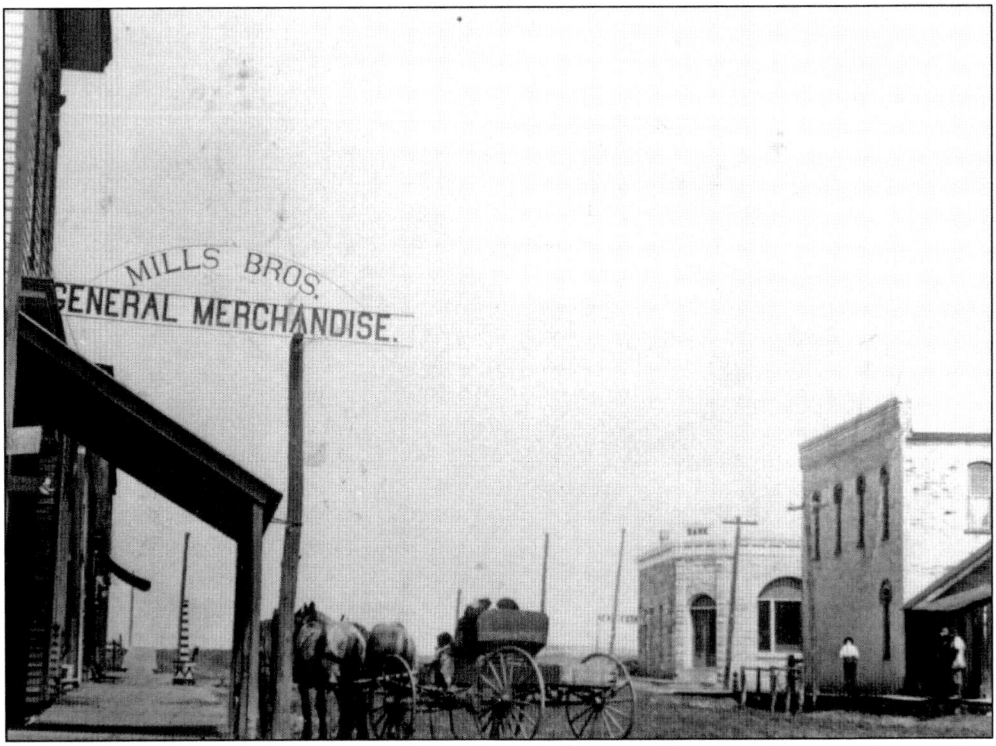

Mills Brothers was owned and operated by Billy and Chet. In addition to the general store, they had a meat market and delivered goods with a wagon to the miners on Battle Creek. In later years, they moved the business to Rapid City, where it was expanded and known as Mills Drug Stores. (Courtesy of Rick Mills.)

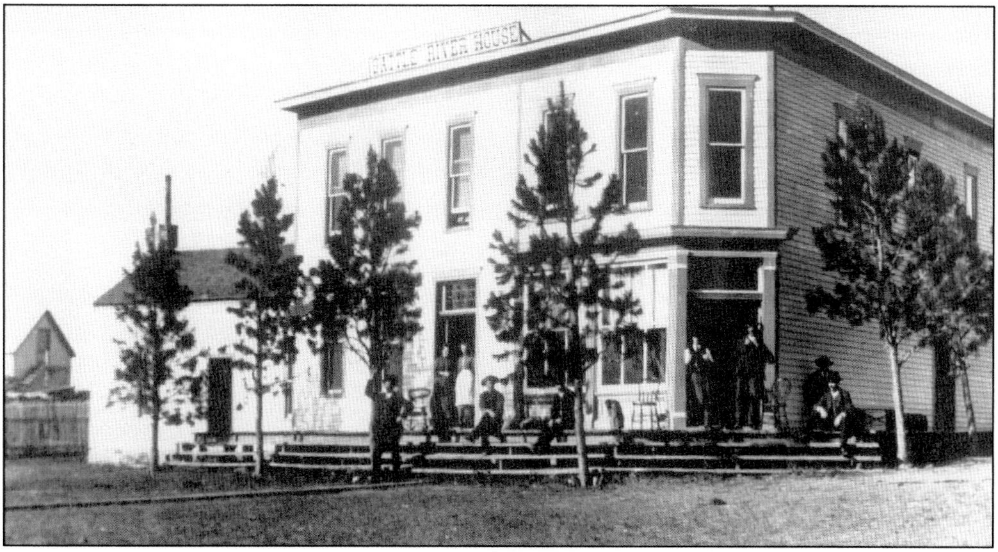

The Battle River House was one of three hotels that opened in Hermosa the first year the town was established (1886). It was run by Ed Stenger. The advertisement to the right was placed in 1888. (Courtesy of the Hermosa Arts and History Association.)

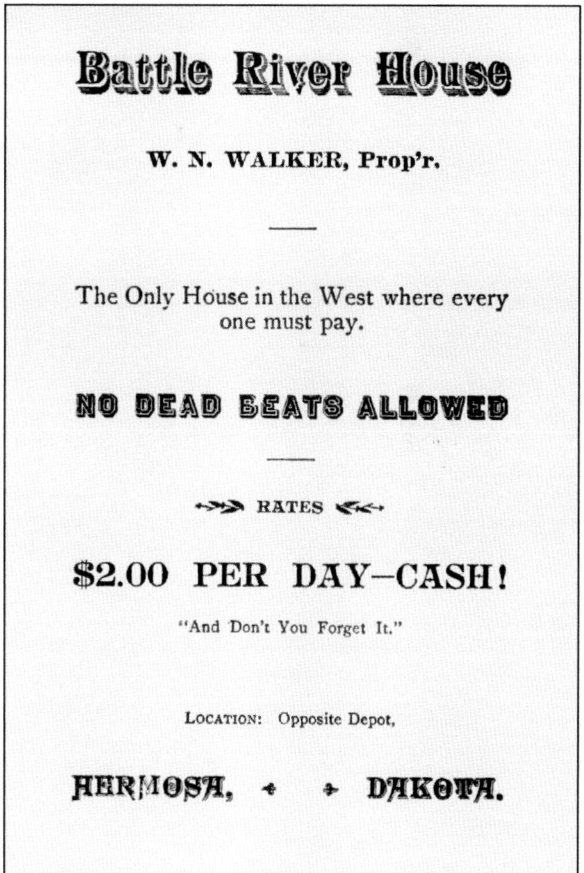

Battle River House

W. N. WALKER, Prop'r.

The Only House in the West where every one must pay.

NO DEAD BEATS ALLOWED

RATES

$2.00 PER DAY—CASH!

"And Don't You Forget It."

LOCATION: Opposite Depot,

HERMOSA, DAKOTA.

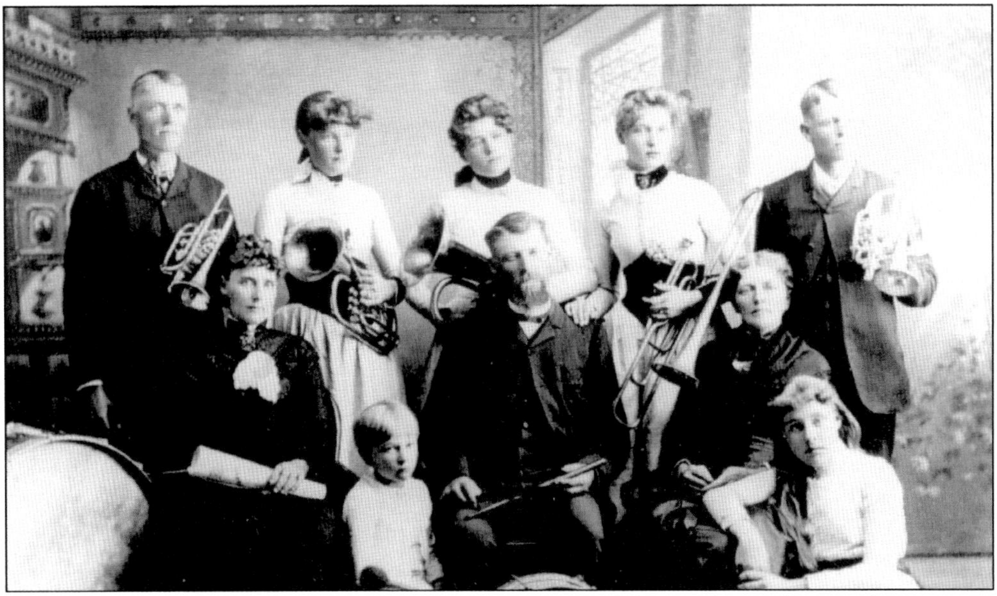

The members of the Bower Family Band pose here. From left to right are (first row) Laura and Quinnie; (second row) Rhoda Alice (who was called Od because the younger children had difficulty saying her name), and the parents, Keziah and John Bower; (third row) Sidney, Nettie, Lulu, Rose, and Mayo. Laura Bower Van Nuys, from Rapid City, wrote *The Family Band from the Missouri to the Black Hills 1881–1900* (published in 1961). The book was later made into the Disney film *The One and Only Genuine Original Family Band*, which debuted in Rapid City. (Courtesy of the Hermosa Arts and History Association.)

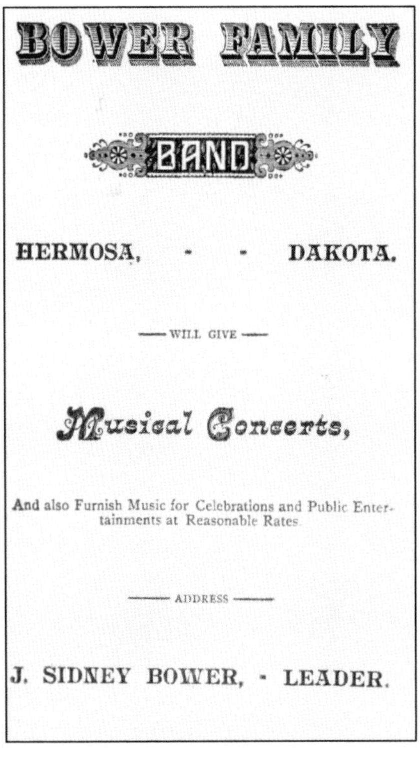

This advertisement was placed by the Bower Family Band in 1888 to generate singing business. In 1891, the family spent the summer in Hot Springs at the behest of Fred Evans. The family lived in a spacious building at the chautauqua grounds at the upper end of town. They played at Evans Plunge, Cascade Springs, and for the first commencement of Black Hills College, among other venues, during their sojourn. (Courtesy of the Hermosa Arts and History Association.)

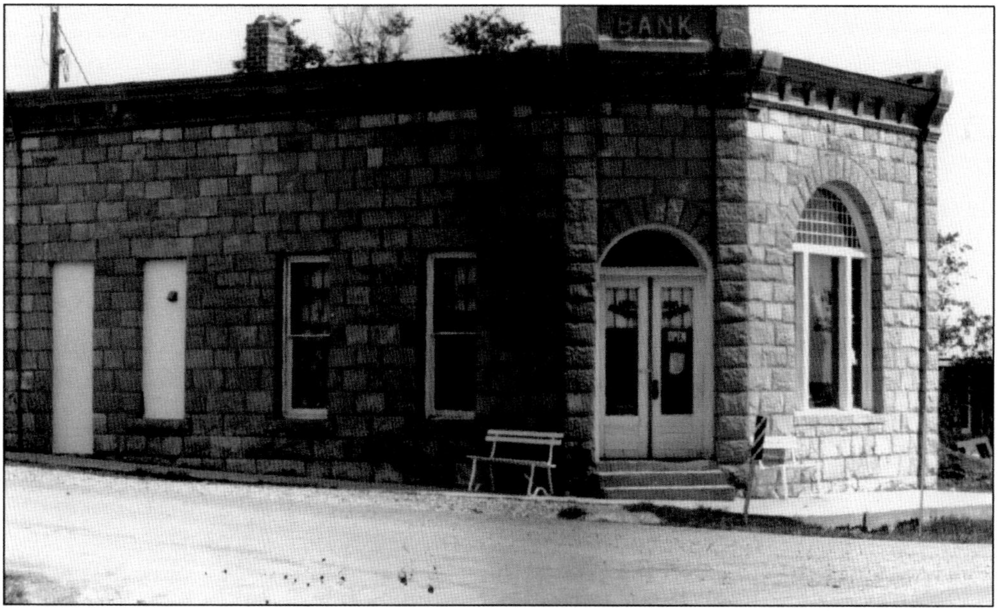

Arsene Hesnard started the Hermosa State Bank. When it was built in 1910, the stone was quarried locally just west of Hermosa. (Courtesy of the Hermosa Arts and History Association.)

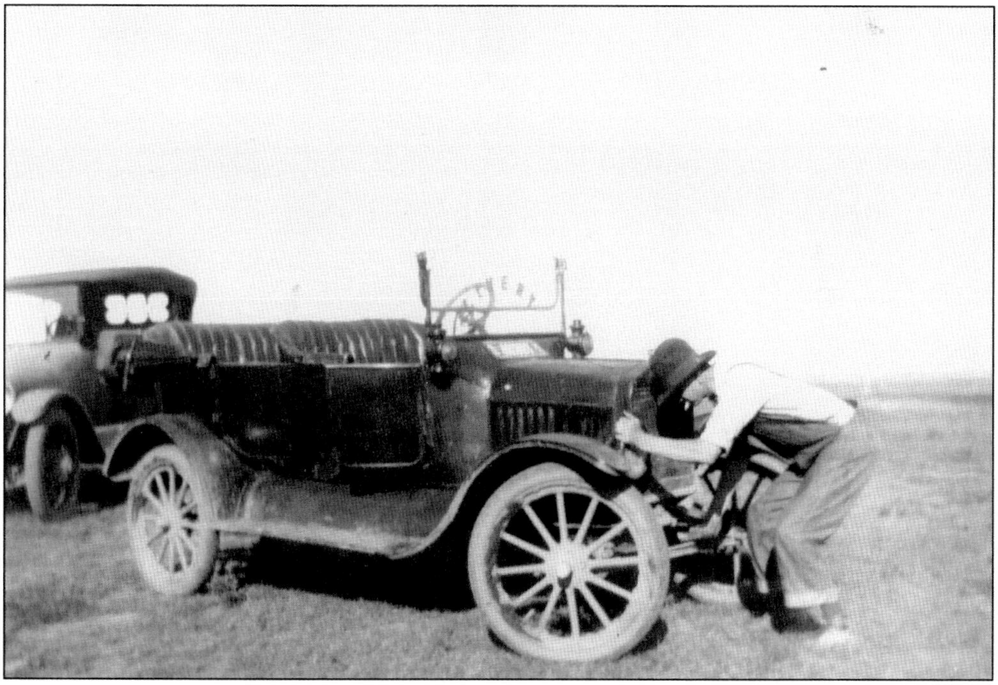

Lewis Mills is seen cranking his Ford to start it. Perhaps he is on his way to deliver mail along a rural mail route, a job someone from the Mills family carried out in the local area for 112 years. Jesse L. Mills was the first, followed by Lewis, then Wayne, and Arlene, Wayne's wife. Jesse's earliest route was from Hermosa to the Etta Mine. One delivery day, when he reached Etta, no one was there. He was told the town had moved three miles to the west; the town is now known as Keystone. (Courtesy of Rick Mills.)

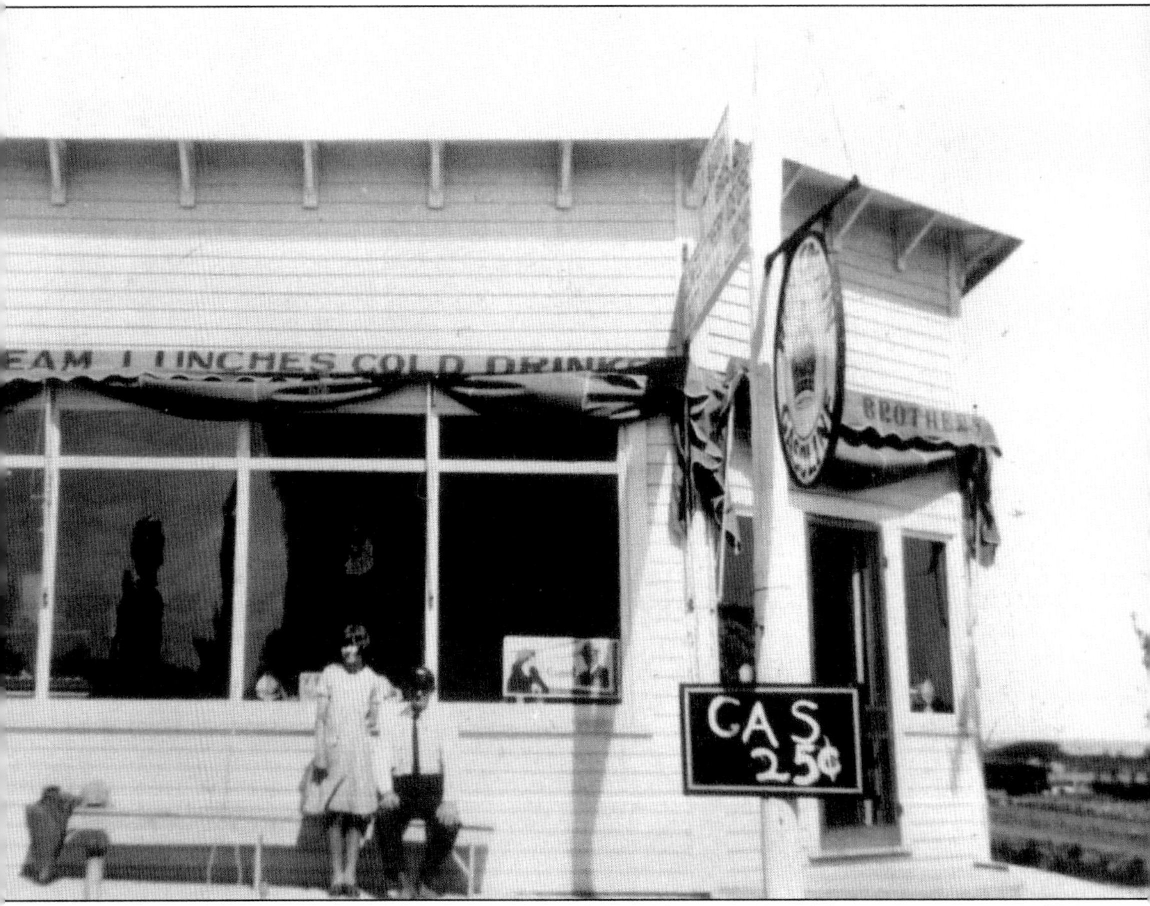

In the 1920s, gasoline at the Hermosa gas station cost the same as it did in 1970—25¢ per gallon. The station was what we would now call a convenience store, as it had a café and post office within. (Courtesy of Hermosa Arts and History Association.)

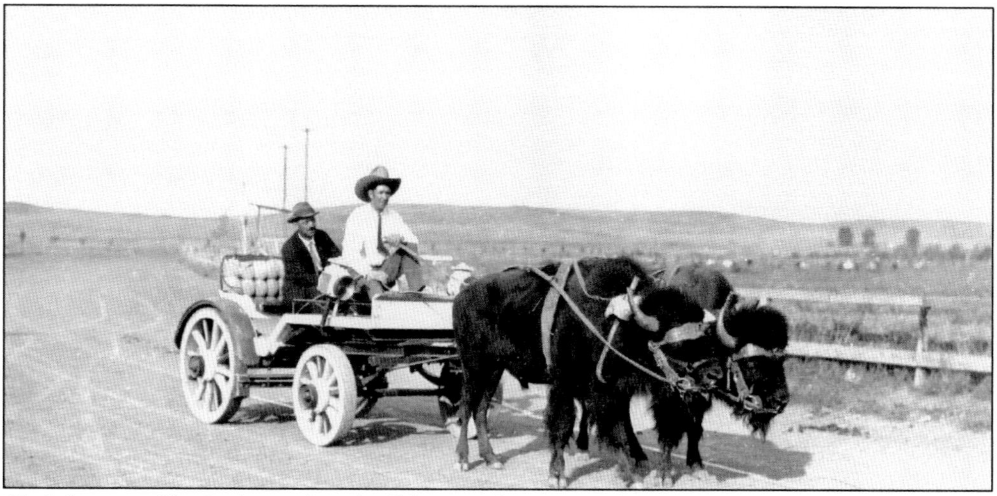

Clyde Jones and his broke-to-drive buffalo team drive around the Hermosa fairgrounds. (Courtesy of Nelda Carroll.)

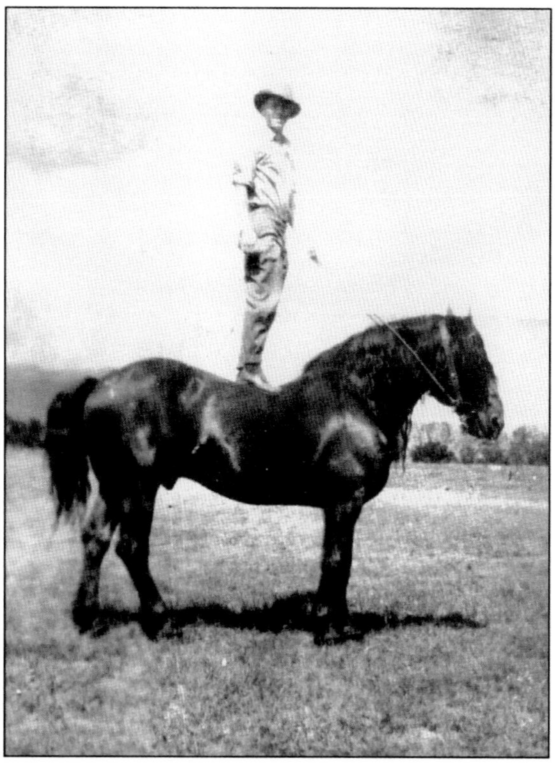

Carl Dow is standing on the back of his workhorse, just having fun. (Courtesy of Nelda Carroll.)

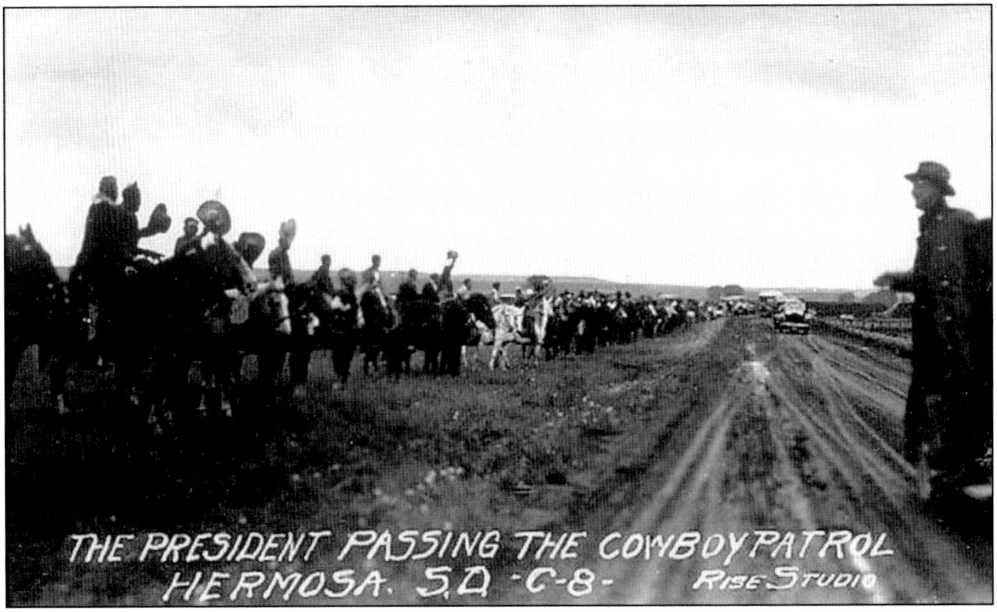

In 1927, Pres. Calvin Coolidge came to the Black Hills for his summer vacation, arriving on a train from Washington, D.C., on June 13. These Hermosa cowboys, led by Ed Stenger and George Kimball, gave the presidential party a warm welcome and escorted them into town. (Author's collection.)

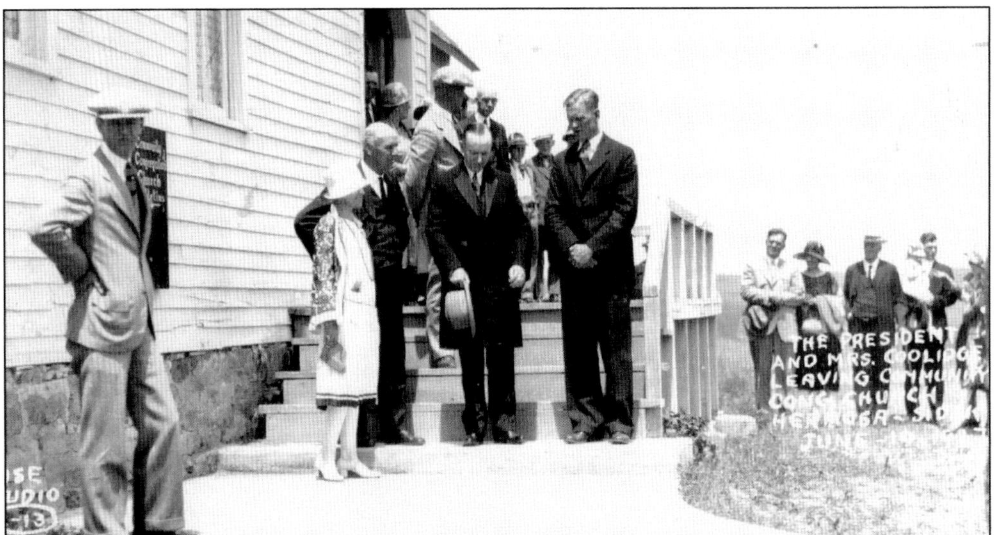

Coolidge attended the Congregational church in Hermosa during his summer stay. The pastor was Ralph Lium, a 20-year-old medical missionary student. The story goes that on the day of Coolidge's first attendance, Lium preached his first sermon ever. (Courtesy of Hermosa Arts and History Association.)

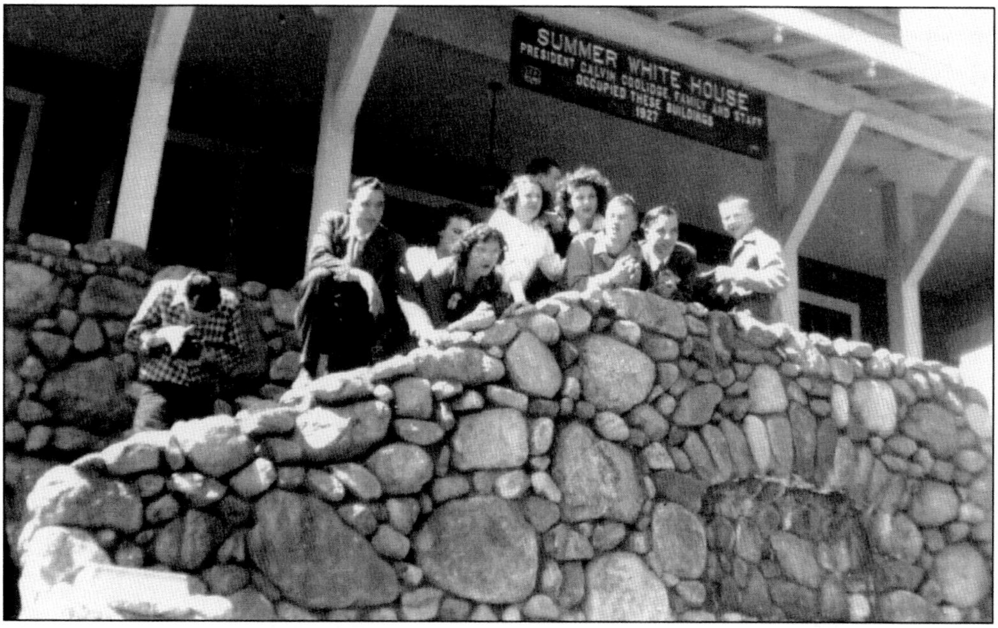

The State Game Lodge, also known as the Coolidge Inn, was home for Calvin and Grace Coolidge and family. Including staff and detail people, approximately 80 people were in the Coolidge party. From the lodge where they headquartered, they did a good deal of touring of the Black Hills. On July 4, 1927, Sen. Peter Norbeck and his wife, Lydia, boarded the presidential train in Rapid City and went along to the Tri-State Round Up at Belle Fourche. (Author's collection.)

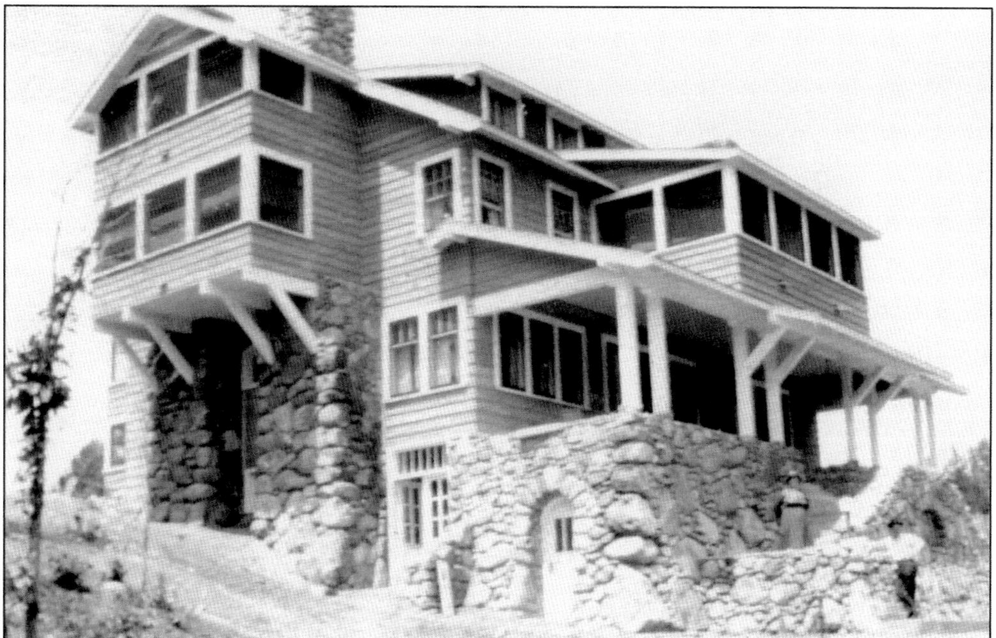

The Coolidge Inn was the summer White House in 1927, although President Coolidge had his office in the new Central High School building in Rapid City. During his summer stay on August 10, 1927, "Silent Cal," as he was known, dedicated Mount Rushmore. The president and his party departed Rapid City by train on September 9, 1927. (Author's collection.)

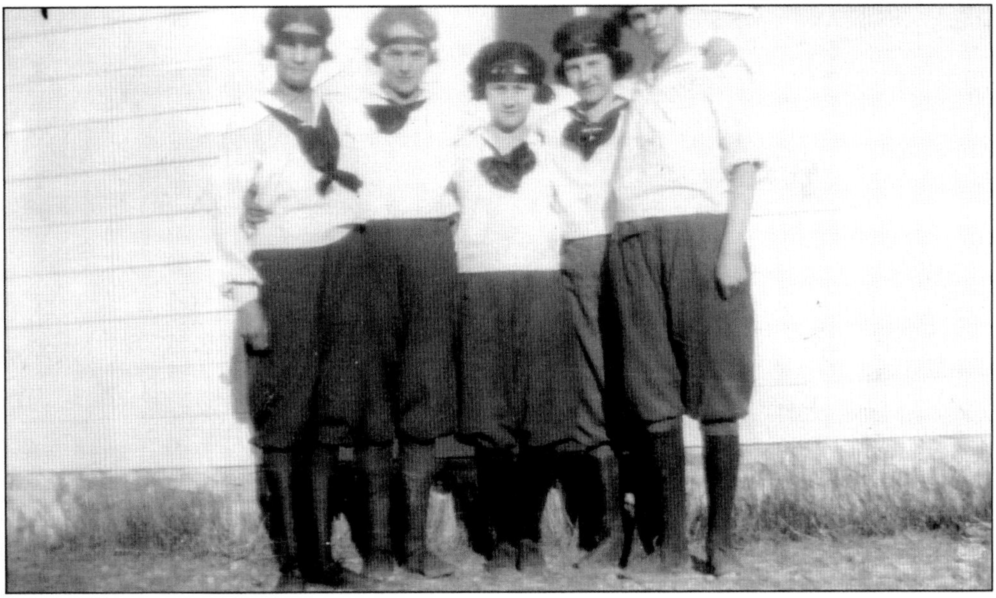

This Hermosa girls basketball team includes, from left to right, Balie Walton, Grazelda Phoenix, Doris Lintz, Sis Kimball, and M. Bodenner. One story goes that during one game, when the Fairburn team did not have enough girls to field a team, Miss Shoemaker of Hermosa volunteered to play for Fairburn so the game could go on. After she was injured, Miss Hanlon, also of Hermosa, stepped forward to take her place. (Above, courtesy of Rick Mills; below, courtesy of the Hermosa Arts and History Association.)

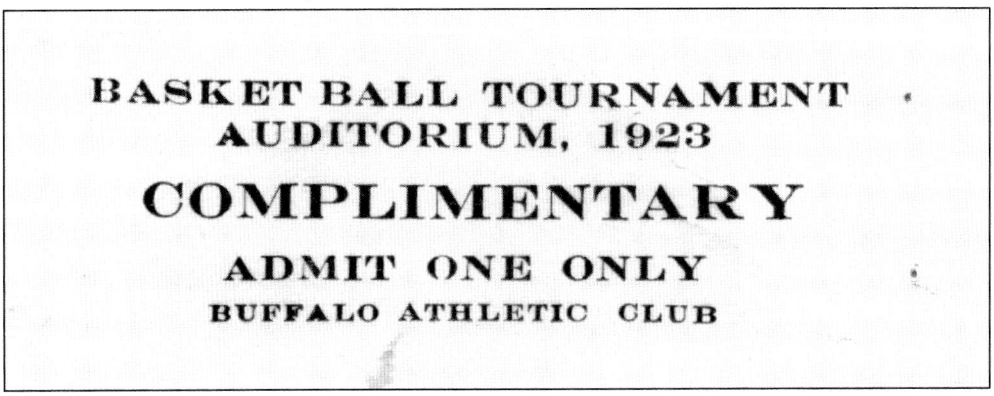

BASKET BALL TOURNAMENT
AUDITORIUM, 1923

COMPLIMENTARY

ADMIT ONE ONLY

BUFFALO ATHLETIC CLUB

Six

Changing Faces

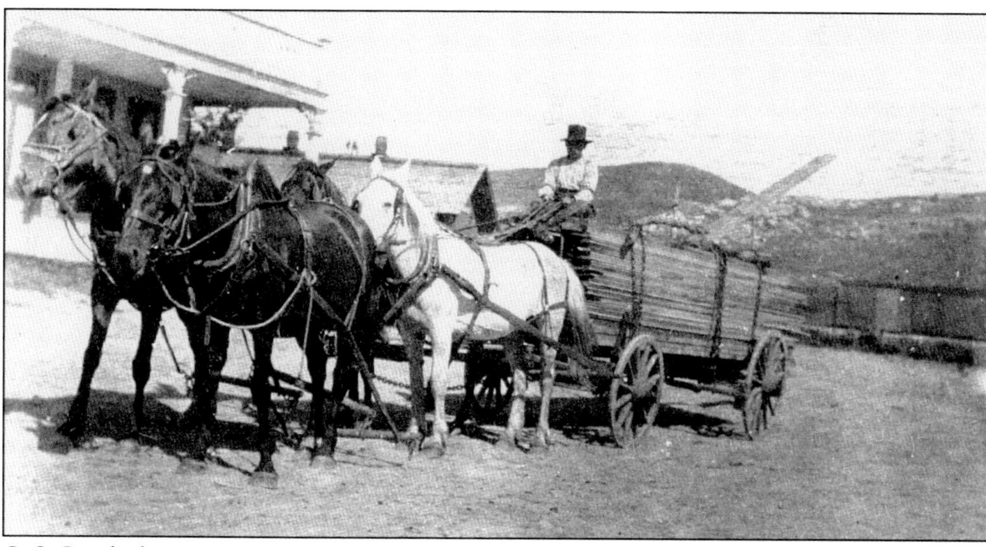

C. J. Smith, known to everyone as Chunky, is seen here with a load of lumber in front of a Fairburn hotel. (Courtesy of Nelda Carroll.)

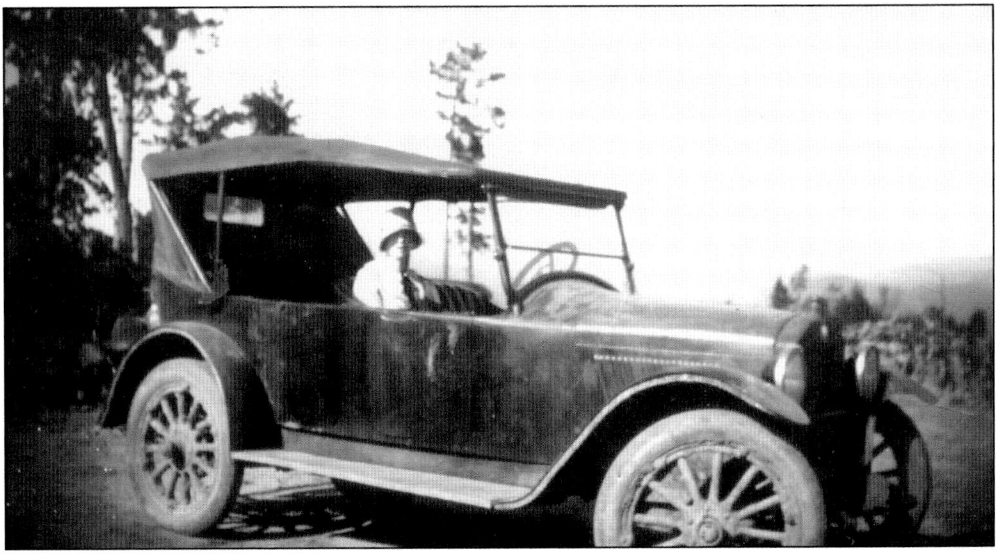

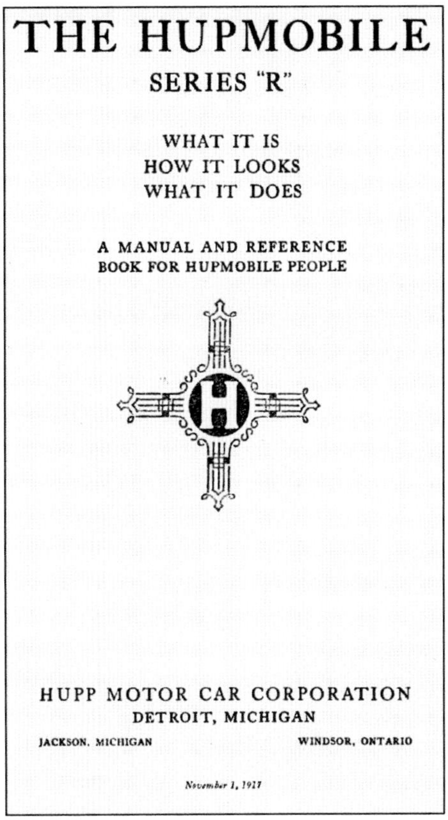

THE HUPMOBILE

SERIES "R"

WHAT IT IS
HOW IT LOOKS
WHAT IT DOES

A MANUAL AND REFERENCE BOOK FOR HUPMOBILE PEOPLE

HUPP MOTOR CAR CORPORATION
DETROIT, MICHIGAN

JACKSON, MICHIGAN WINDSOR, ONTARIO

November 1, 1917

Vern Smith's Hupmobile had long, sleek lines. (Courtesy of Glen Smith.)

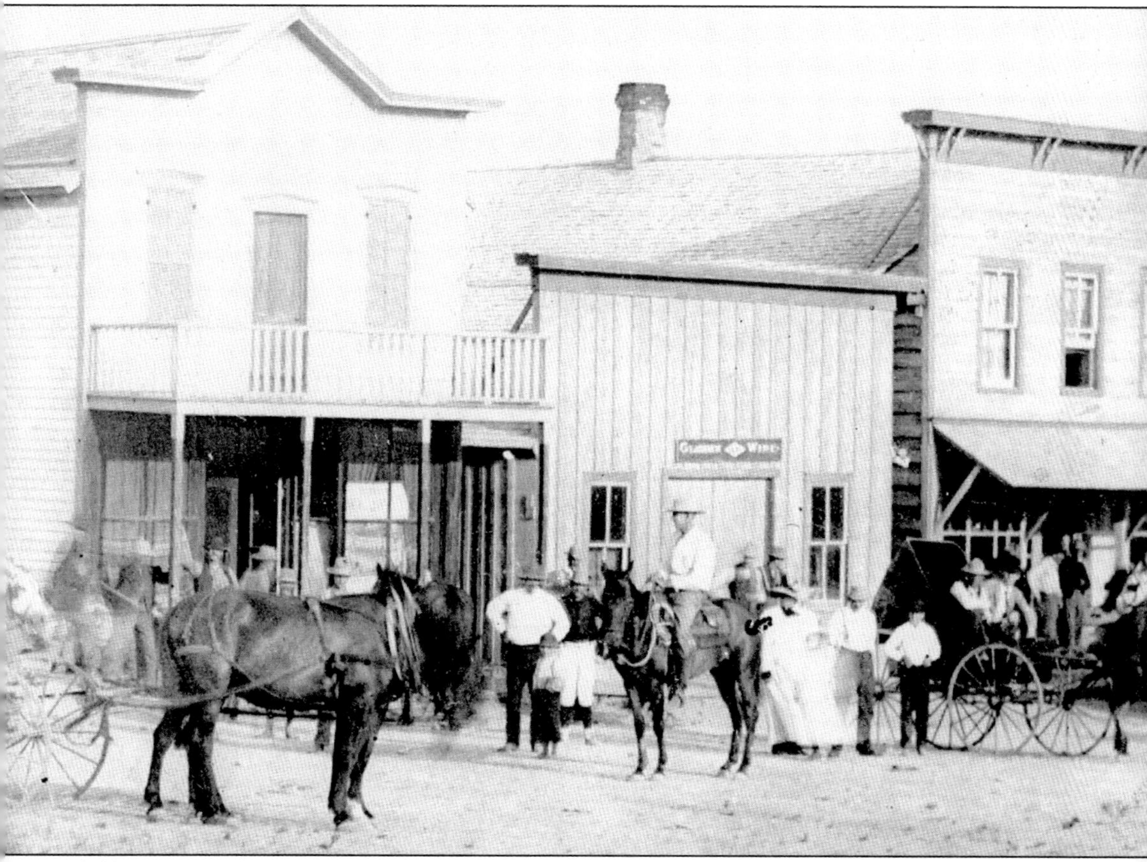

Glidden Wire is the sign on this store in downtown Fairburn. (Courtesy of Nelda Carroll.)

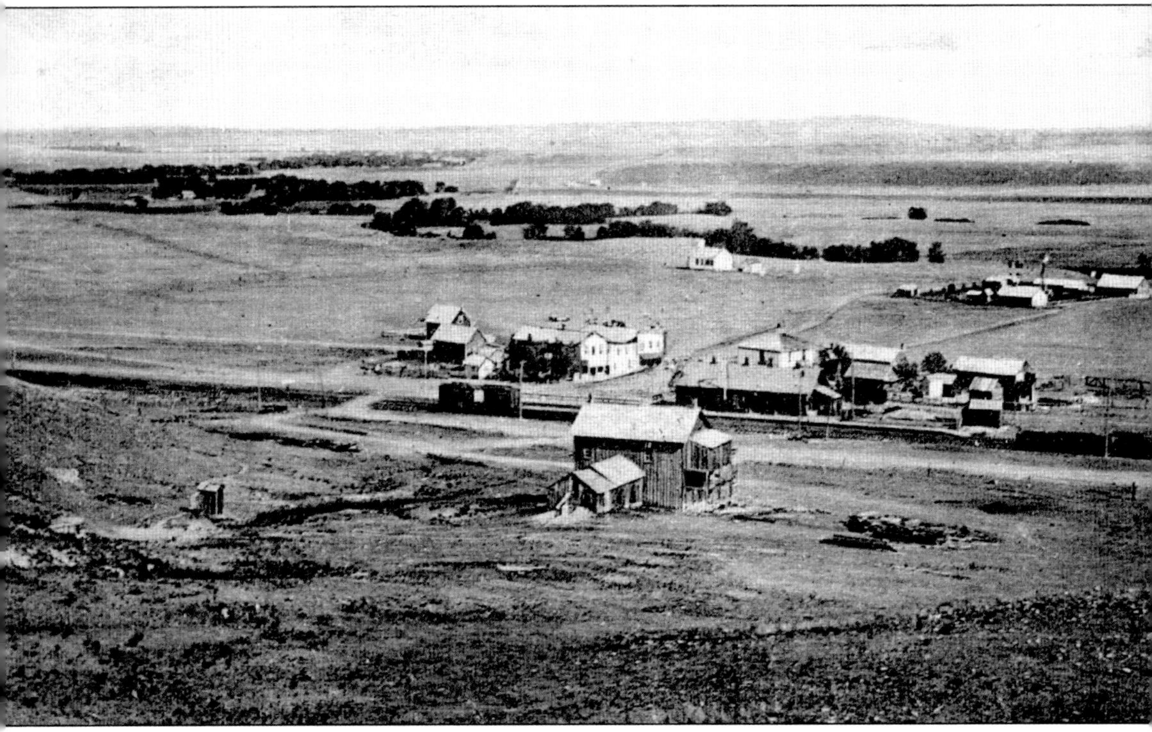
In 1912, Fairburn was a bustling community. (Courtesy of Nelda Carroll.)

The Fairburn School is pictured in 1905 with the town in the background. The school later became the Catholic church. (Courtesy of Glen Smith.)

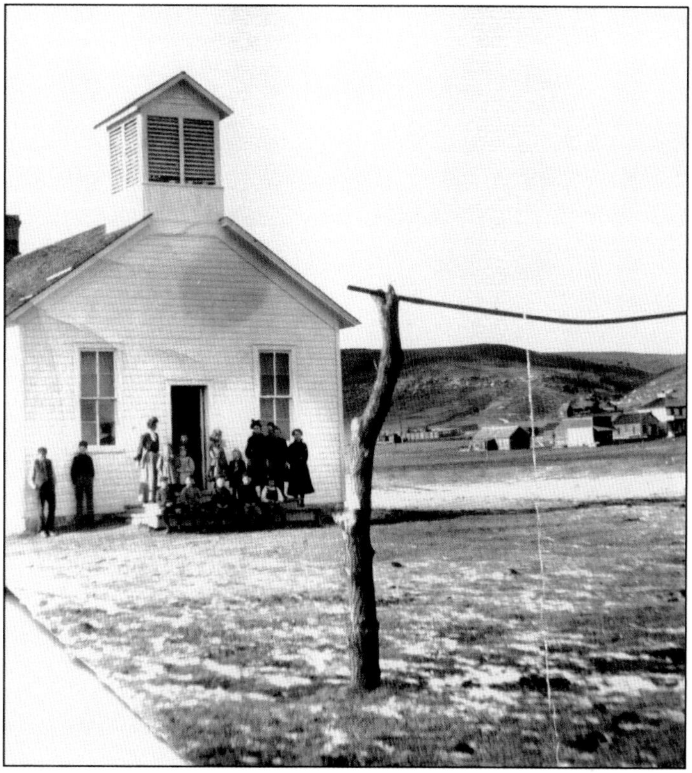

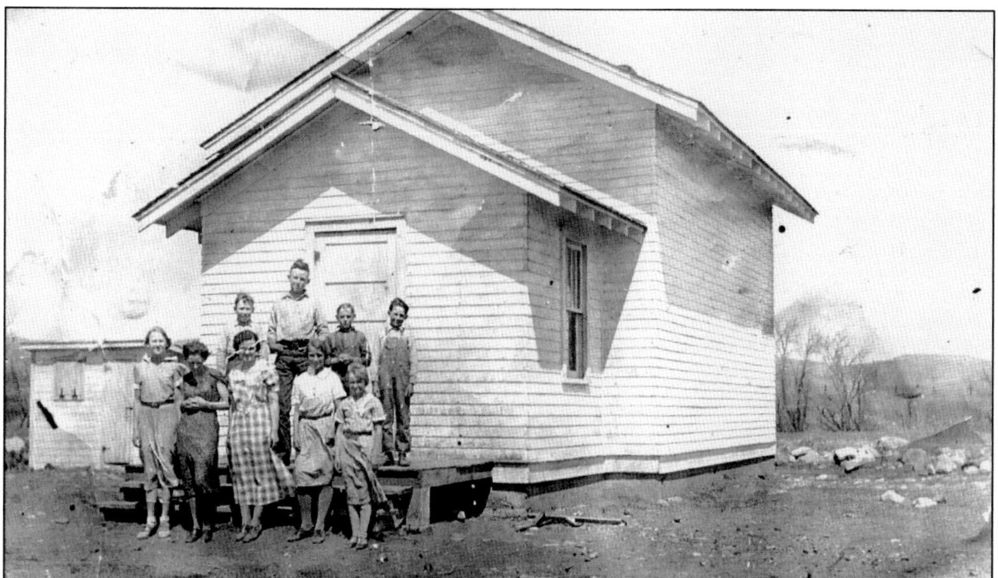

Students in the Downen School south of Fairburn include Alma Downen, Deana Downen, Jeanny Hawkens, Billy Mills, Betty Mills, Wendell Downen, Maynard Downen, and Glen R. Smith. (Courtesy of Nelda Carroll.)

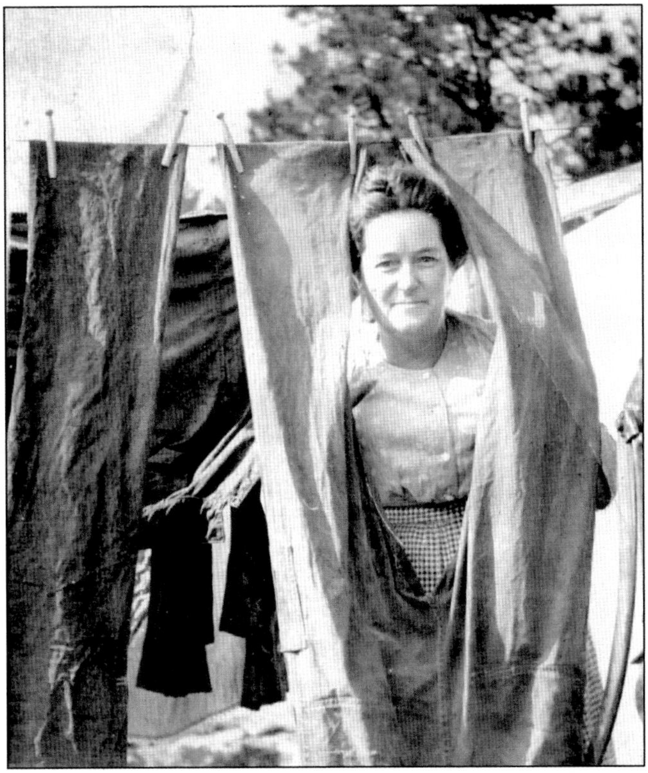

This unidentified woman and her smiling face are framed by the laundry on the line. (Author's collection.)

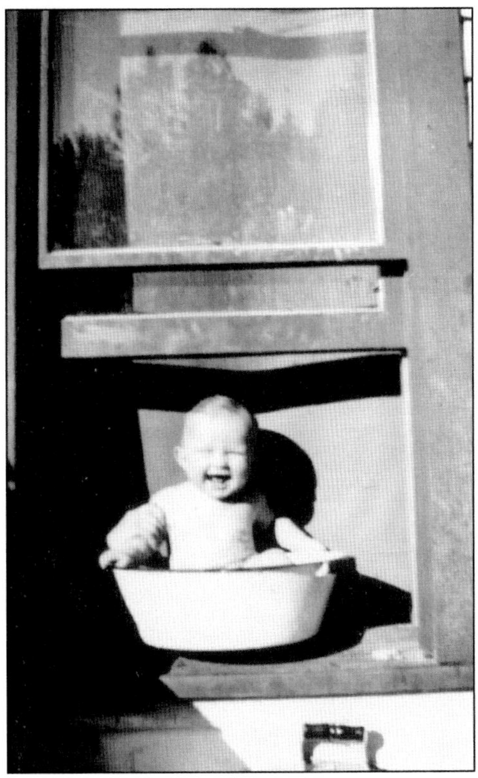

Larry Gorsuch seems to be happy in his bath. (Courtesy Mary Brady.)

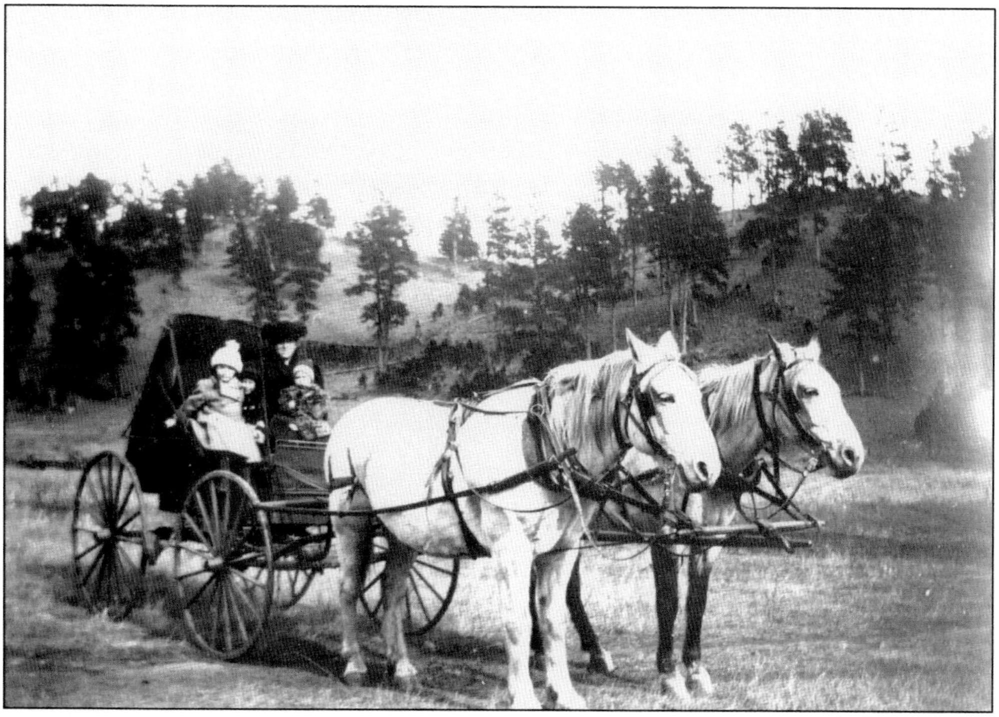

Seen here is Francis Havens driving the buggy with her children Dexter, Eva, and Cora. (Courtesy of Nelda Carroll.)

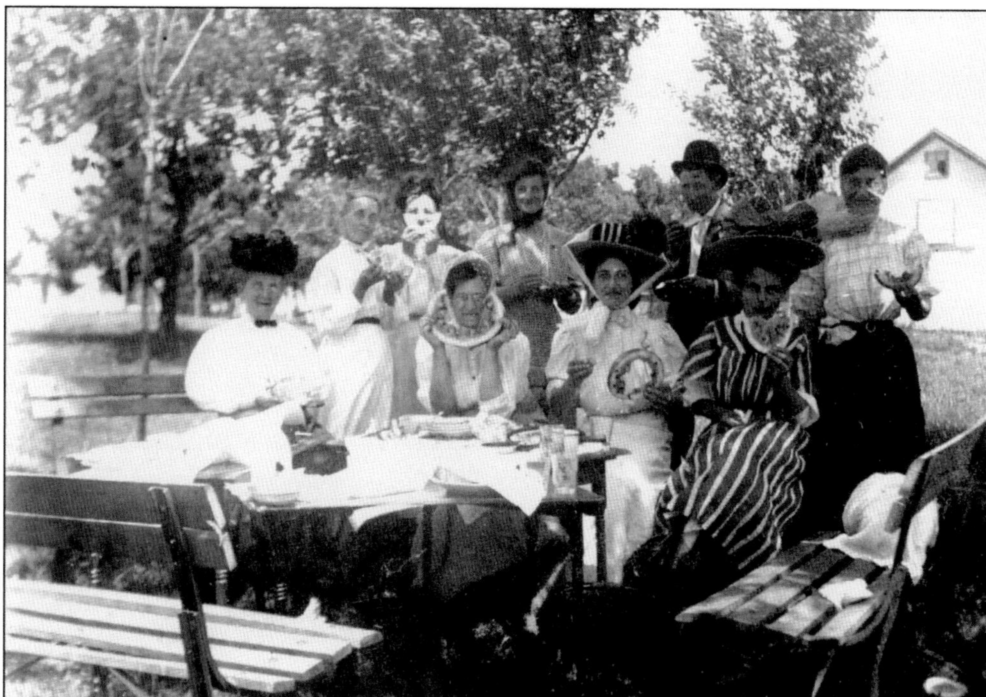

This watermelon party seems to be an excuse for getting together and having fun. (Courtesy of Irv and Geraldine Evans.)

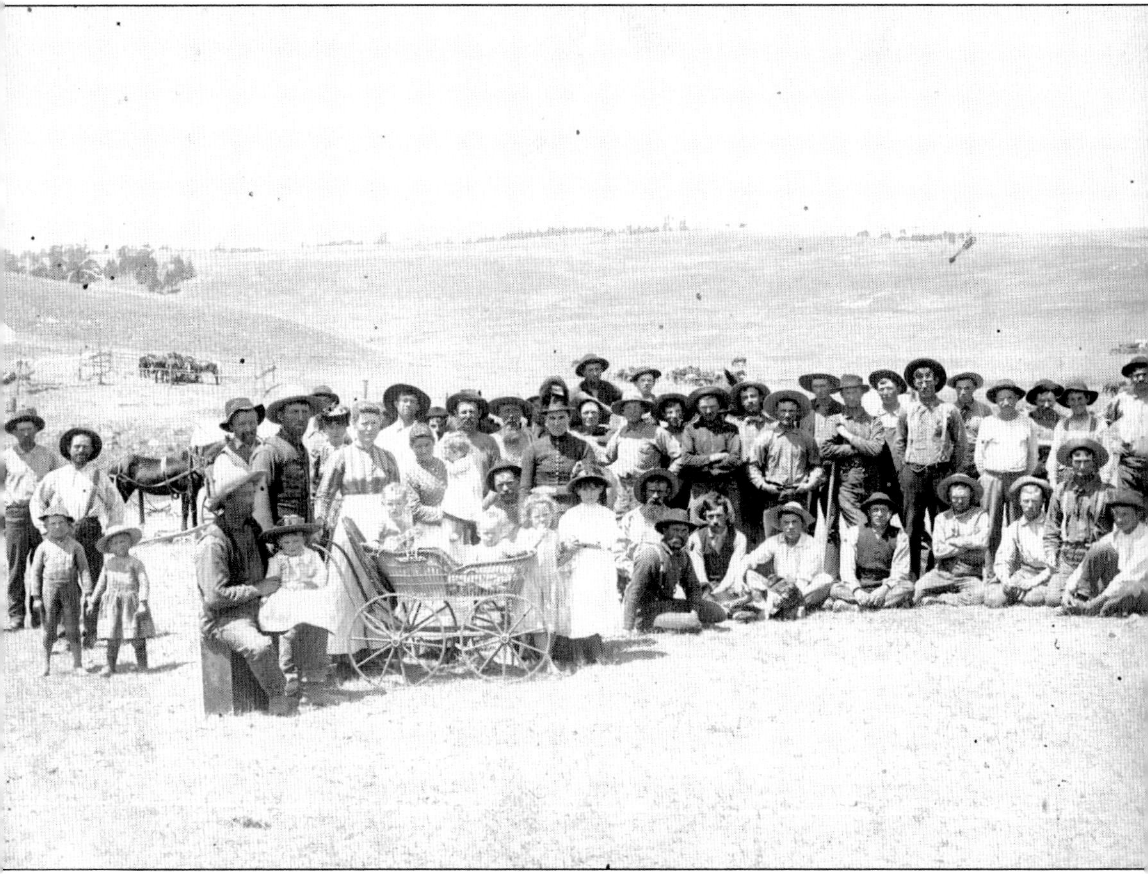

Members of a railroad construction crew and their families gather at Argyle in 1890. The man nearly in the center with the long beard (two men behind the right side of the baby carriage) is Martin Rasmussen, the great-uncle of Wayne Kewley. (Courtesy of Wayne Kewley.)

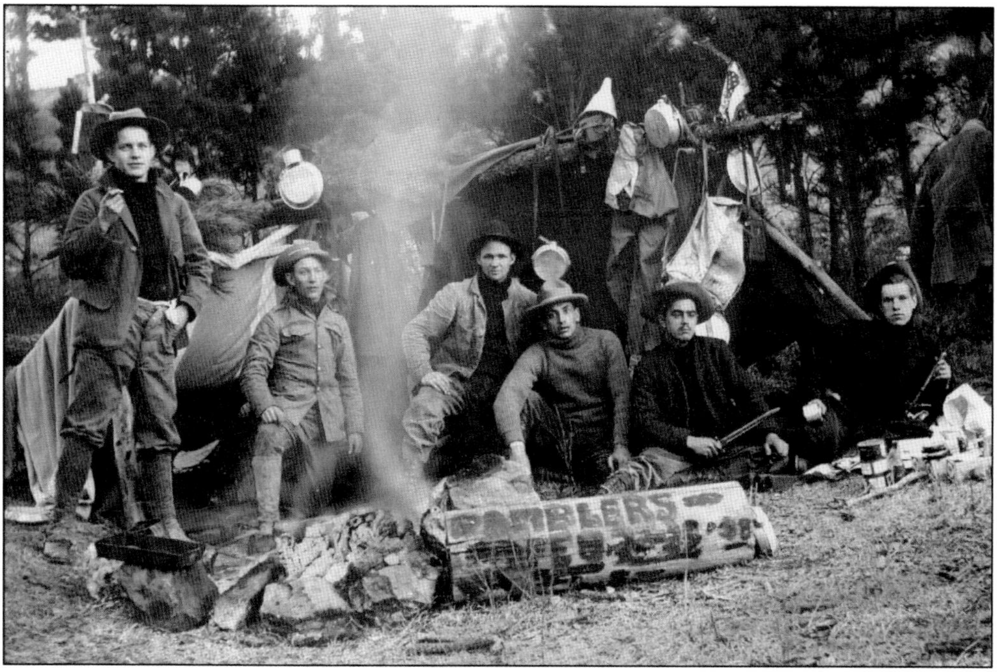

The next two photographs show the Ramblers, a loosely organized men's group from Hot Springs, at the onyx mine near Argyle. (Courtesy of Fall River County Pioneer Museum.)

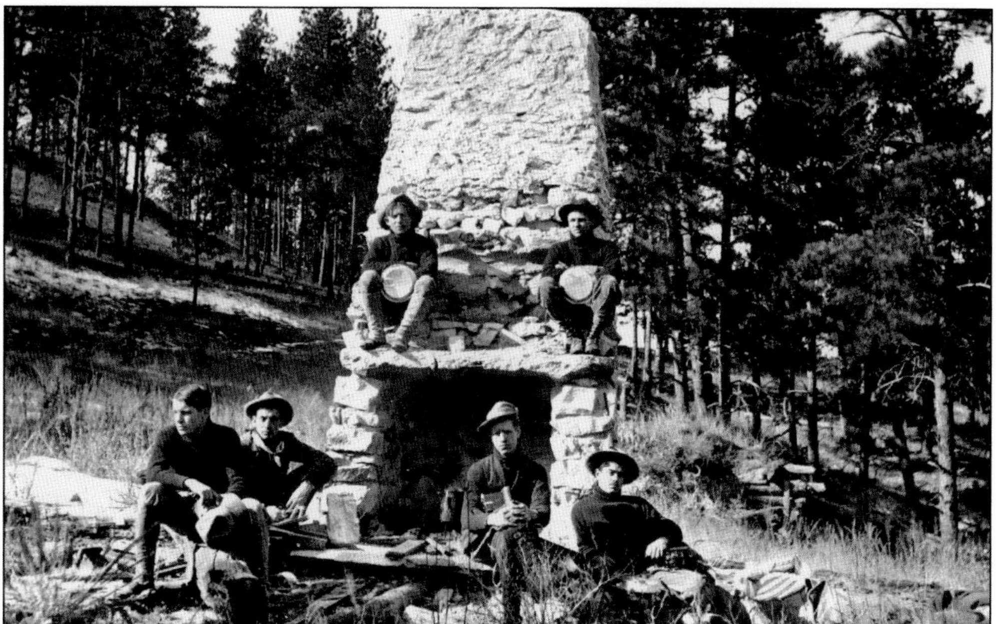

At one time, there was a hotel at the onyx mine, and this fireplace was all that was left after the hotel burned. (Courtesy of Fall River County Pioneer Museum.)

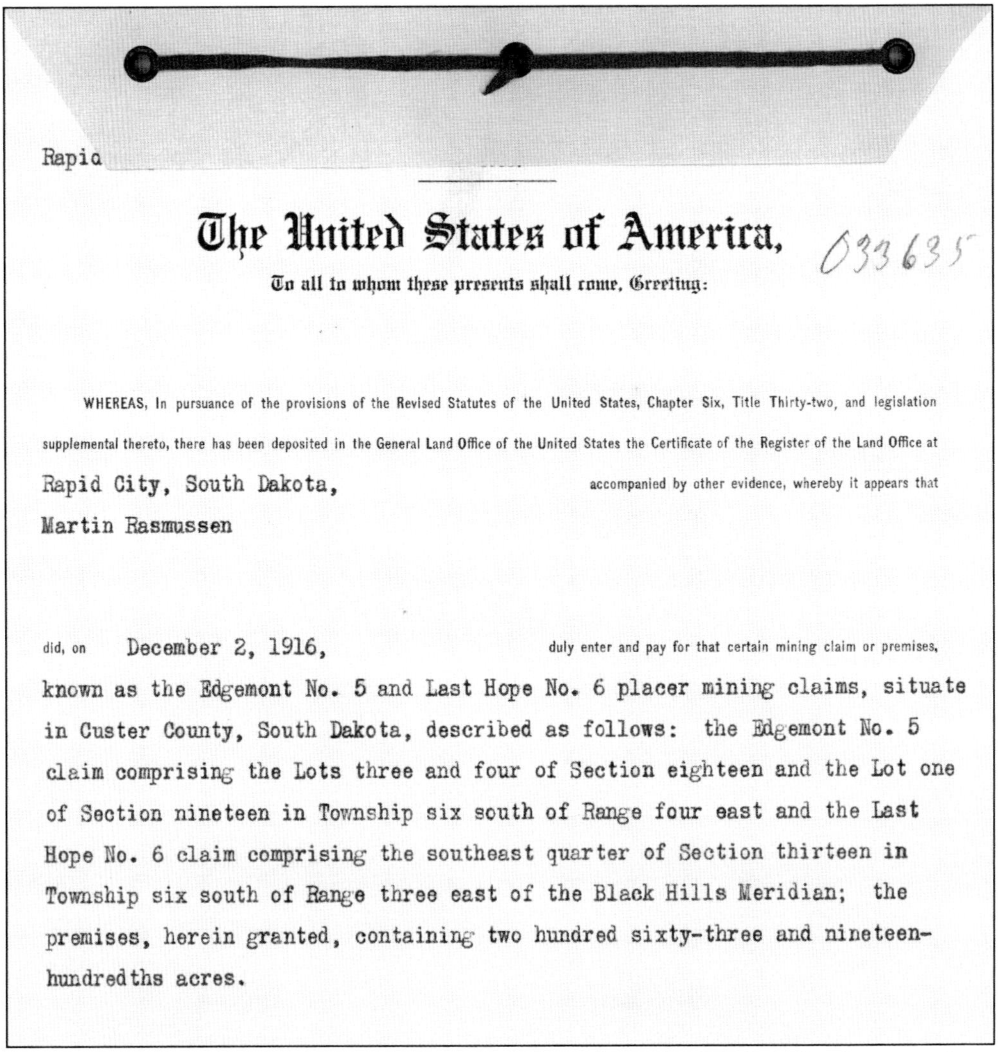

Rapid

The United States of America,

033635

To all to whom these presents shall come, Greeting:

WHEREAS, In pursuance of the provisions of the Revised Statutes of the United States, Chapter Six, Title Thirty-two, and legislation supplemental thereto, there has been deposited in the General Land Office of the United States the Certificate of the Register of the Land Office at Rapid City, South Dakota, accompanied by other evidence, whereby it appears that Martin Rasmussen

did, on December 2, 1916, duly enter and pay for that certain mining claim or premises, known as the Edgemont No. 5 and Last Hope No. 6 placer mining claims, situate in Custer County, South Dakota, described as follows: the Edgemont No. 5 claim comprising the Lots three and four of Section eighteen and the Lot one of Section nineteen in Township six south of Range four east and the Last Hope No. 6 claim comprising the southeast quarter of Section thirteen in Township six south of Range three east of the Black Hills Meridian; the premises, herein granted, containing two hundred sixty-three and nineteen-hundredths acres.

Mining claims abounded in Custer County and throughout the Black Hills. Among others, claims were for gold, silver, tin, iron, copper, mica, onyx, and tungsten. Placer mining is mining done on the surface of the earth as opposed to underground.

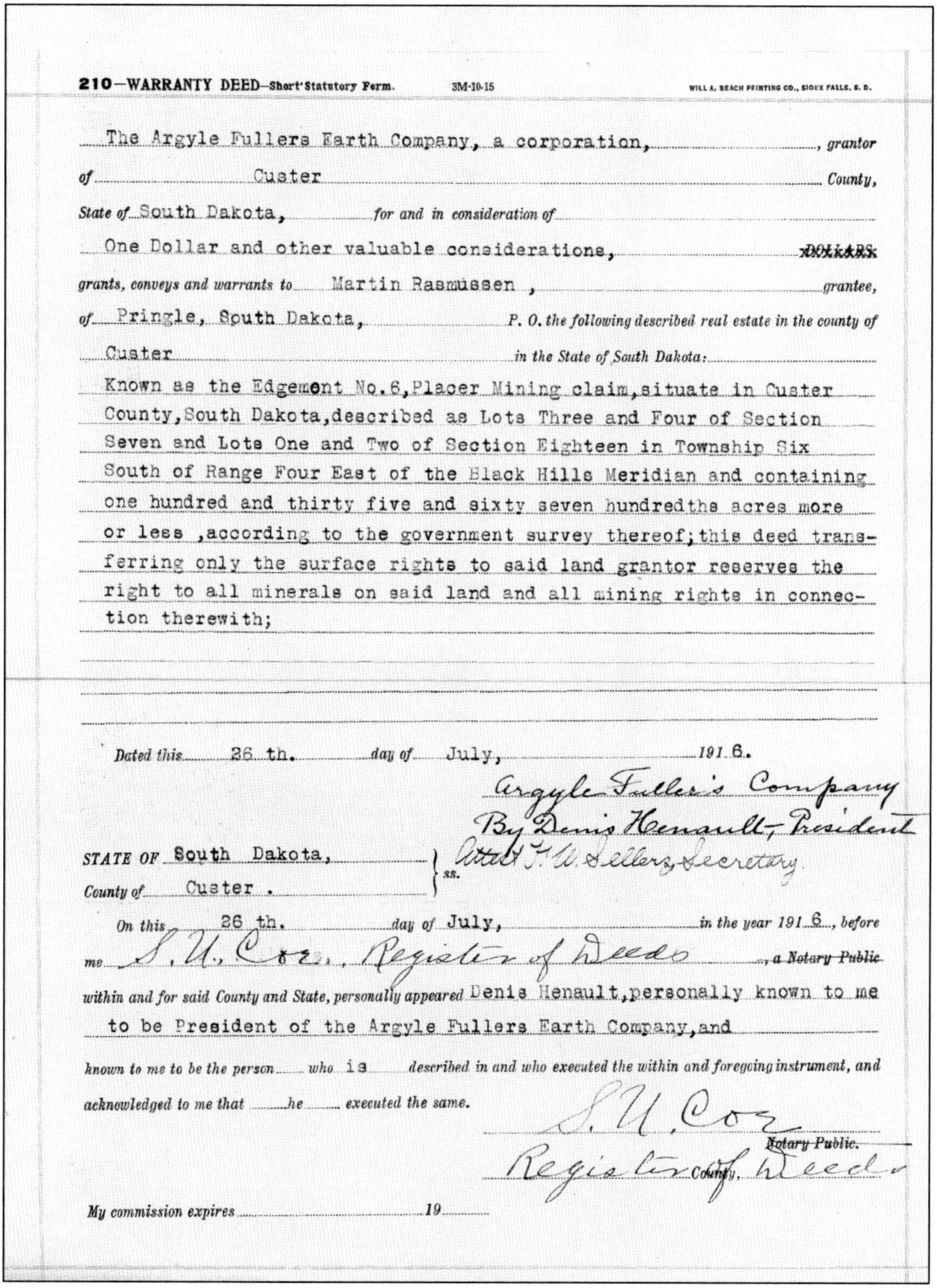

210—WARRANTY DEED—Short Statutory Form. 3M-10-15 WILL A. BEACH PRINTING CO., SIOUX FALLS, S. D.

The Argyle Fullers Earth Company, a corporation, grantor of Custer County, State of South Dakota, for and in consideration of One Dollar and other valuable considerations, ~~DOLLARS~~ grants, conveys and warrants to Martin Rasmussen, grantee, of Pringle, South Dakota, P. O. the following described real estate in the county of Custer in the State of South Dakota:

Known as the Edgement No.6,Placer Mining claim,situate in Custer County,South Dakota,described as Lots Three and Four of Section Seven and Lots One and Two of Section Eighteen in Township Six South of Range Four East of the Black Hills Meridian and containing one hundred and thirty five and sixty seven hundredths acres more or less ,according to the government survey thereof;this deed transferring only the surface rights to said land grantor reserves the right to all minerals on said land and all mining rights in connection therewith;

Dated this 26 th. day of July, 1916.

Argyle Fuller's Company
By Denis Henault, President
Attest F. W. Sellers, Secretary

STATE OF South Dakota,
County of Custer. } ss.

On this 26 th. day of July, in the year 1916, before me S. U. Coe, Register of Deeds, ~~a Notary Public~~ within and for said County and State, personally appeared Denis Henault,personally known to me to be President of the Argyle Fullers Earth Company,and known to me to be the person who is described in and who executed the within and foregoing instrument, and acknowledged to me that he executed the same.

S. U. Coe
~~Notary Public.~~
Register of Deeds County,

My commission expires 19

The Argyle Fullers Earth Company mined Henault pumice sand, named after the company's president, Denis Henault. Analysis showed that the pumice was 92 percent silica, 2 percent iron, and 6 percent mica and manganese. The pumice bed on this property was four feet thick. Once it was mined, it was sold as an abrasive.

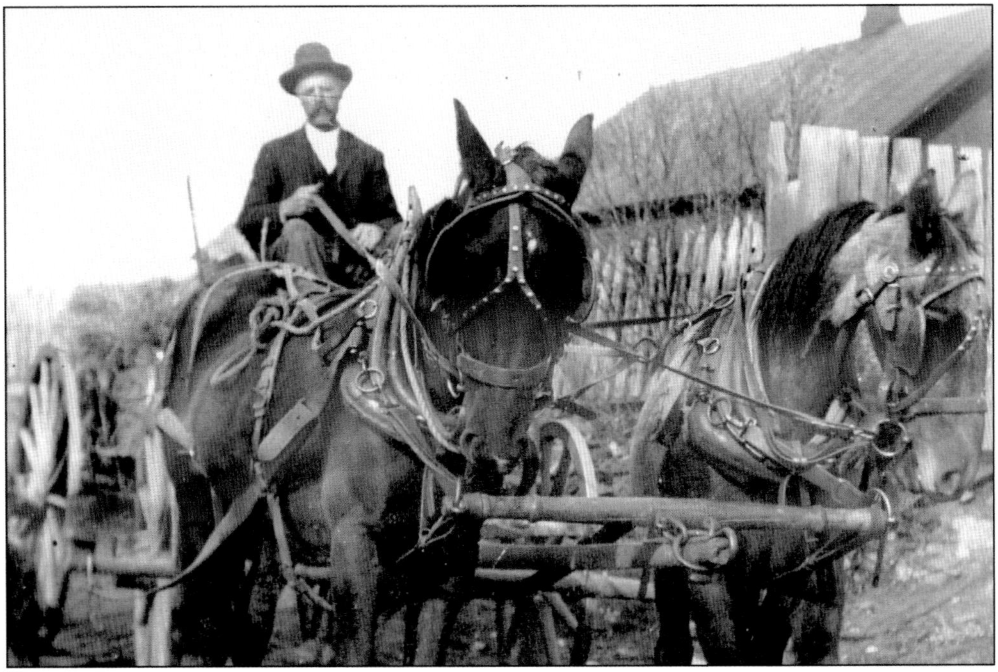

Anton Nelson is shown with his team near Argyle. (Courtesy of Wayne Kewley.)

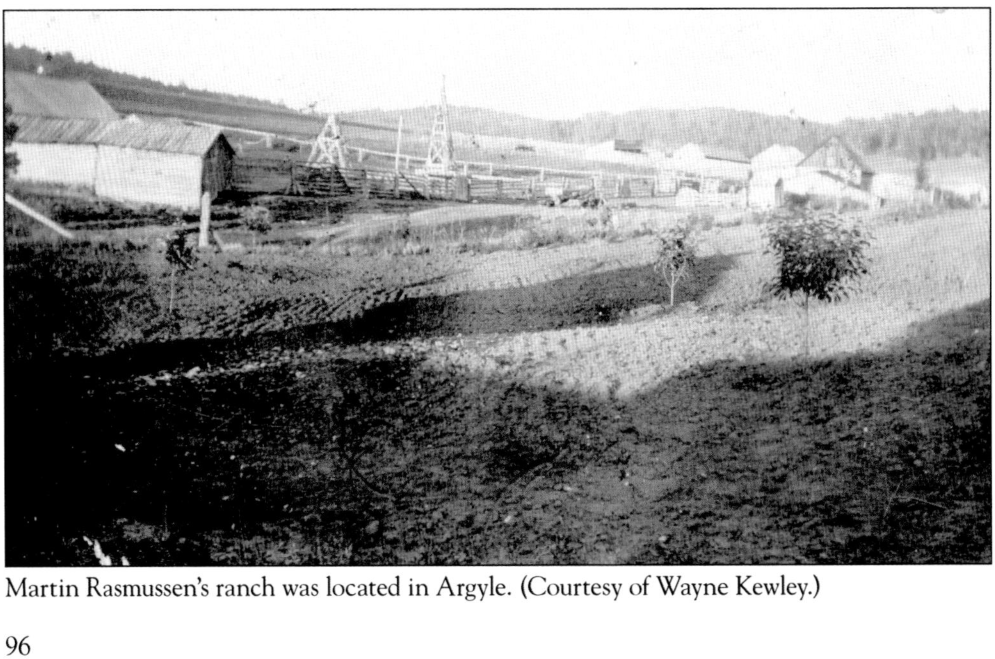

Martin Rasmussen's ranch was located in Argyle. (Courtesy of Wayne Kewley.)

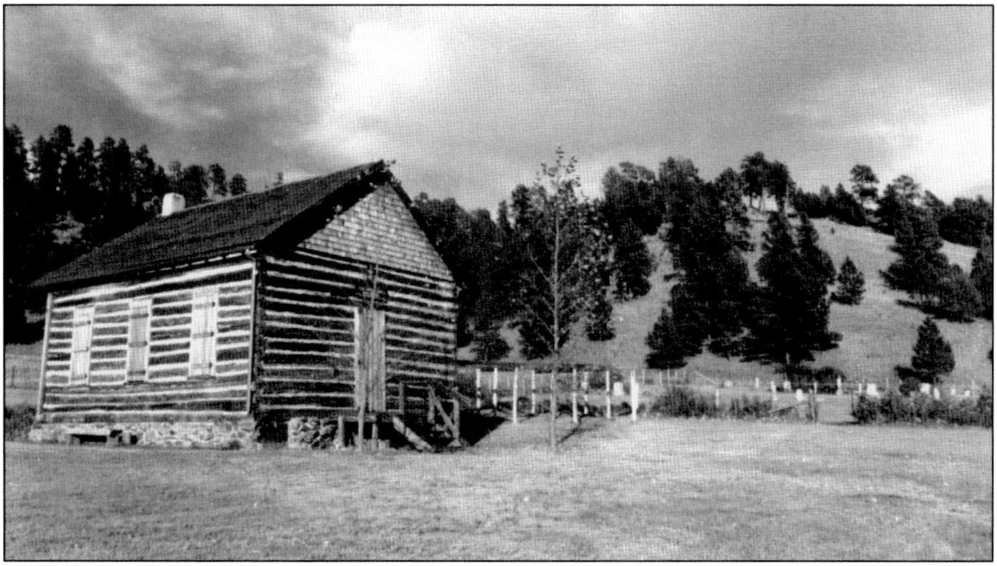

The Cold Springs School House was added to the National Register of Historic Places in 1973 after a group of concerned area citizens decided to renovate and keep it in good repair. The Cold Springs Historical Society meets at the schoolhouse during the summer months. (Courtesy of Gladys Reed.)

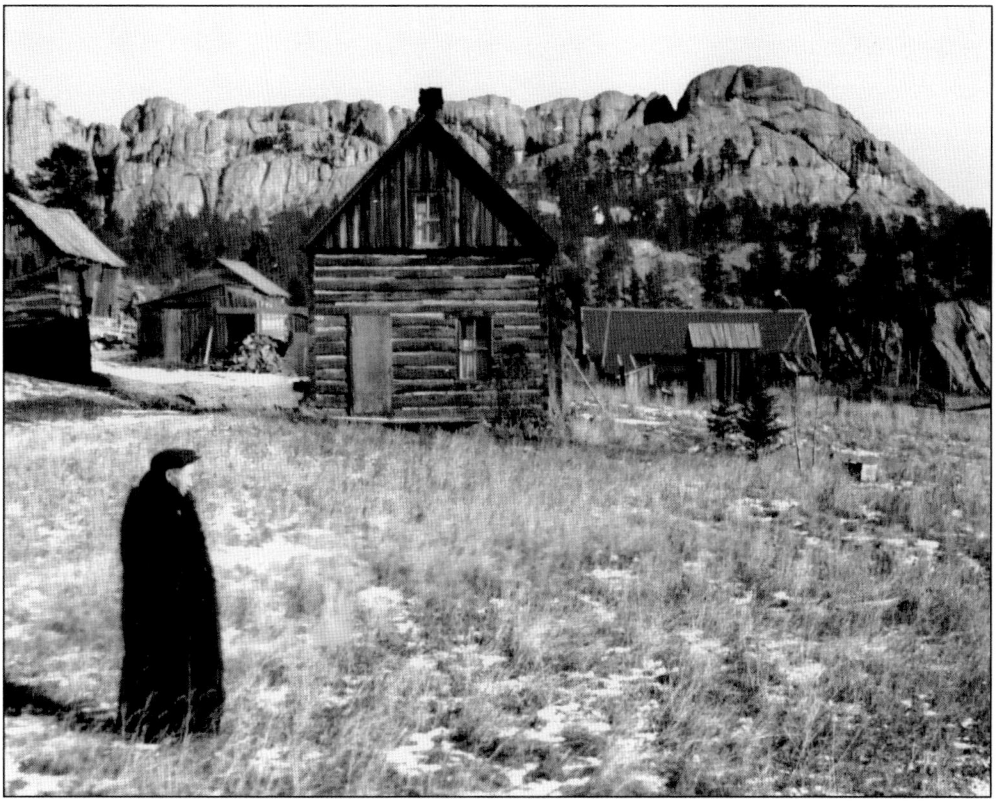

C. J. Smith is pictured wearing his buffalo robe coat. Calamity Peak is in the background. (Identification and photograph courtesy of Nelda Carroll.)

7-11 7-11

Home Coming Game

Hot Springs, S. D., Friday, October 3, 1941

HOT SPRINGS	
64—Aaberg, end	150
60—Craft, halfback	160
66—Eastlick, guard	148
67—Kelly, tackle	160
69—Hanson, end	152
70—Beswick, fullback	200
68—Krutsch, quarterback	168
65—Getty, fullback	150
61—Taylor, halfback	160
41—Hopper, fullback	132
23—Skaggs, quarterback	150
56—Jansen, end	140
59—McClure, tackle	140
63—Menuey, center	145
45—H. Miller, center	148
50—Peters, guard	150
51—Pfeiler, end	138
20—Rooney, halfback	130
25—Larive, halfback	144
58—Renz, guard	140
71—Salmon, guard	180
62—Waugh, tackle	155
47—Weber, tackle	160
49—Sieg, tackle	130
21—Wilcox, center	130
24—P. Miller, guard	135
43—Hamlin, tackle	134

CUSTER	
40—Brigham, end	144
41—Davidson, tackle	139
42—Harley, guard	151
43—Evans, guard	135
44—Walton, end	169
45—Blaine, guard	158
46—McClaren, tackle	150
47—Morris, guard	131
48—Snodgrass, center	123
49—Sherrill, end	156
50—Byers, halfback	125
51—Callan, center	136
52—Peters, tackle	221
53—Roetzel, F., guard	136
54—Staehnke, guard	141
55—Carter, end	136
56—Farrell, fullback	126
57—Roetzel, C., tackle	150
58—Kautz, halfback	122
59—Bostwick, quarterback	132
60—Burrows, quarterback	140
61—Johnson, fullback	160
62—Nystrom, halfback	143
63—Duncan, halfback	136

COMPLIMENTS OF

7-11 RANCH DAIRY

F. O. BUTLER, OWNER

F. O. Butler was a great supporter of youth, as is demonstrated by his sponsorship of this program. His 7-11 Ranch east of Buffalo Gap was known for its registered Hereford cattle herd and polo ponies. Butler donated a large parcel of land in Hot Springs for a recreation area and park. (Courtesy of Pat Roseland.)

Seven

ANCHORS OF THE COUNTY

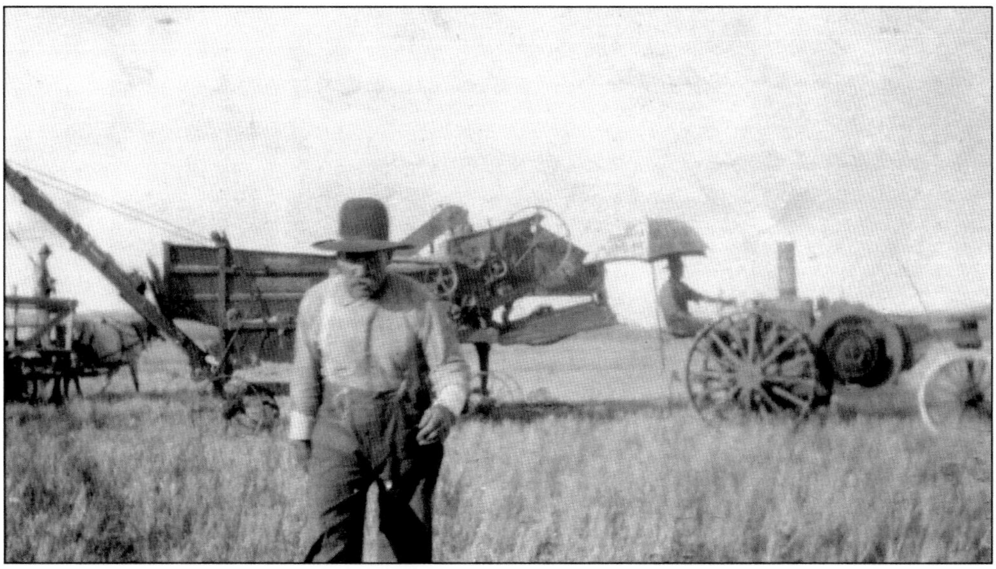

C. J. Smith is seen in front of the straw carrier and threshing setup. (Courtesy of Nelda Carroll.)

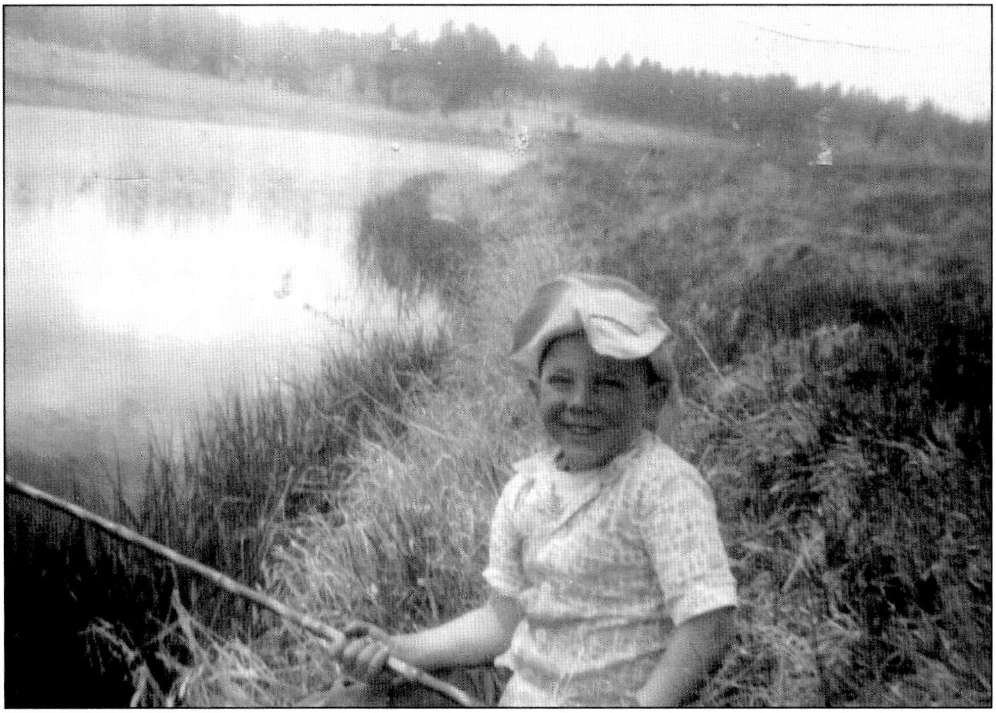

Scott Phillips tries out his fishing pole at Stockade Lake, also known as Doran Lake. The state purchased most of the Doran family ranch as a place to build a lake and had the Civilian Conservation Corps excavate the site and build the lake. The CCC camp was called Camp Doran—hence the two names, Doran and Stockade, for the same lake. (Courtesy of Joyce Phillips.)

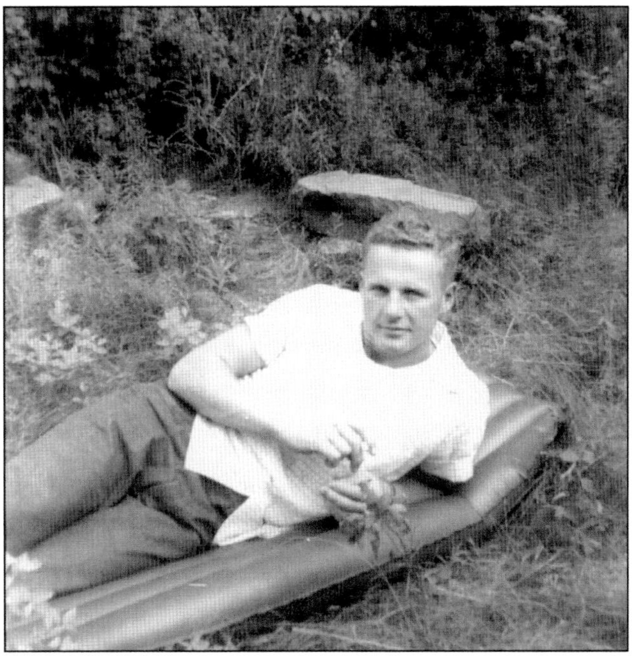

Bob Harley enjoys a day off in this 1956 photograph. (Courtesy of Bob and Carol Harley.)

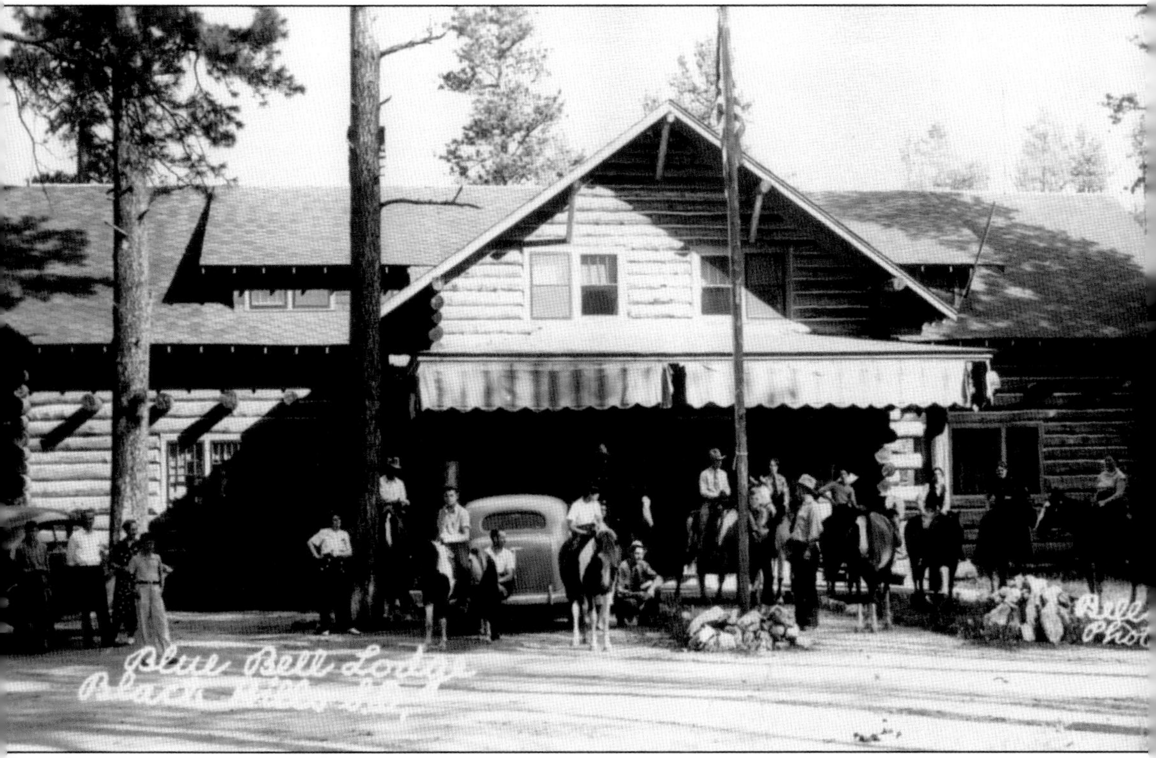

Blue Bell Lodge was built by Chris Jensen. A letter written by Leslie Jensen (son of Chris) on March 30, 1954, to Walter F. Little of Igloo reads, "My late father, C. L. [Chris] Jensen, started building Blue Bell Lodge in the fall of 1926. He had a crew of men living in portable houses. They worked through the winter locating and cutting the large trees and skidding them on the snow to the site where they were peeled and left to season. He started laying up logs in 1927 and I recall that when the President visited the Hills that summer the roof was on and carpenters were framing the openings and working on the interior. A Mr. Berglund Burg, a man still in the Hills, the best man I've ever seen with an adz, was in charge of the log work and derricks were used to lift the large logs into place." (Photograph and letter excerpt courtesy of Chris Jensen, great-grandson of C. L. Jensen.)

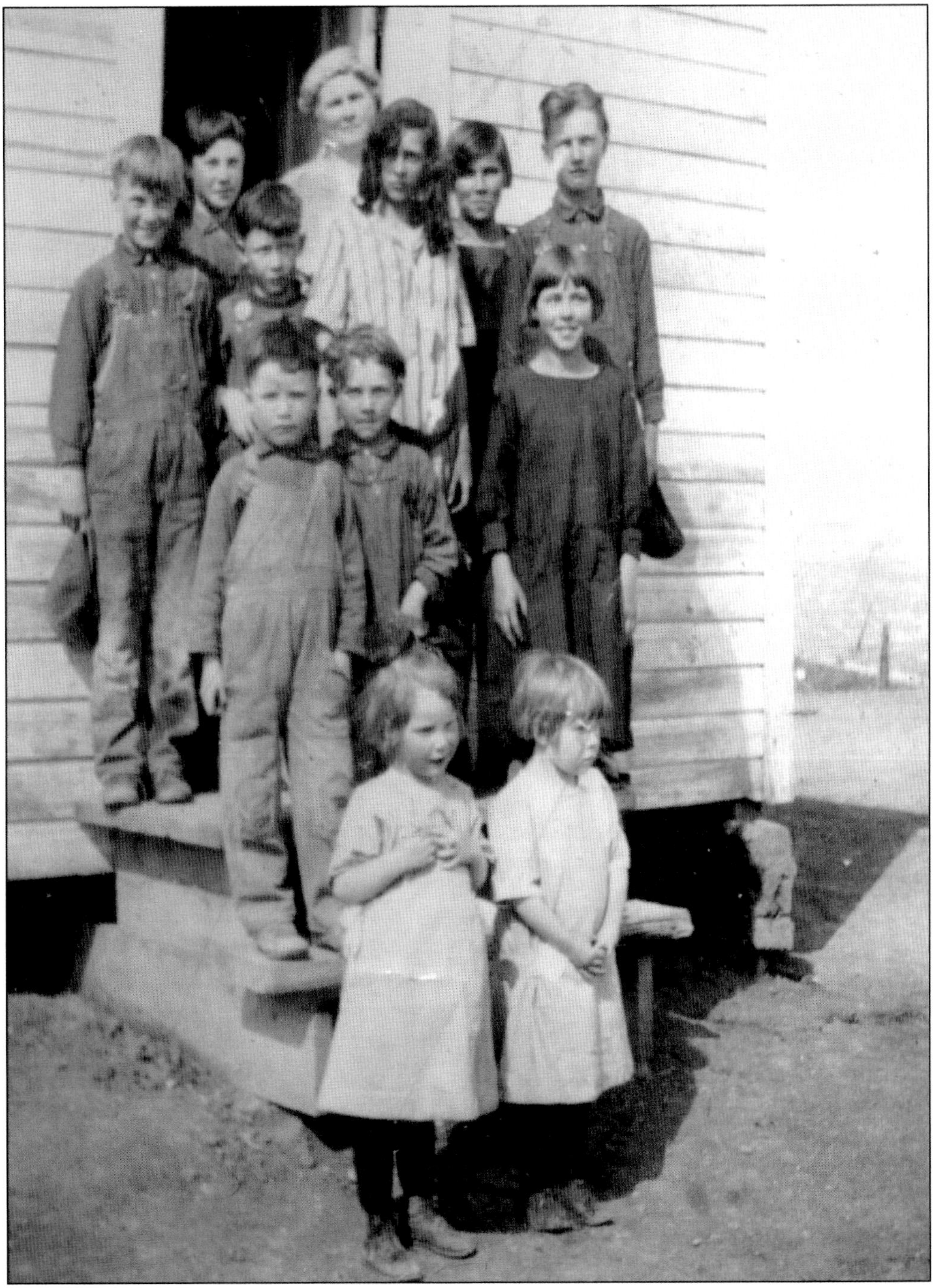

The Melvin School was a country school in the area of Buffalo Gap. Posing in 1925 are, from left to right, the following: (first row) Anna Marie (Johnson) Nordstrom and Marcella (Roberts) Ayres; (second row) Bill Degnan, Floyd Roberts, and Marian (Roberts) O'Bryan; (third row) Ed Johnson, Buryl Degnan, Marie (Peterson) Wilson, and Walt Johnson; (fourth row) Edwin Johnson, Bert Van Pelt, teacher Mrs. Miller, Dorothy (Roberts) Harmon, and Walt Johnson. (Courtesy Shortie Gallentine.)

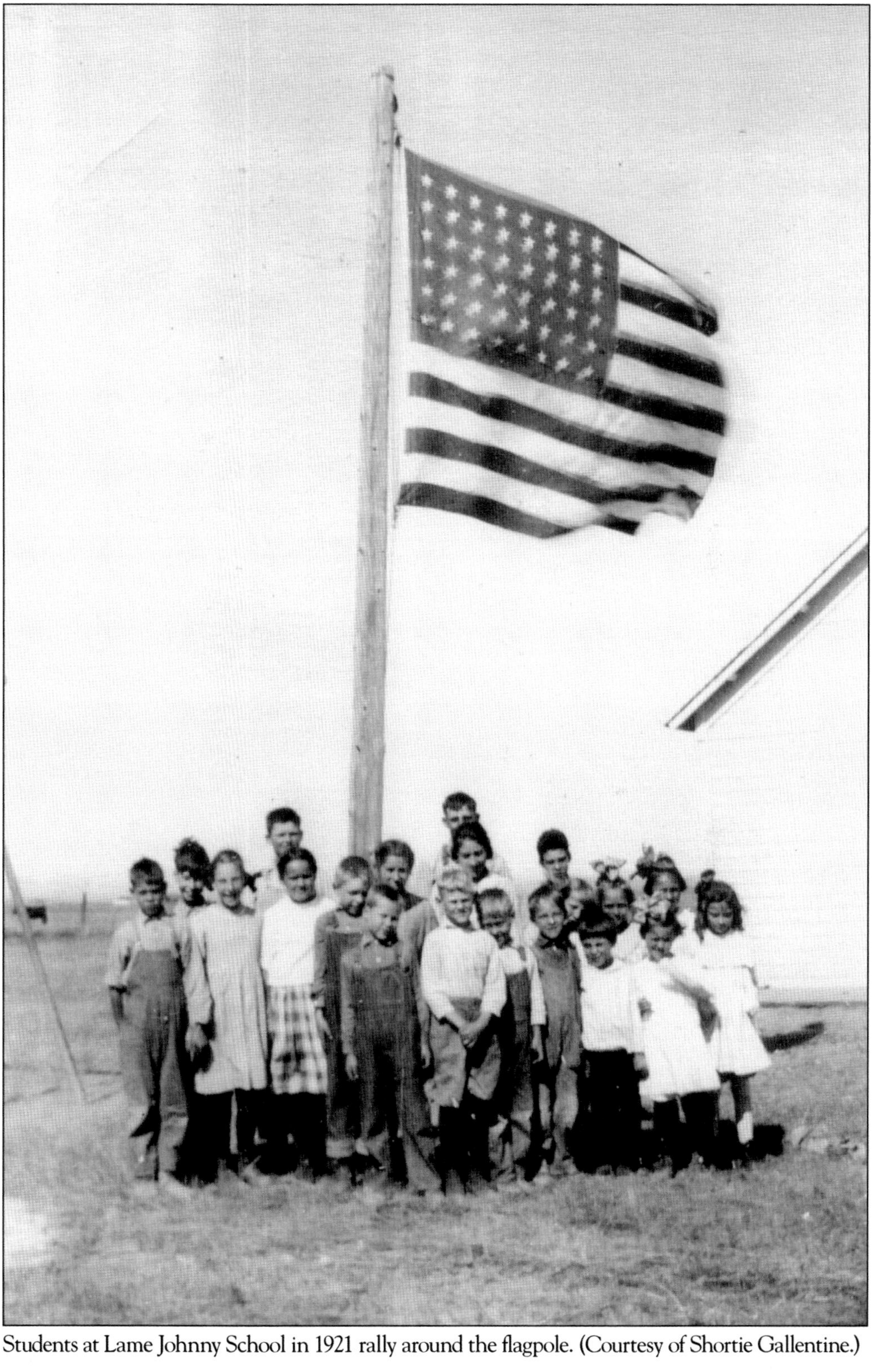
Students at Lame Johnny School in 1921 rally around the flagpole. (Courtesy of Shortie Gallentine.)

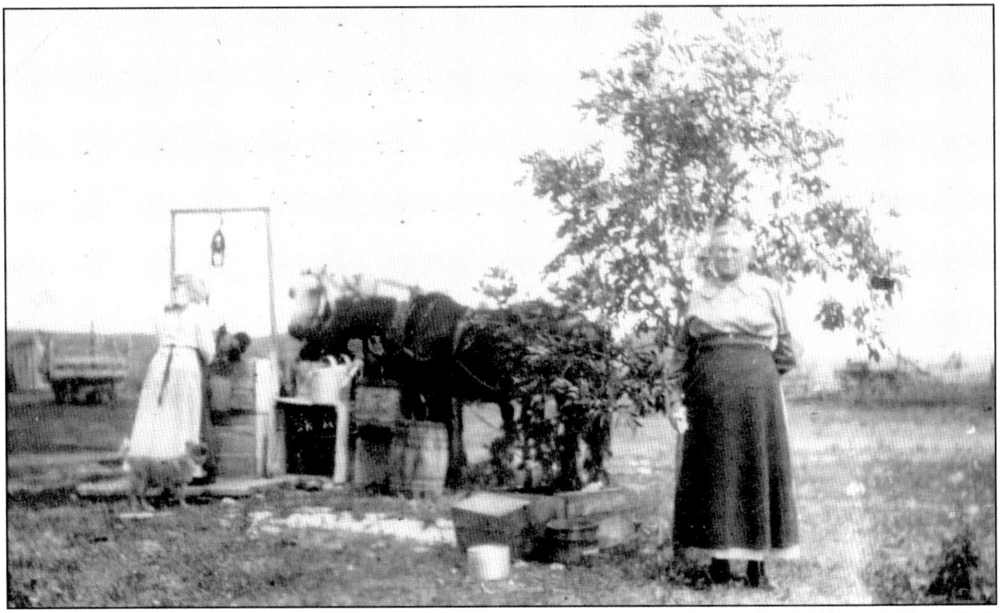

Teresa Smith is on the right in this 1912 photograph. The woman at the well is unidentified. (Courtesy of Nelda Carroll.)

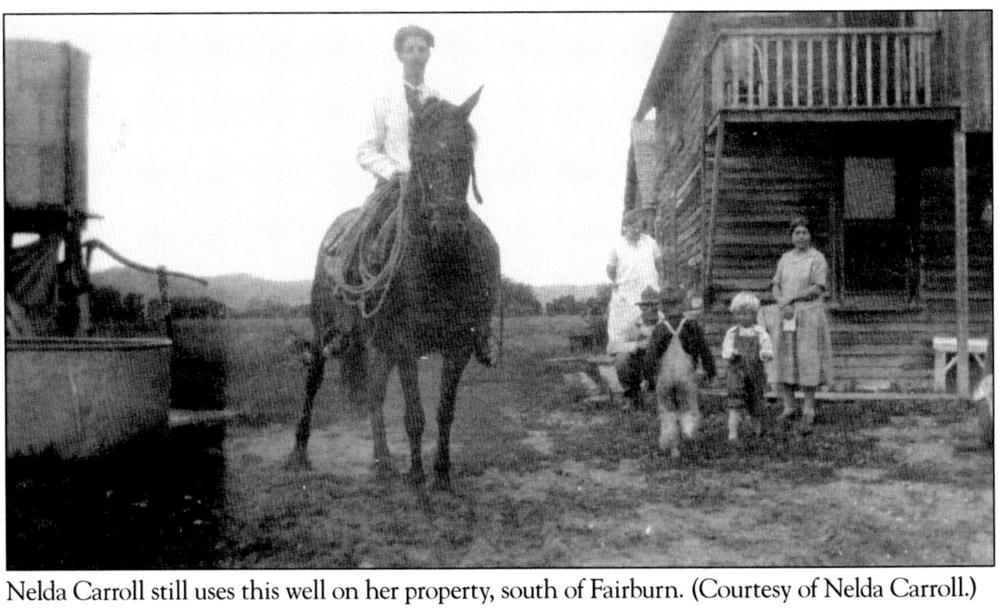

Nelda Carroll still uses this well on her property, south of Fairburn. (Courtesy of Nelda Carroll.)

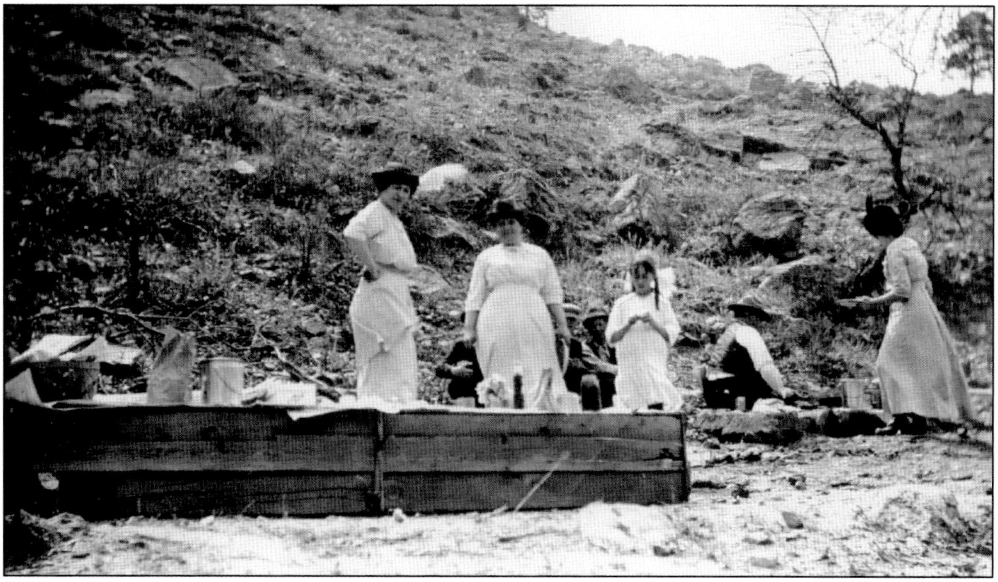

Members of the Stabler family are seen on a 1915 outing at Calico Canyon. (Courtesy of Jim and Marlene Galloway.)

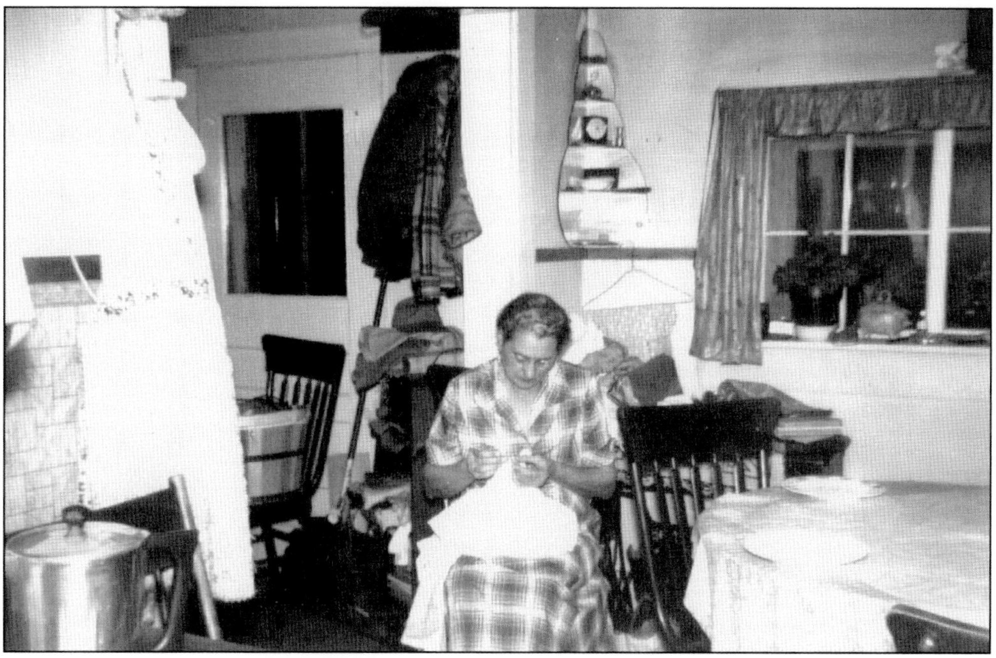

There is never an idle moment with Louise Dumke, who is shown doing handwork in her kitchen. (Courtesy of Joyce Phillips.)

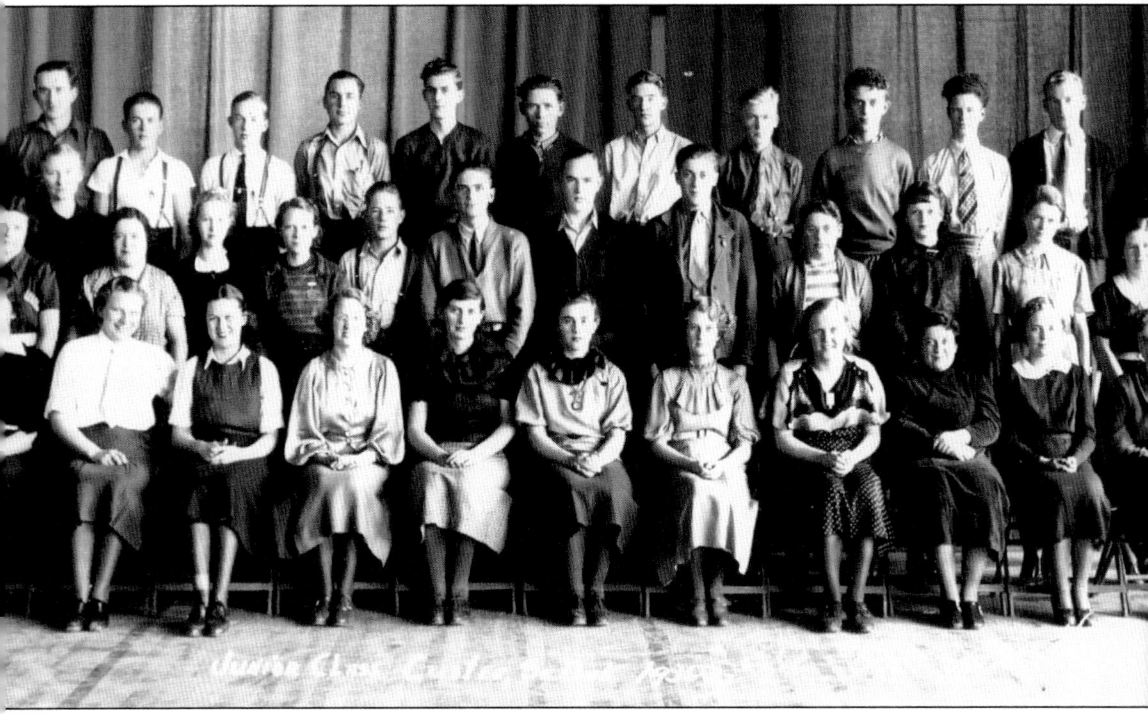

The junior class of Custer in 1936–1937 poses here. From left to right are the following: (first row) H. Brauner, W. Larsen, L. Carlson, R. Anderson, P. Mildner, A. Pinkle, R. Pithan, L. Manary, J. Markley, R. Gordon, G. LaFollette, and H. Kautz; (second row) D. Greenen, Miss Nelson, R. Daily, J. Sturm, B. Jones, L. Fall, L. O'Laughlin, F. Sellers, I. Harris, J. Weidensee, M. Staehnke, F. Stratton, and M. Jackson; (third row) F. Kidwell, L. Neilson, D. Freeland, A. Nystrom, I. Matt, E. Matt, M. Burgess, N. L. O'Connell, V. Ackley, I. Fowler, and M. Jerred. (Courtesy of Mary Brady.)

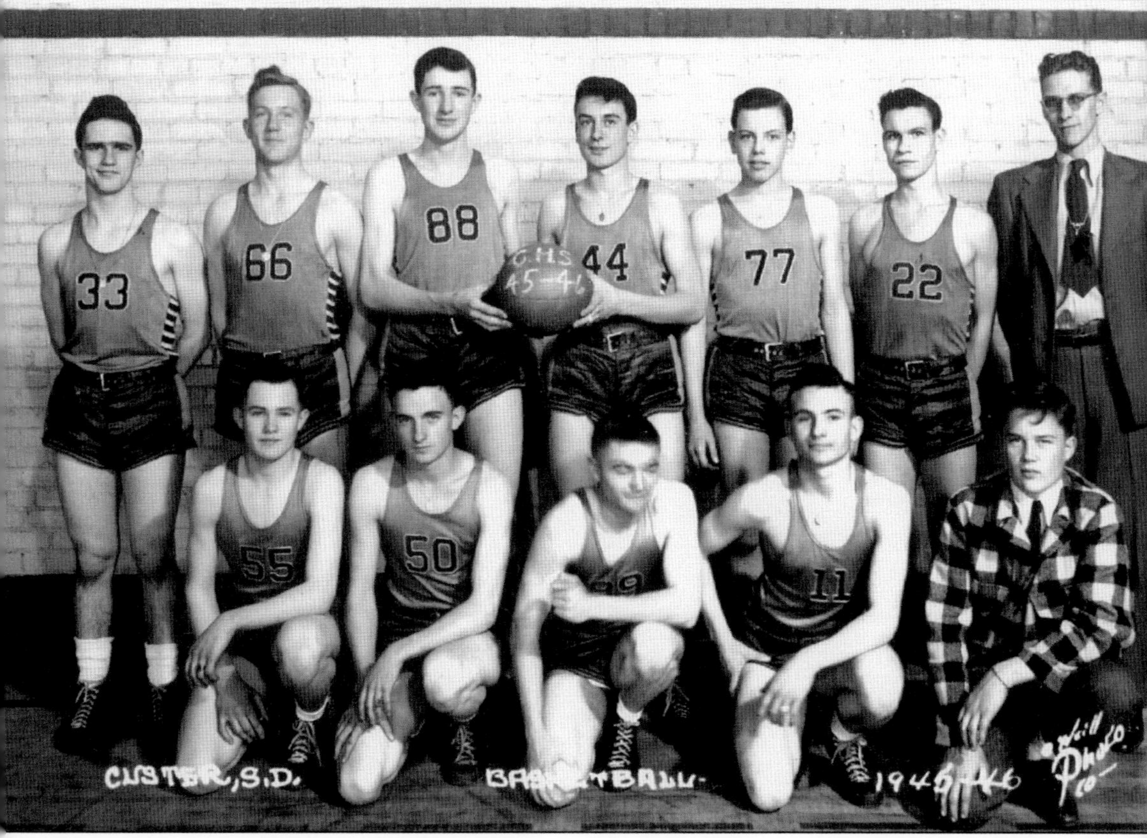

Here is the Custer High School basketball team for the 1945–1946 year. (Author's collection.)

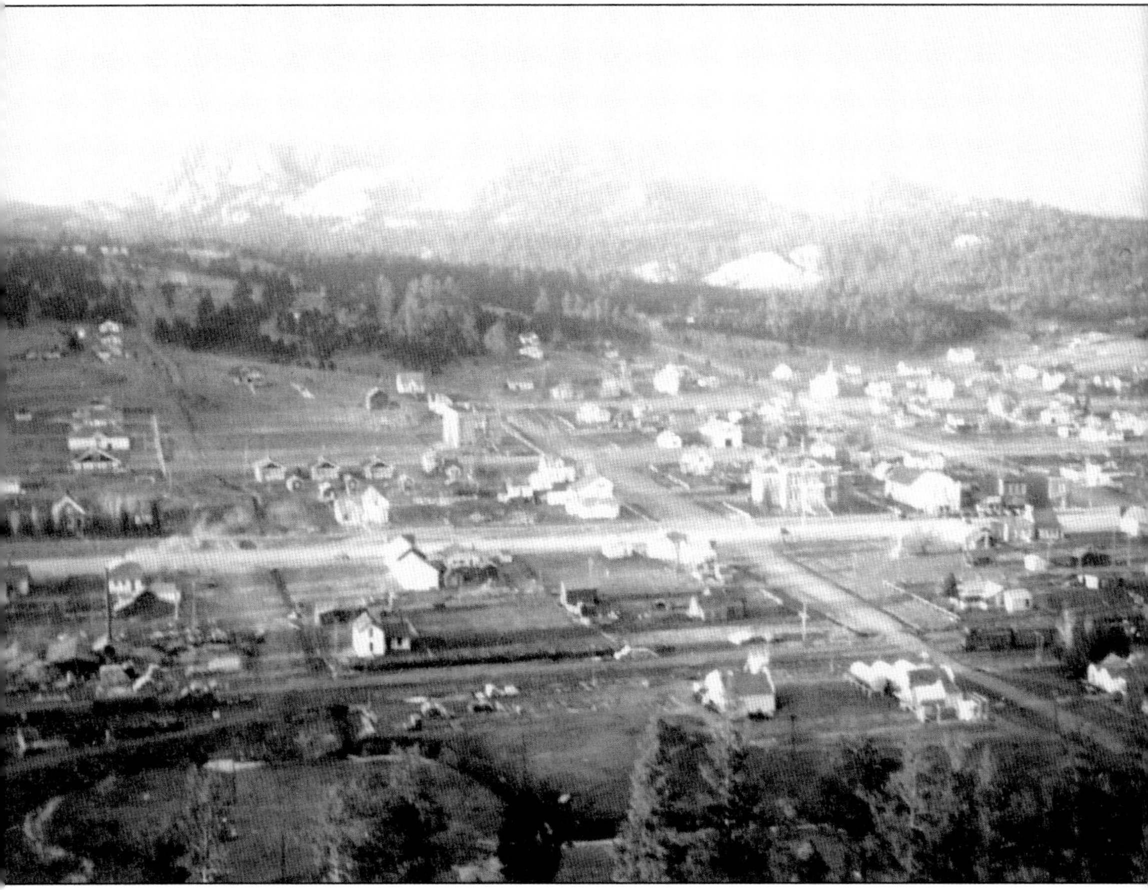

This photograph of Custer was taken in 1934 or 1935 by George Dobesh when he was serving in the Civilian Conservation Corps with Company 1791 at Camp Custer F-12. (Courtesy of Barbara [Dobesh] Robinson.)

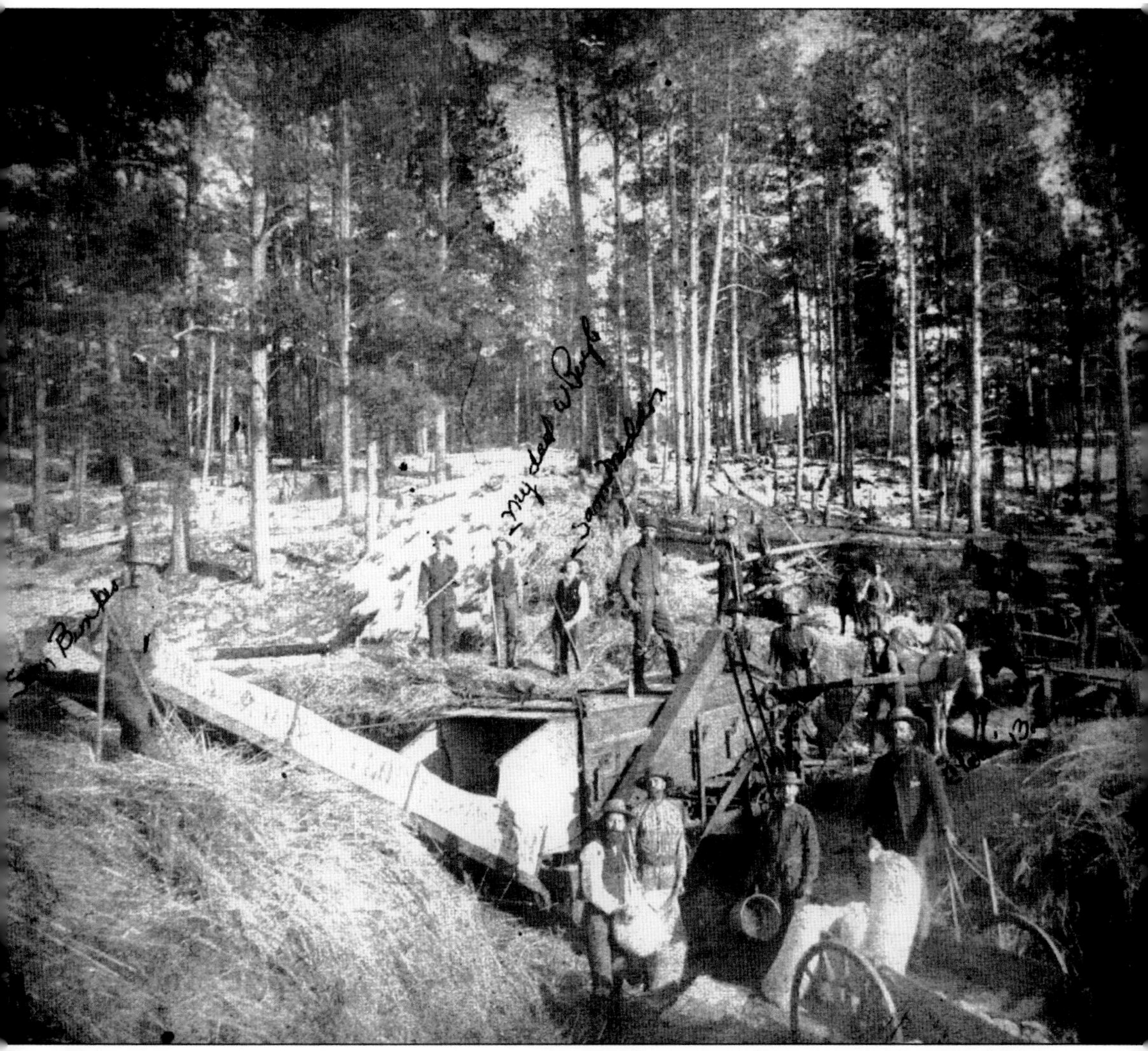

The Aultman-Taylor thresher was popular around 1910. The names of the men appear to read Sam Bunks, W. Pringle, Sam Maddox, and Charlie Zulke. (Courtesy of Leonard and Oonagh Wood.)

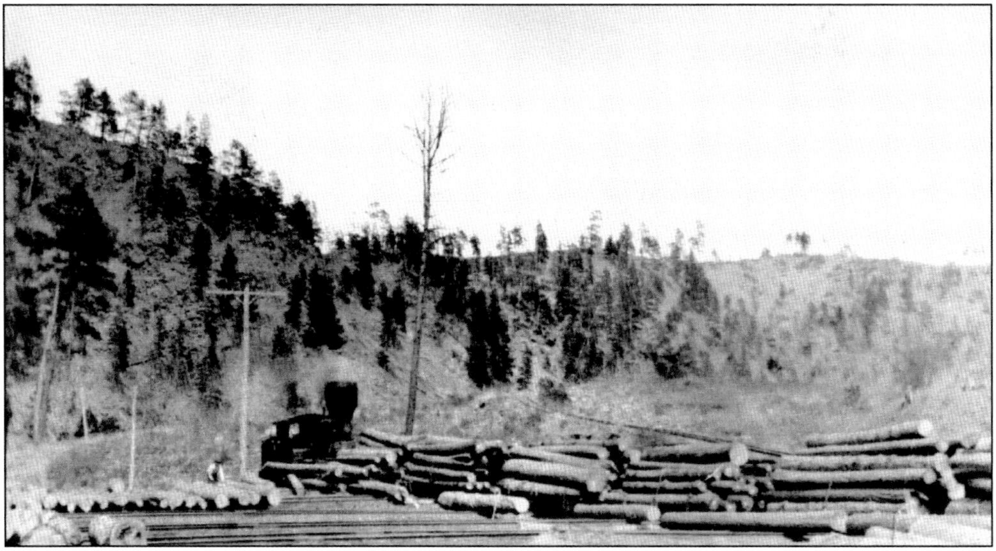

Logging and forestry has always been a big part of the economy in Custer County. This narrow-gauge railroad, owned by the Warren Lamb Lumber Company, brought logs from the Galena area and Custer State Park to Fairburn. The logs were then put onto Chicago and North Western Railroad cars for transport to Rapid City. When Furman Smith was an engineer on the narrow gauge, he and his family lived at Galena. (Courtesy of Glen Smith.)

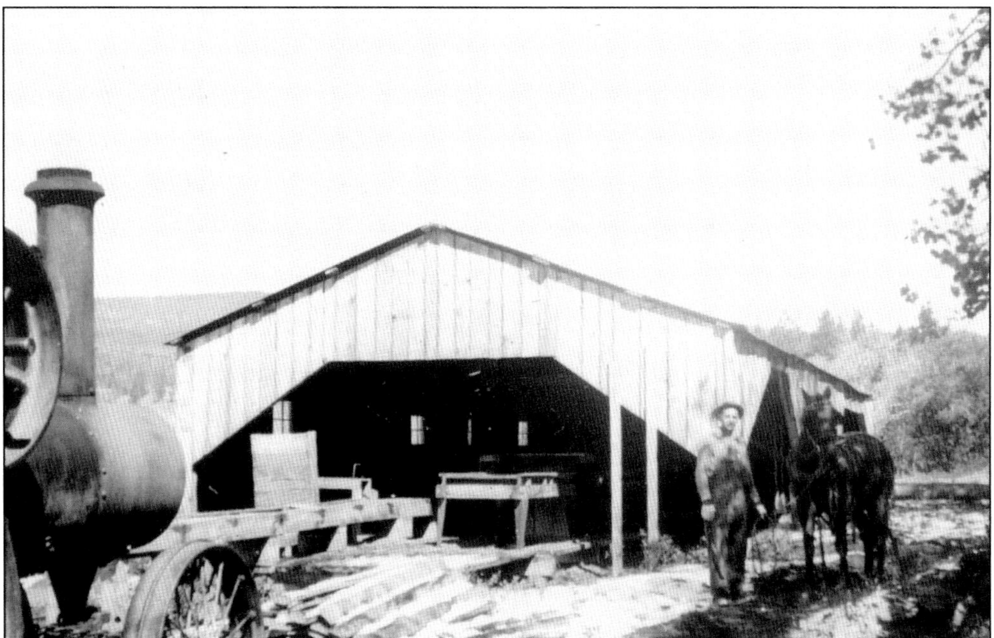

August Doll's sawmill was one of many independent mills that operated in the area. It was located northwest of Custer, near the Civilian Conservation Corps' Camp Custer. (Photograph by George Dobesh; courtesy of Barbara [Dobesh] Robinson.)

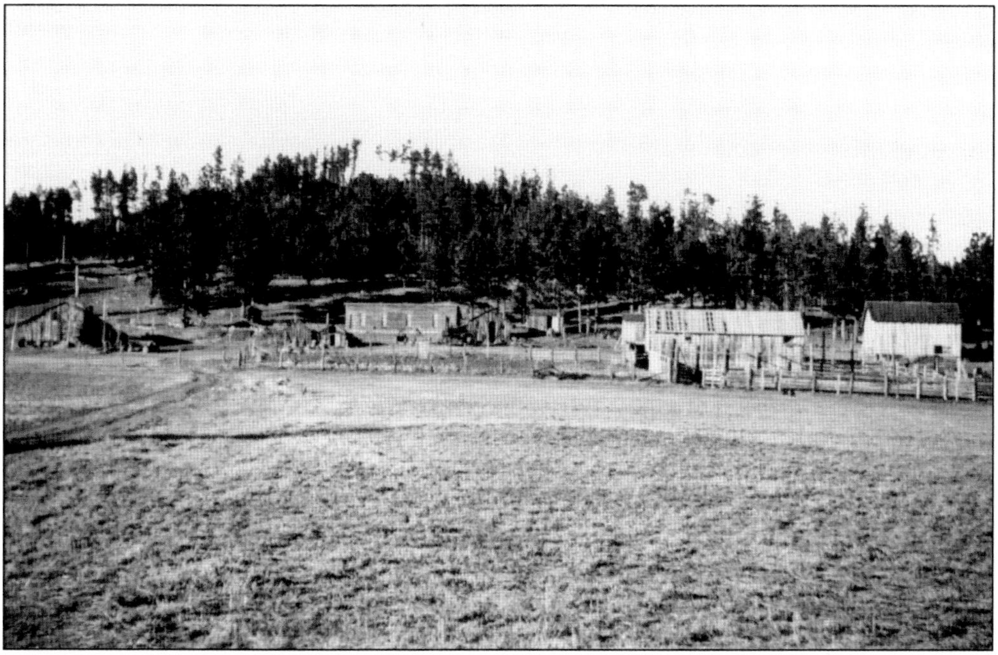

This photograph shows some of the buildings on August Doll's ranch, near Camp Custer. (Photograph by George Dobesh; courtesy of Barbara [Dobesh] Robinson.)

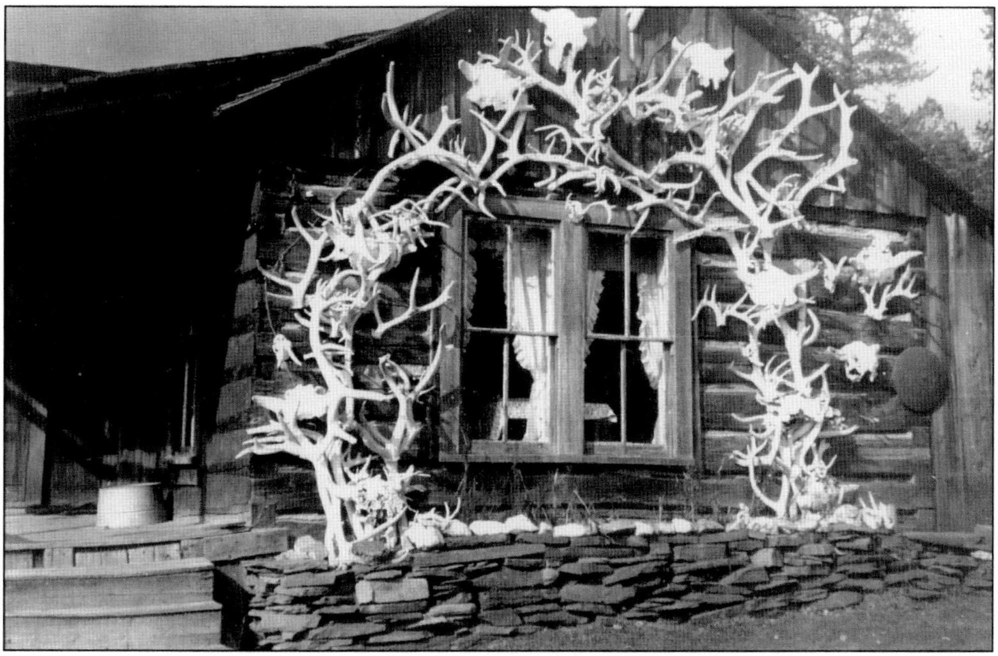

A popular type of decoration used on houses in the Black Hills is shown on what is believed to be the Strause home, near Camp Custer. (Photograph by George Dobesh; courtesy of Barbara [Dobesh] Robinson.)

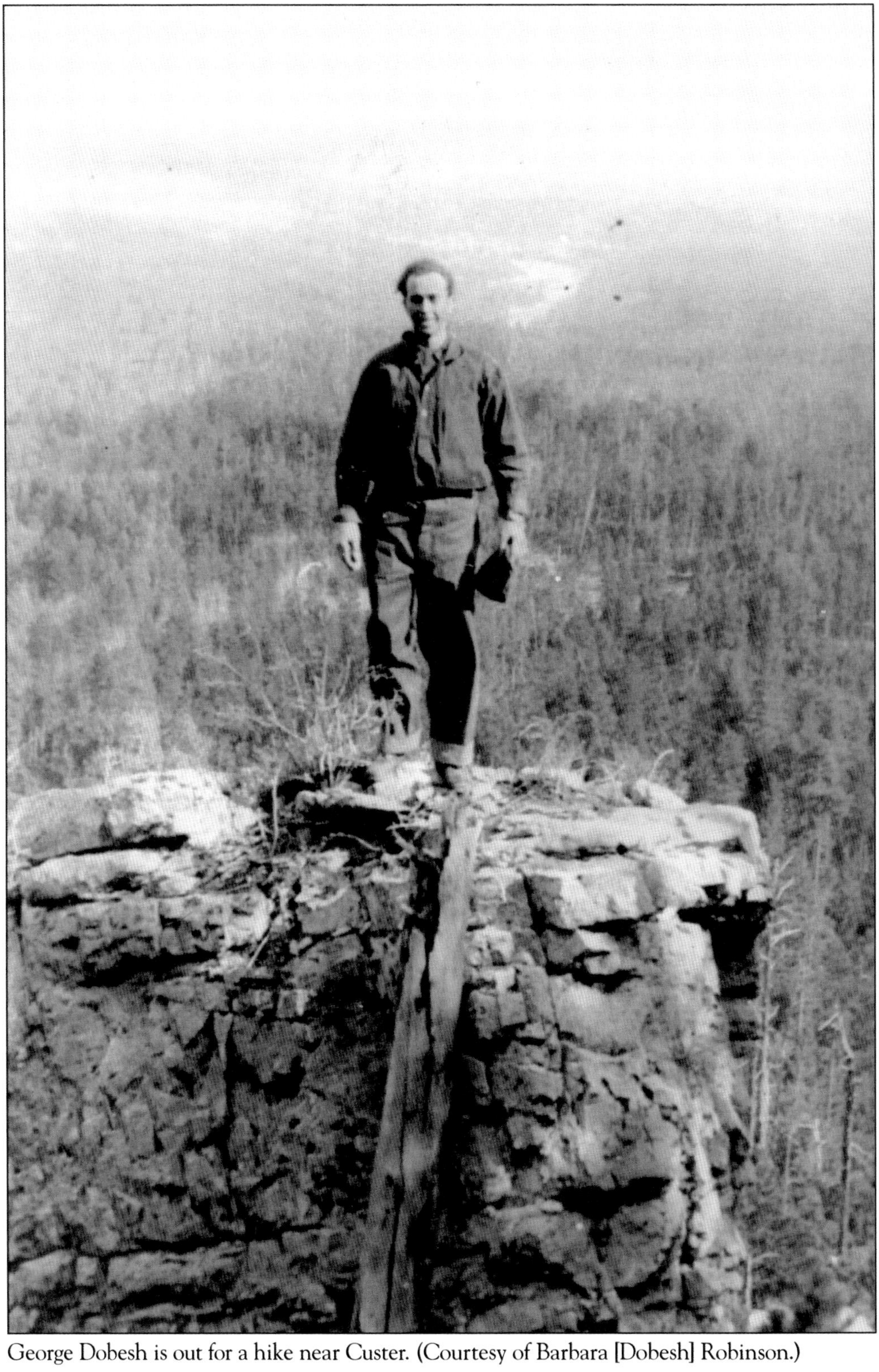

George Dobesh is out for a hike near Custer. (Courtesy of Barbara [Dobesh] Robinson.)

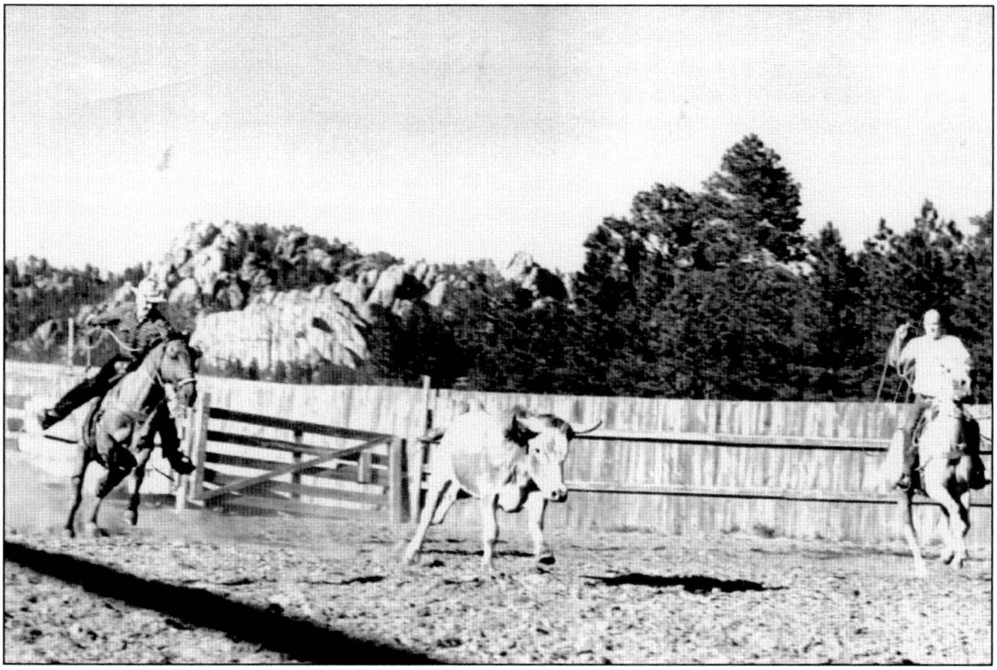

Gene Phillips and Tony Wahle are team roping at the Boot Hill Arena west of Custer. (Courtesy of Joyce Phillips.)

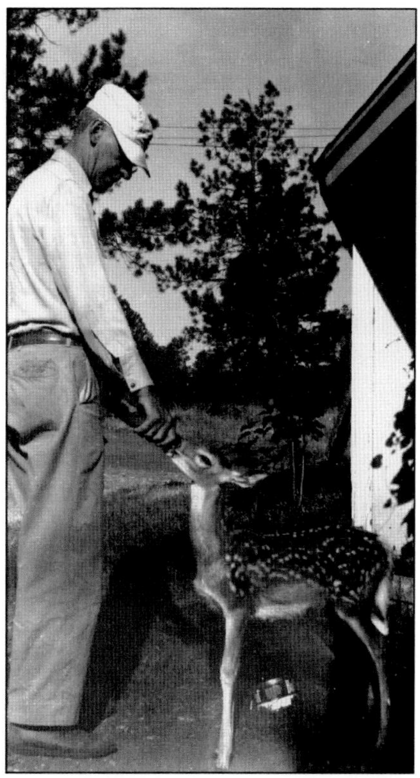

With wildlife all around his place, Les Phillips has made a pet out of this fawn by feeding it a bottle of cooked oatmeal. (Courtesy of Joyce Phillips.)

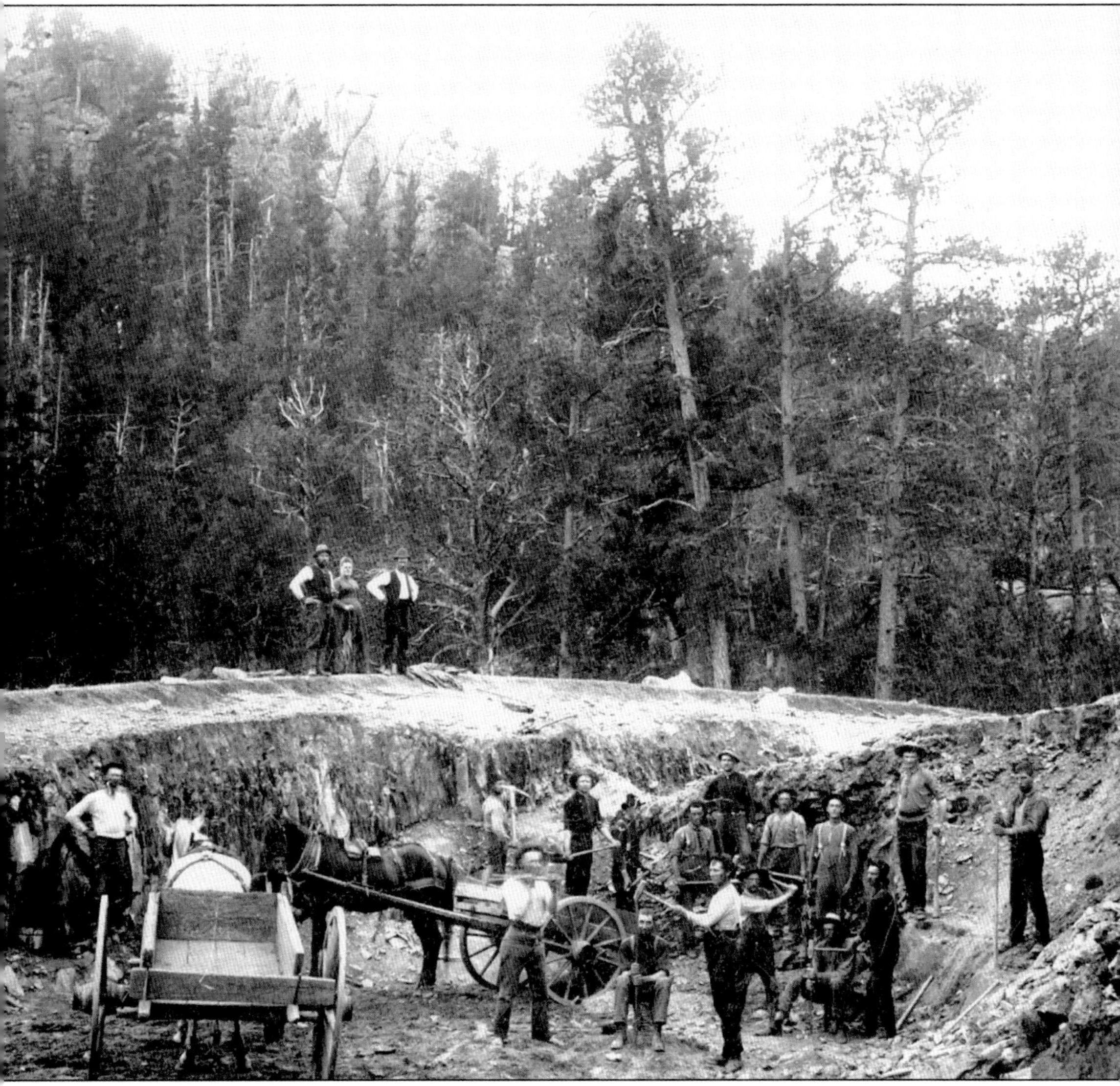

These men are putting in the railroad north of Pringle. The year is 1890. (Courtesy of Leonard and Oonagh Wood.)

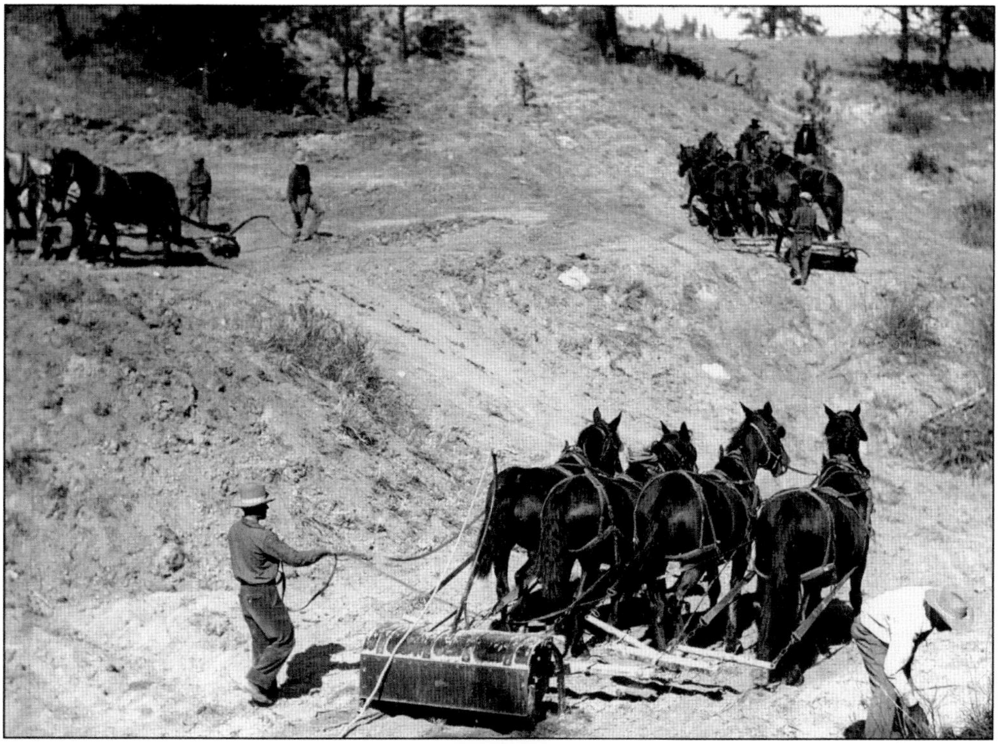

Stock dams and roads were built by teams and fresnoes, dirt-moving equipment. (Author's collection.)

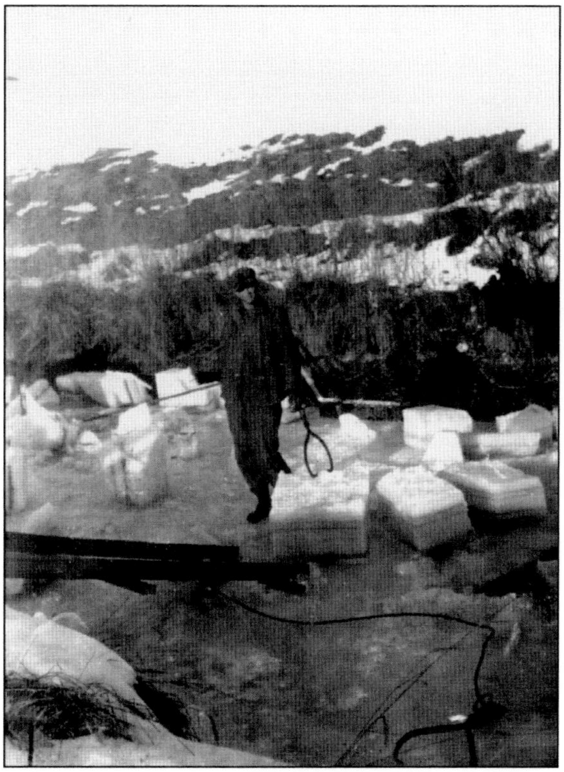

Before there were refrigerators, people harvested chunks of ice, insulated it with layers of sawdust in the icehouse, and used or sold it as needed. (Courtesy of Hermosa Arts and History Association.)

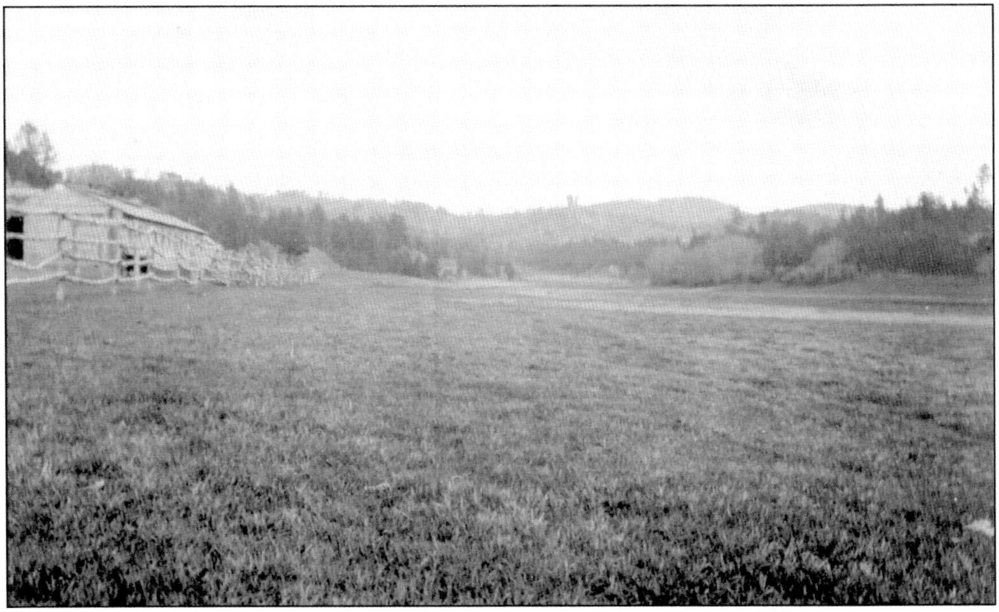

This view of Beecher's Rock is from Camp Mayo. (Courtesy of Edna Wulff.)

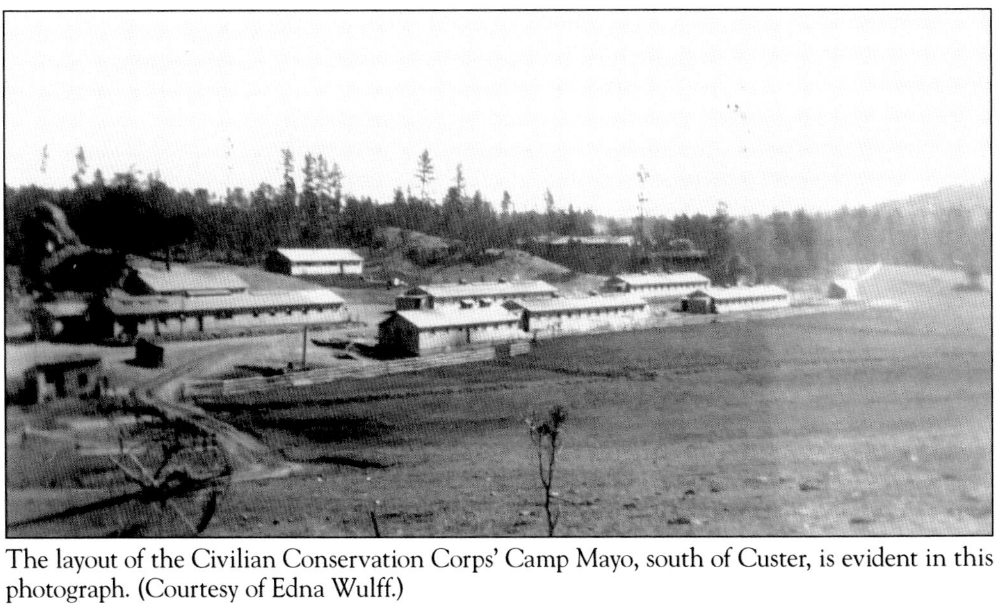

The layout of the Civilian Conservation Corps' Camp Mayo, south of Custer, is evident in this photograph. (Courtesy of Edna Wulff.)

As a forest service employee, Paul R. Lewis of Pringle was a side camp foreman with Camp Custer. (Author's collection.)

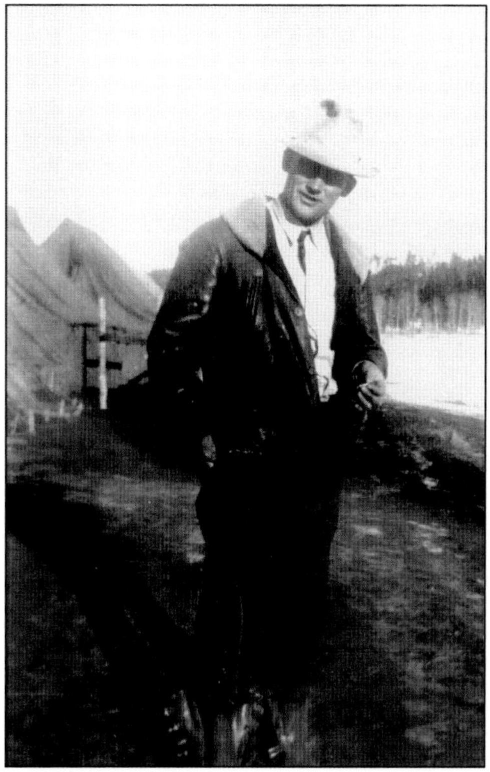

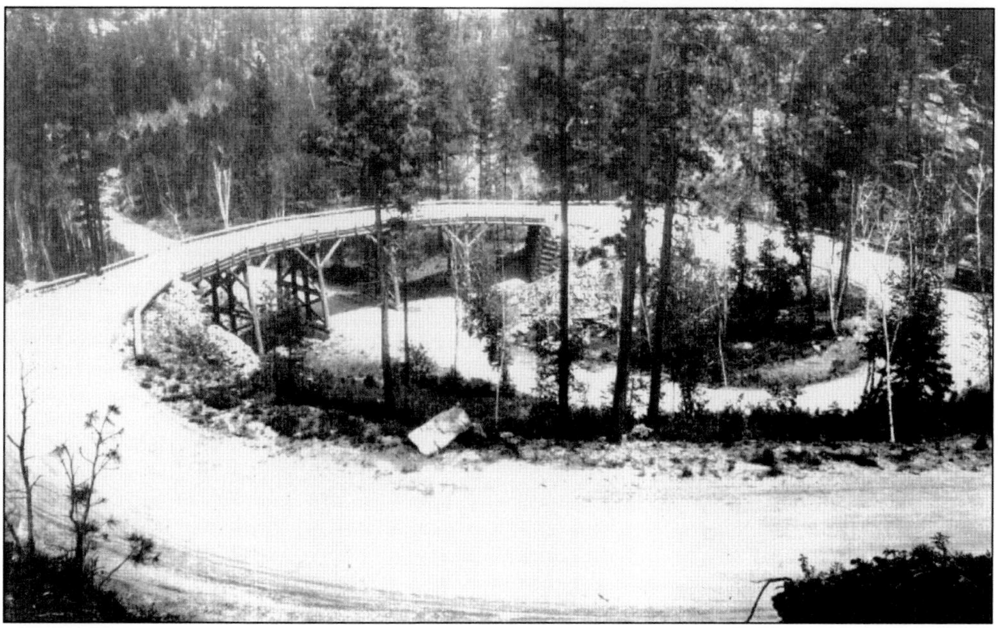

The corkscrew, or pigtail, bridges were the brainchild of South Dakota's Peter Norbeck, who was a U.S. senator from 1921 until his death in 1936. (Author's collection.)

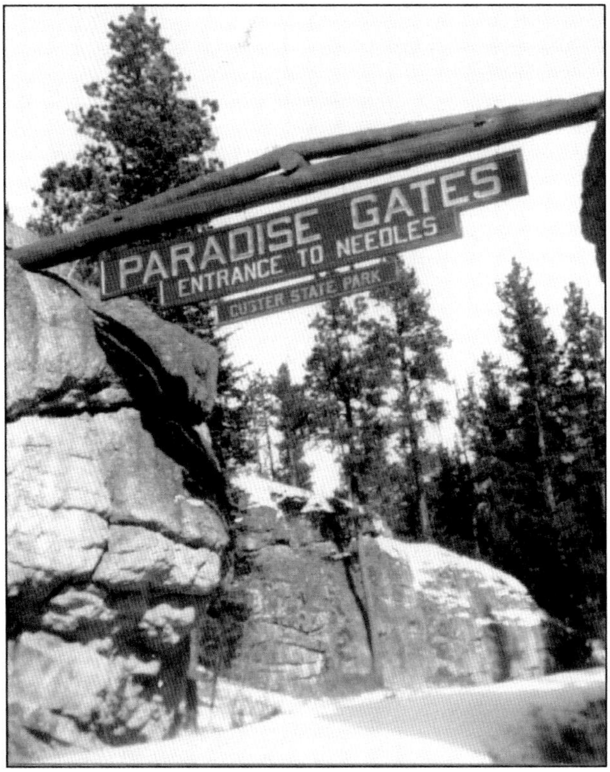

Seen here is the sign over the entrance to the Needles Highway in Custer State Park. (Author's collection.)

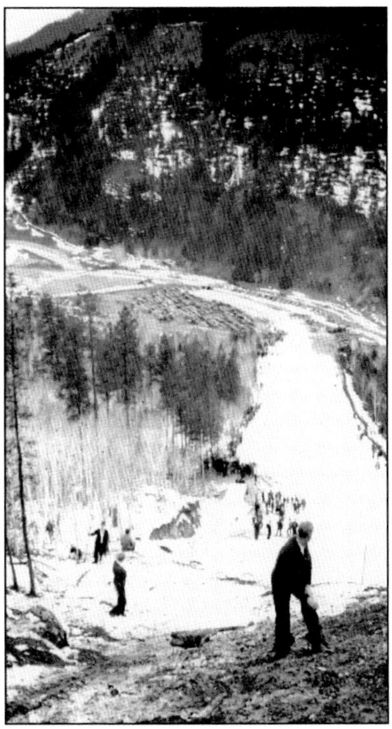

The Civilian Conservation Corps built this ski jump by Sylvan Lake. (Courtesy of Helen Van Nice.)

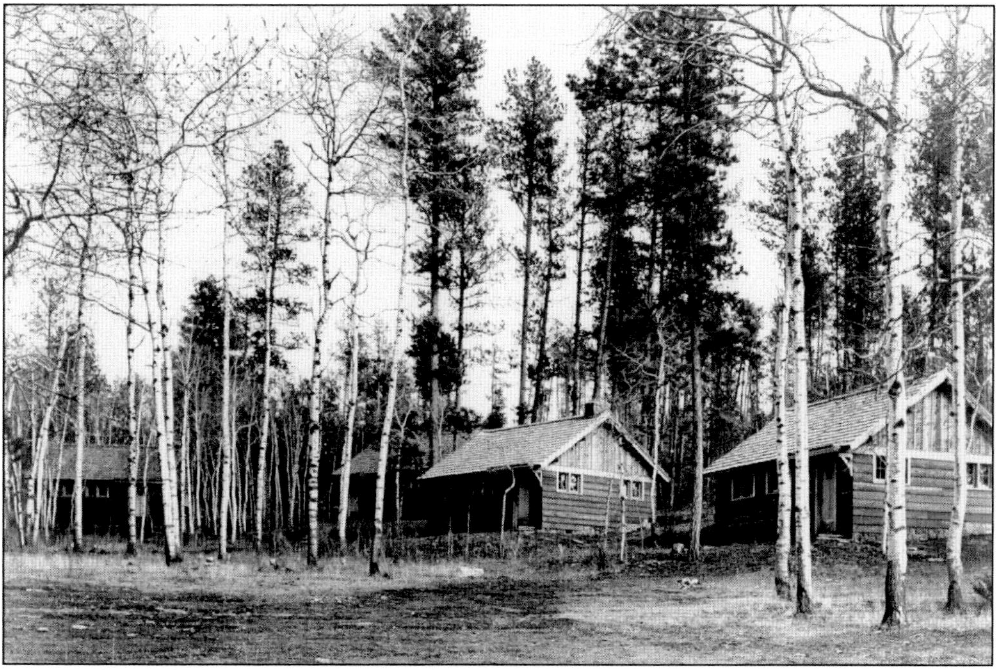

Camp Bob Marshall was built by the Civilian Conservation Corps for the Forest Service during the years 1938–1940 to be used as a youth camp. It was never occupied by the CCC. (Courtesy of Gary Holst, manager of Camp Bob Marshall.)

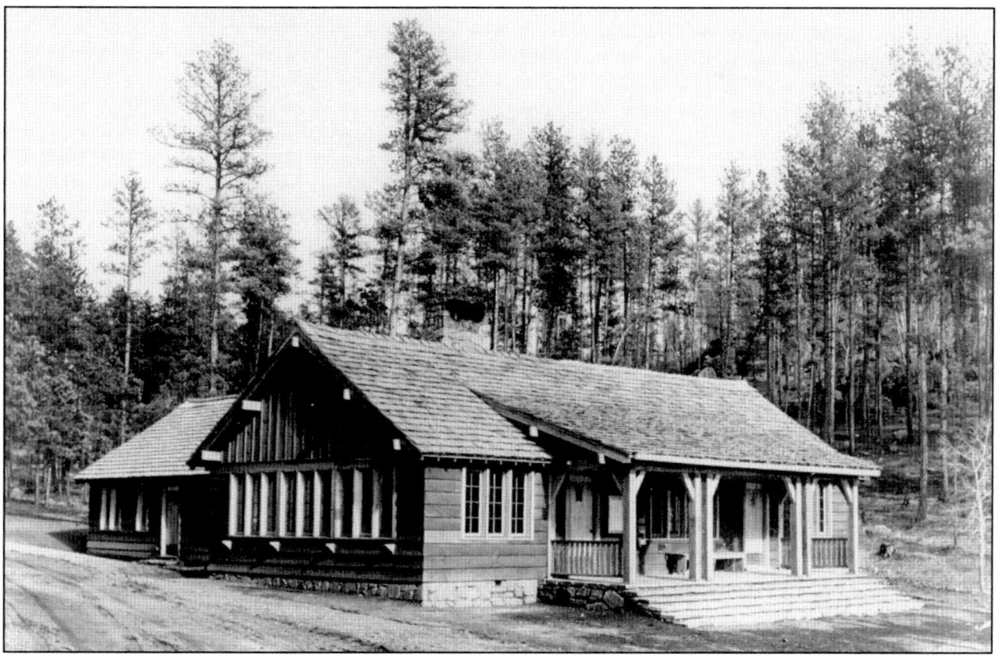

Camp Bob Marshall is currently operated by the Western Dakota 4-H Camp Association. (Courtesy of Gary Holst, manager of Camp Bob Marshall.)

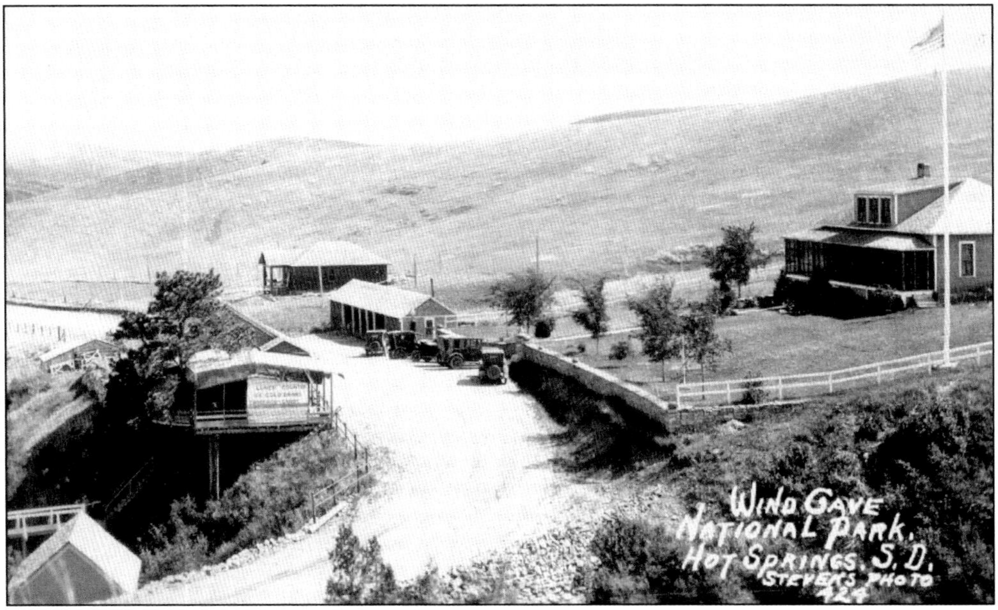

Wind Cave National Park has been in the hands of the federal government for over 100 years. The sign on the old concession stand reads, "Lunch Counter, Ice Cold Drinks, Groceries and Candy." (Author's collection.)

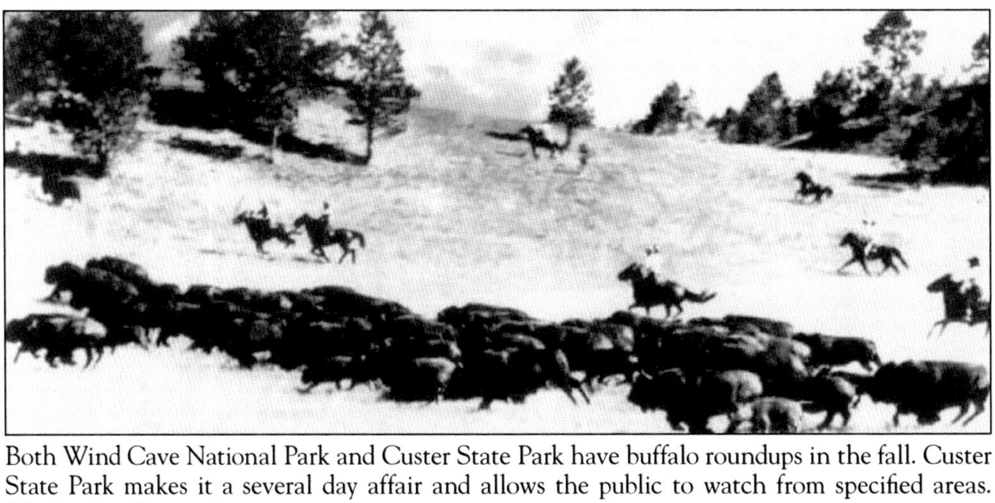

Both Wind Cave National Park and Custer State Park have buffalo roundups in the fall. Custer State Park makes it a several day affair and allows the public to watch from specified areas. (Author's collection.)

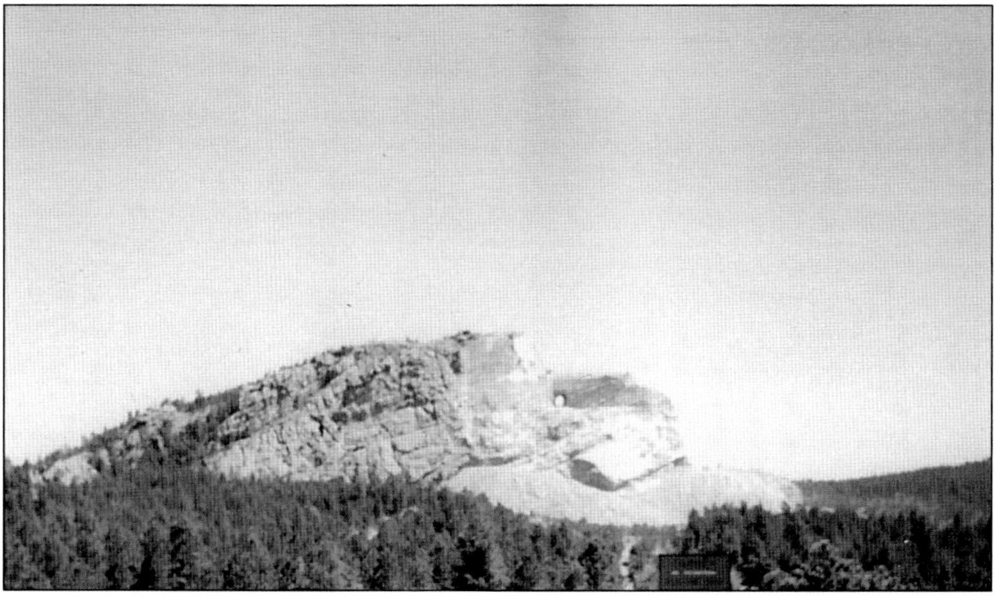

In 1939, sculptor Korczak Ziolkowski was invited by Lakota Indian chiefs to carve Crazy Horse in the Black Hills. The first blast at the memorial took place on June 3, 1948. By 1985, the amount of rock that had been removed since the first blast was eight million tons. (Courtesy of Donovin Sprague.)

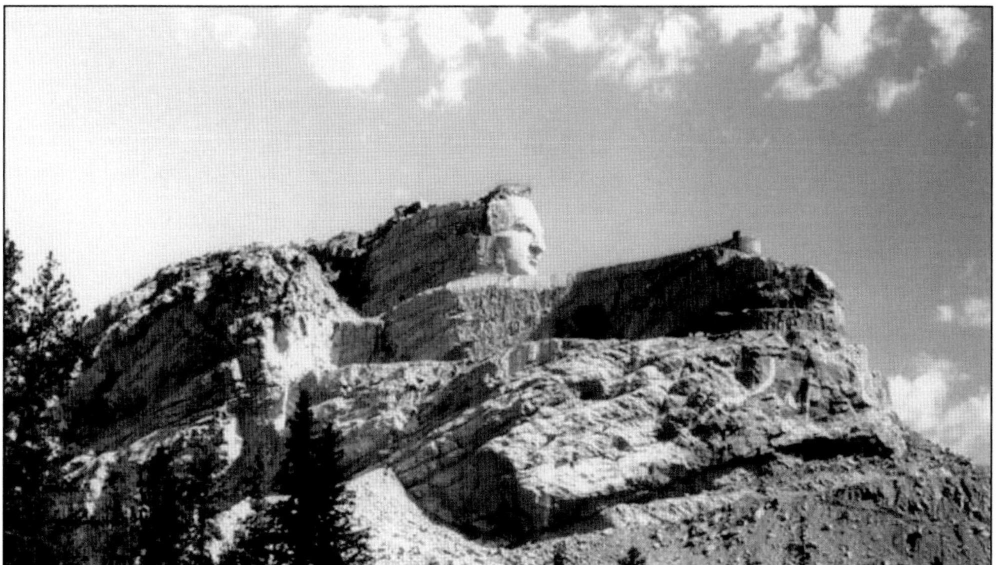

The face of Crazy Horse was completed in 1998, and work continues on the mountain. When completed, the horse's head is planned to be 219 feet. Every year on the first weekend in June, the public is invited to walk up to the sculpture. As many as 15,000 people have walked the trail during a single weekend. (Courtesy of Donovin Sprague.)

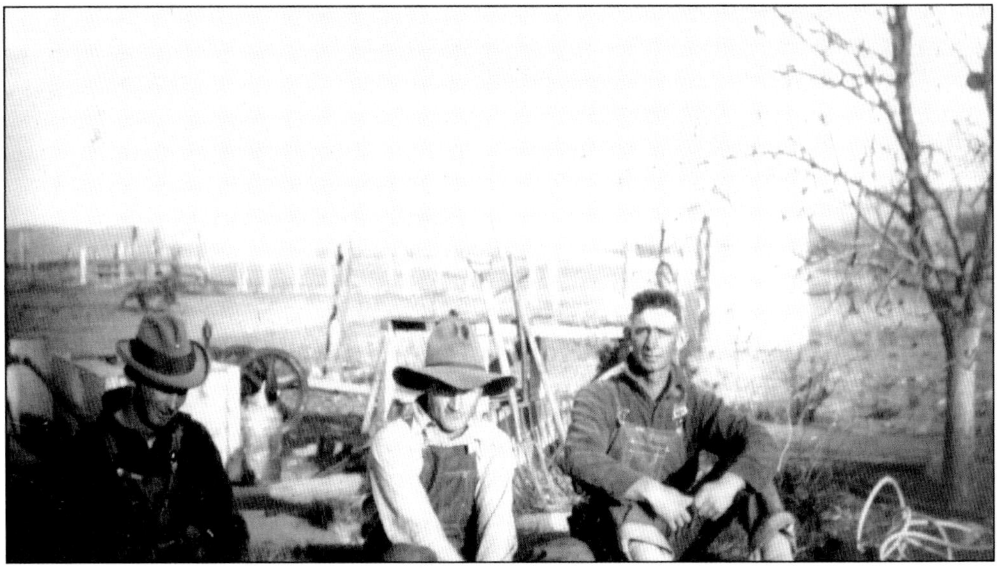

Resting after a hard day's cattle working are, from left to right, Leo, Leonard, and Bill Gregerson. (Courtesy of Nelda Carroll.)

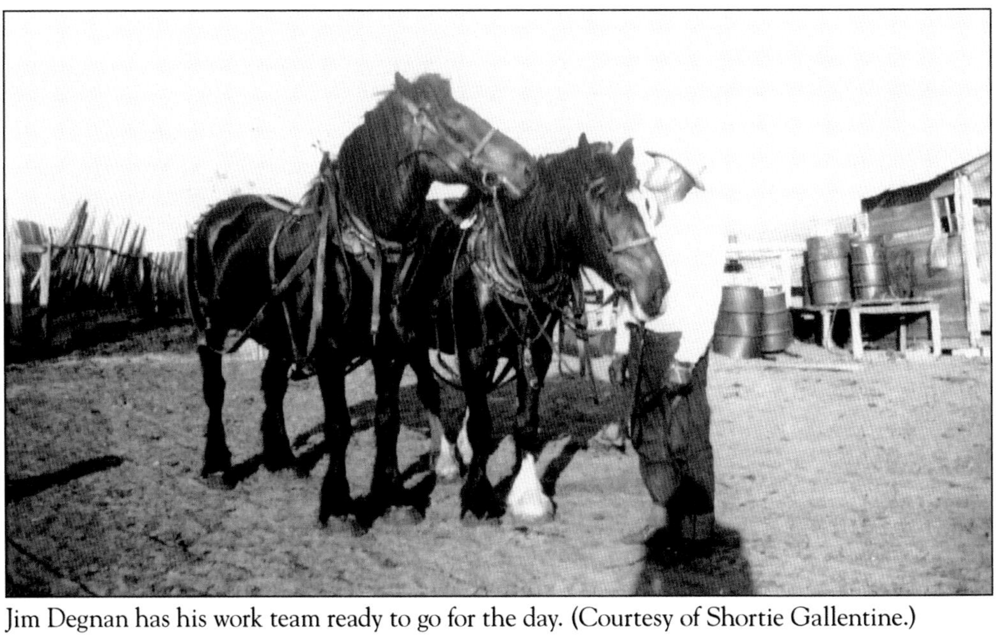

Jim Degnan has his work team ready to go for the day. (Courtesy of Shortie Gallentine.)

Born in Nebraska on May 2, 1899, Wiley McClaren later moved to South Dakota and ultimately ranched north of Pringle. (Courtesy of Charlotte McClaren.)

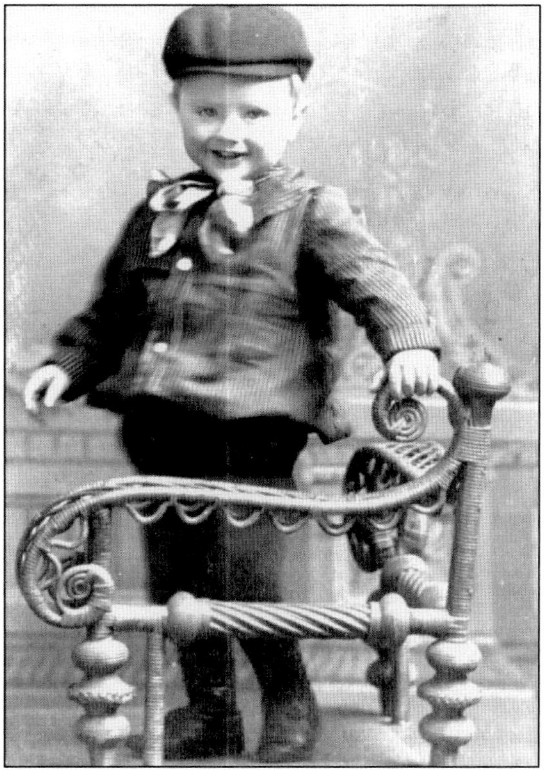

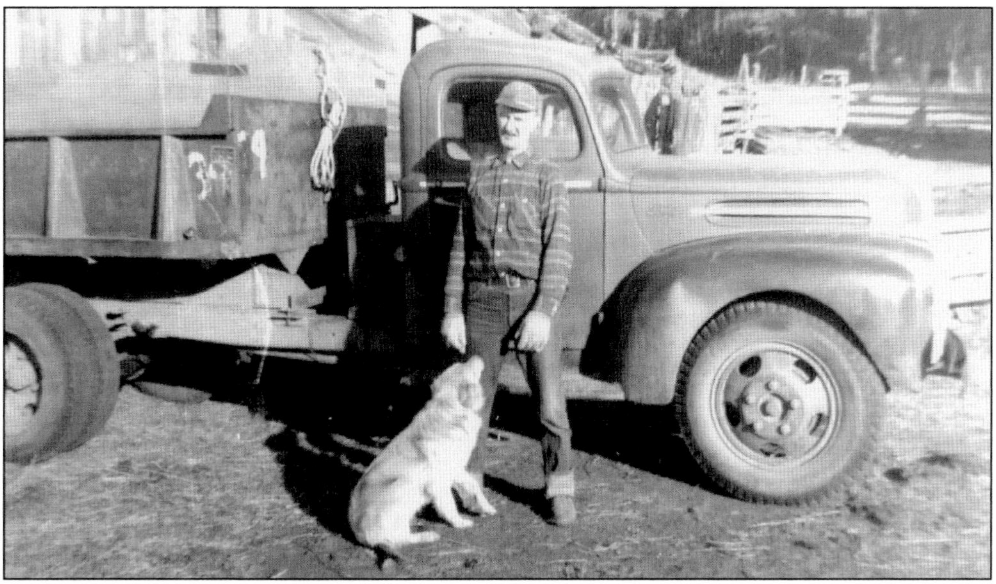

Wiley McClaren continued the ranch operation throughout his life. He is pictured with his dog King. (Courtesy of Charlotte McClaren.)

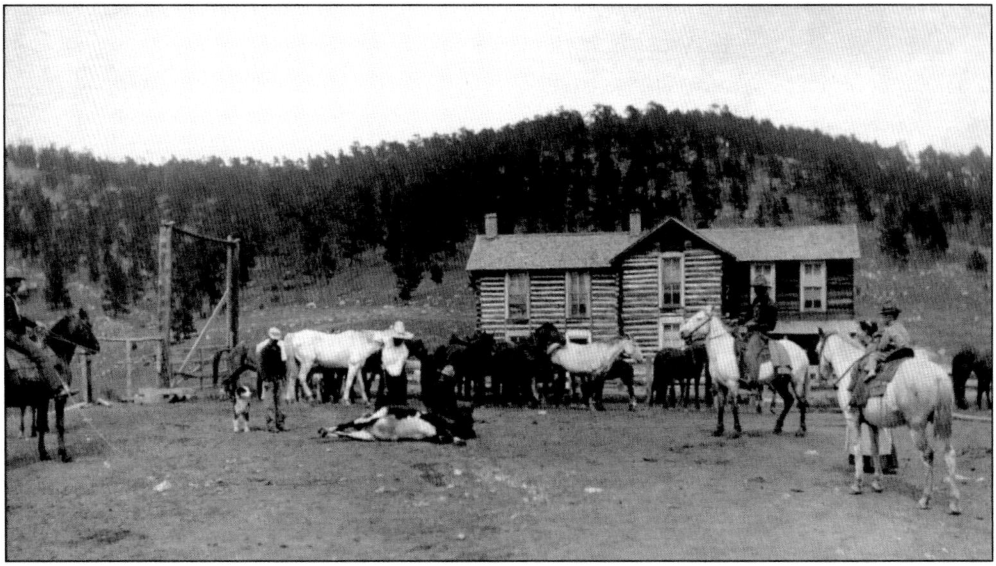

This branding is on the Nelson place near Pringle. Grandson Jack Nelson is on the far right horse, and Mrs. Nelson is standing at the horse's front side. A brand shows ownership just as license plates do on a car. (Courtesy of Leonard and Oonagh Wood.)

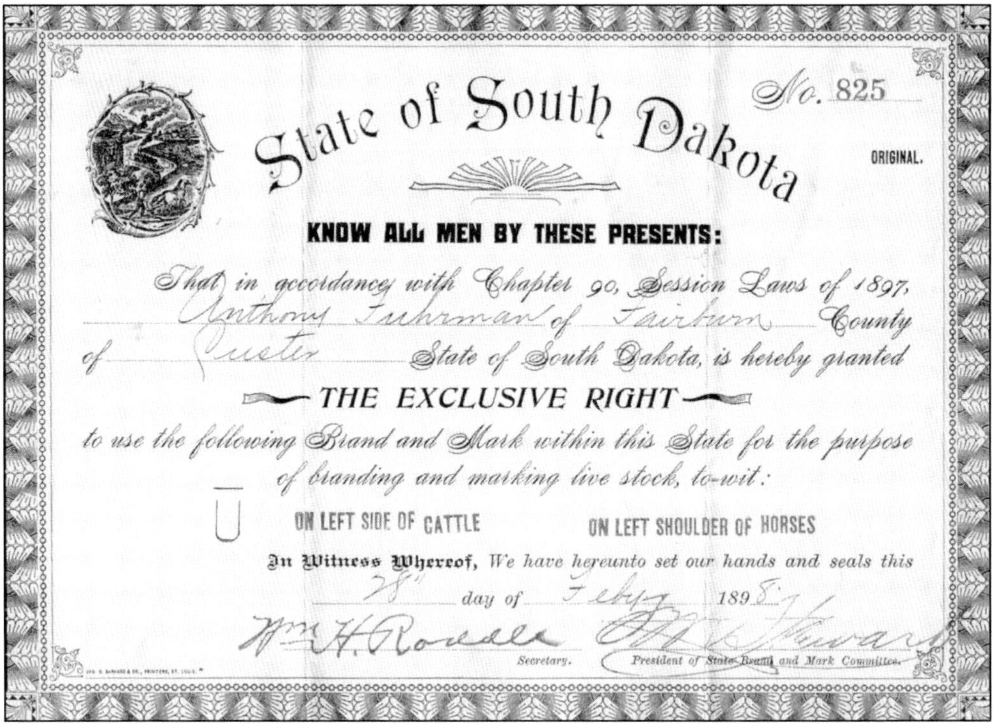

No. 825

State of South Dakota

ORIGINAL.

KNOW ALL MEN BY THESE PRESENTS:

That in accordance with Chapter 90, Session Laws of 1897, Anthony Fuhrman of Fairburn County of Custer State of South Dakota, is hereby granted

THE EXCLUSIVE RIGHT

to use the following Brand and Mark within this State for the purpose of branding and marking live stock, to-wit:

ON LEFT SIDE OF CATTLE ON LEFT SHOULDER OF HORSES

In Witness Whereof, We have hereunto set our hands and seals this 28th day of Feby 1898

Secretary. President of State Brand and Mark Committee.

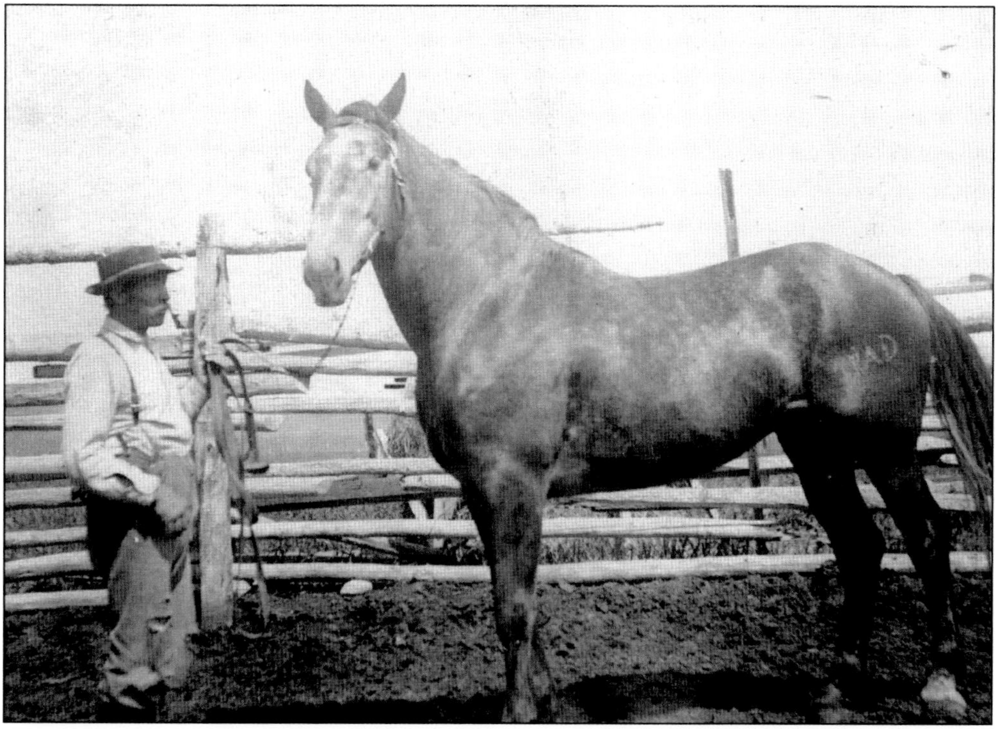

Vern Smith poses with a horse named Pete. Notice that horses were also branded. (Courtesy of Glen Smith.)

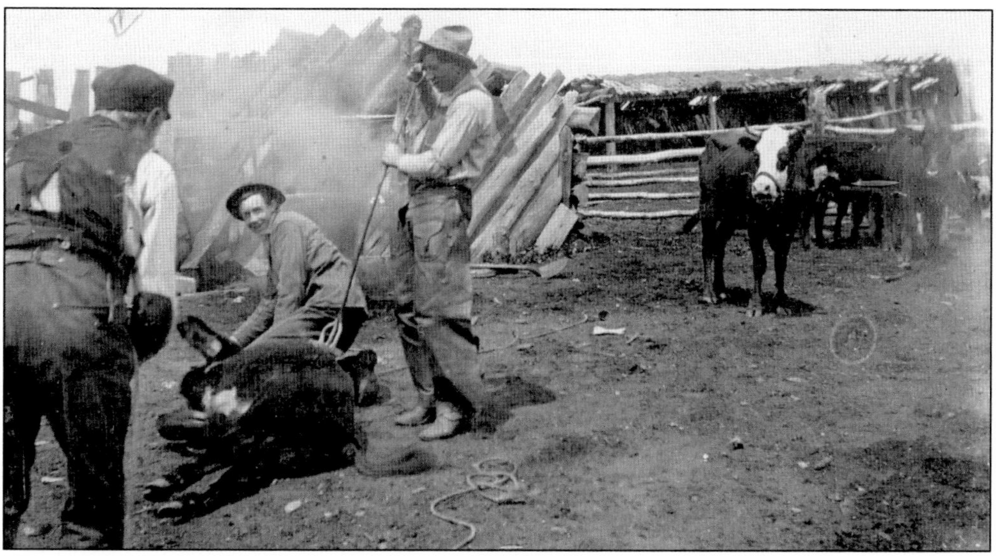

Mike Rasmussen is using a branding iron at the Rasmussen ranch near Argyle. (Courtesy of Wayne Kewley.)

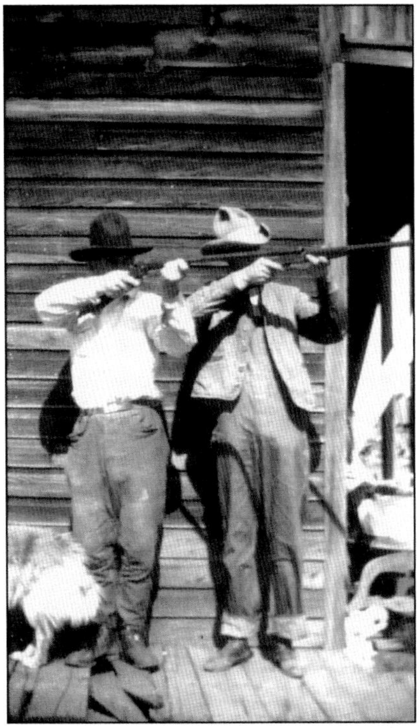

Vern Smith and Bill Gregerson are hamming it up for the camera. (Courtesy of Glen Smith.)

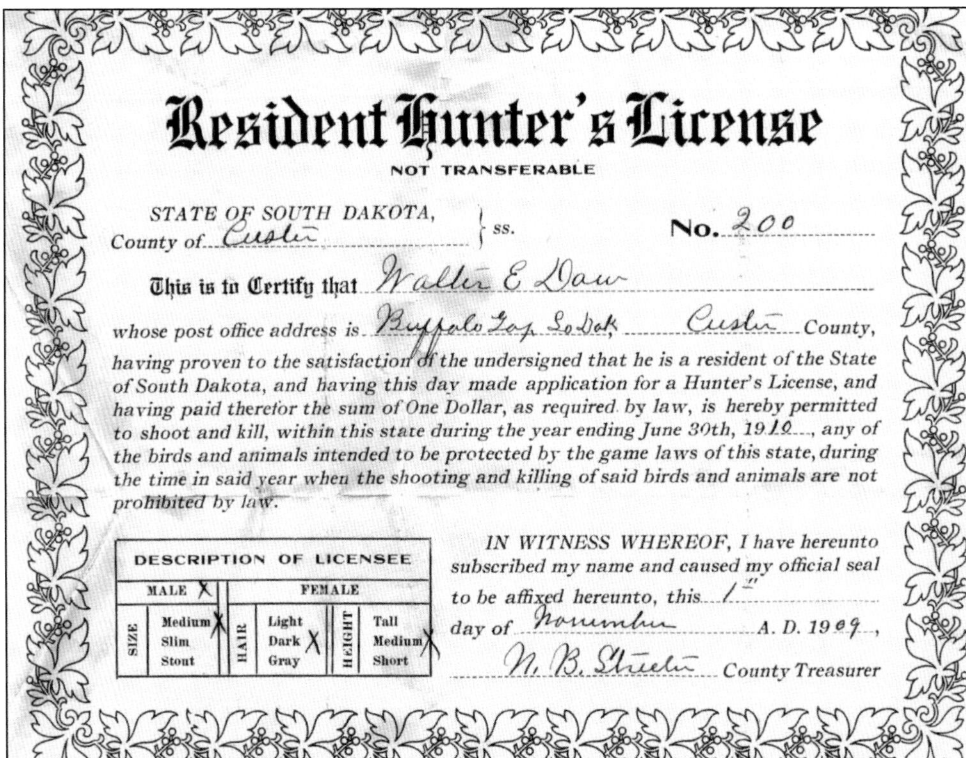

Resident Hunter's License

NOT TRANSFERABLE

STATE OF SOUTH DAKOTA, }
County of Custer } ss. No. 200

This is to Certify that Walter E Daw

whose post office address is Buffalo Gap So Dak Custer County, having proven to the satisfaction of the undersigned that he is a resident of the State of South Dakota, and having this day made application for a Hunter's License, and having paid therefor the sum of One Dollar, as required by law, is hereby permitted to shoot and kill, within this state during the year ending June 30th, 1910, any of the birds and animals intended to be protected by the game laws of this state, during the time in said year when the shooting and killing of said birds and animals are not prohibited by law.

DESCRIPTION OF LICENSEE					
MALE X			FEMALE		
SIZE	Medium X Slim Stout	HAIR	Light Dark X Gray	HEIGHT	Tall Medium X Short

IN WITNESS WHEREOF, I have hereunto subscribed my name and caused my official seal to be affixed hereunto, this 1st day of November A. D. 1909,

N. B. Streeter County Treasurer

Walter Dow's 1910 resident hunting license cost him $1, and he could hunt anything that was legal for that fee. (Courtesy of Shortie Gallentine.)

Buryl Degnan received his first rifle, a .22, for Christmas when he was five years old. (Courtesy of Shortie Gallentine.)

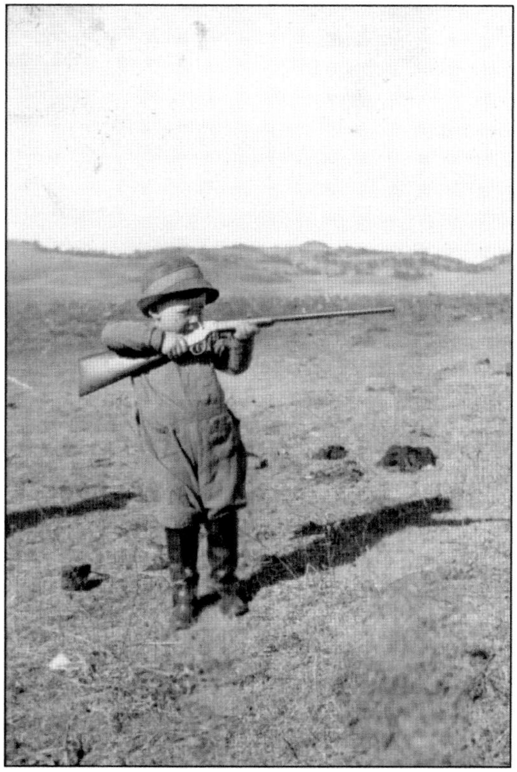

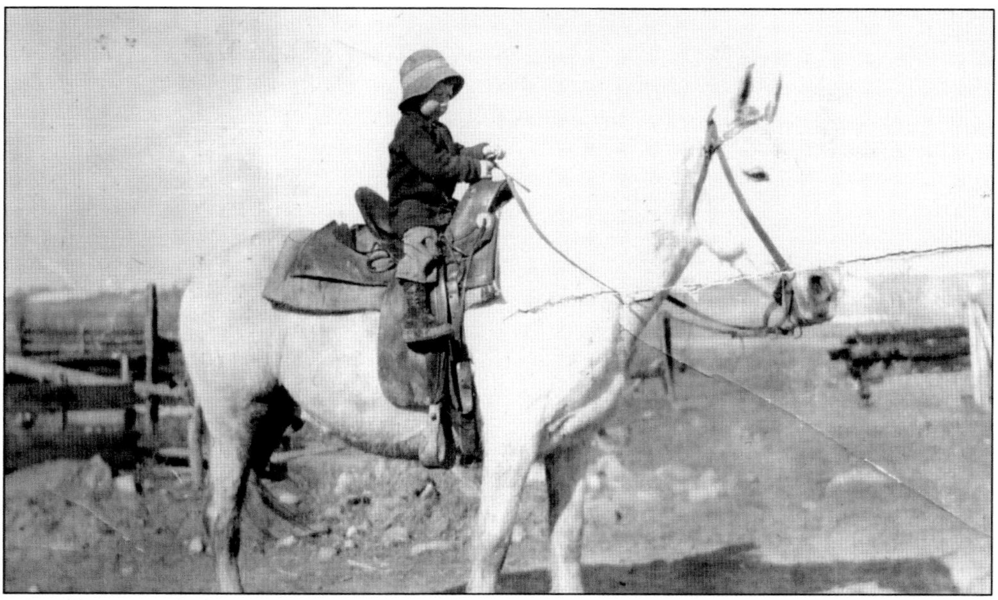

Like all country kids, Buryl Degnan started riding and learning about horses and cattle, taking care of animals, and fulfilling other responsibilities when he was just a small boy. (Courtesy of Shortie Gallentine.)

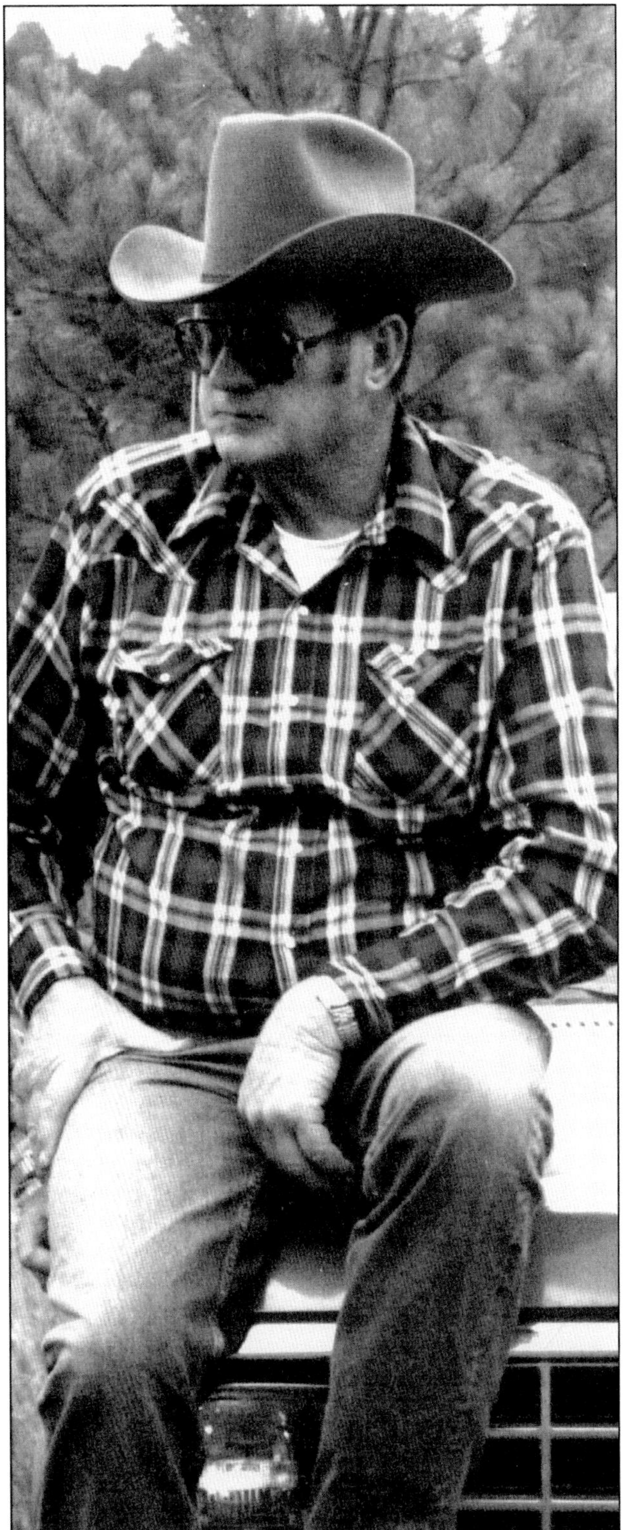

Joe McClaren, son of Wiley McClaren, followed in his father's footsteps by owning and operating their ranch north of Pringle. (Courtesy of Ferol McClaren.)